Lessons in Laughter

Also by the authors
Tales from a Clubroom

Lessons in Laughter

The Autobiography of a Deaf Actor

Bernard Bragg

as signed to EUGENE BERGMAN

Gallaudet University Press
Washington, D.C.

Gallaudet University Press, Washington, DC 20002

First edition

Published 1989. Second printing, 1990.

Printed in the United States of America

Cover photograph by Hal Roth.

Library of Congress Cataloging-in-Publication Data

Bragg, Bernard, 1928—
    Lessons in laughter: the autobiography of a deaf actor / by Bernard Bragg
as signed to Eugene Bergman.
     p. cm.
    ISBN 0-930323-46-7
    1. Bragg, Bernard, 1928-   . 2. Actors—United States—Biography.
3. Deaf—United States—Biography.   4. Authors, American—20th
century—Biography.   I. National Theatre of the Deaf.   II. Bergman,
Eugene.   III. Title.
PN2287.B6827A3   1989   792'.028'092-dc20
[B]   89-1493
                                         CIP

To my mother whose gentleness was her strength,
And to my father who did not go gentle into that good night.

Contents

Preface

I am a storyteller. I don't write stories, I perform them. The very telling of stories is what fascinates me because it involves an audience—a live one. More often than not, the telling can be what makes a story a story—what a story is meant to be—what it has got to be. The facts of a story alone are never completely satisfactory; it is the meshing of the facts with the manner of their telling that breathes life into what otherwise would be merely a straightforward, factual reporting of events.

I see stories in my everyday life. I see them everywhere. I spin stories as I go along. I read stories into nearly everything. Or rather, they unfold themselves right before my eyes. But to me, stories live only when I perform them dramatically in sign and mime before an audience. They disappear into thin air after I have acted them out—except when they are transferred to print.

A longtime friend and colleague of mine, Gene Bergman, has a feel for words and a flair for matching them with my storytelling performance, so by joining forces we were able to produce this book. Each one of my stories is true. Up until now, they have vanished once the curtain has fallen, but no more. Each will live on here.

Bernard Bragg

Acknowledgments

We owe thanks to Edna S. Levine for encouraging us to write this book, and to Harlan Lanc for writing thc Introduction. We also wish to express our appreciation to Ivey Pittle, Bruce White, Pat Hurt-Ritenburg, Ernest Moncada, Catherine Kalbacher, Kathee Christensen, Russell Astley, Martin Sternberg, Donna Chitwood, and Peggy Hansen for their sensitive and probing criticism. Last, but not least, we are in debt to Gene's wife, Claire, for the patience and good humor with which she endured our long hours of working together, and to David Seltzer and Sabrina Bergman for their witty comments, which enlivened our collaboration.

Introduction

Hearing people frequently ask me to explain what constitutes deaf culture. Now I can direct them to this engrossing autobiographical montage of stories told in sign language by America's leading deaf theater artist, Bernard Bragg, and rendered into English with great brio by Eugene Bergman. *Lessons in Laughter* is about deaf culture and it is an artifact of deaf culture at the same time (how right that it should have originated in signed stories, often about communication). Many of the recurrent themes addressed by deaf authors across the centuries, legends rooted in the deaf collective unconscious, are to be found here freshly presented. Listen, for example, to Pierre Desloges, the first deaf man to publish a book (it, too, was autobiographical), as he describes his discovery of the power of French Sign Language.

> *When a deaf person encounters other deaf people more highly educated than he, as I myself have experienced, he learns to combine and improve his signs, which had hitherto been unordered and unconnected. . . . He acquires the supposedly difficult art of depicting and expressing all his thoughts, even those most independent of the senses, using natural signs with as much order and precision as if he understood the rules of grammar.*

Compare Bragg:

> *What electrified and enthralled us about Mr. Panara was his very embodiment of a living breathing revelation of the potential of sign language. . . . In contrast to the choppy, abrupt, and often homemade signs we normally used among ourselves, his signs were a miracle of vividness and eloquence. . . . We had never realized that this, our native language, could be such a powerful vehicle for expressing the richest and subtlest feelings and conveying nuances of meaning as sophisticated as those of the most articulate English speakers and writers.*

Or consider John Kitto, the deaf, English, Bible commentator, writing in the middle of the last century on the medical approach to deafness:

They poured into my tortured ears various infusions hot and cold; they bled me, they blistered me, leeched me, physicked me; and at last they gave it up as a bad case.

Compare Bernard Bragg:

The left side of his face was partially paralyzed owing to an operation done on his ear when he was six by a so-called medical doctor who thought he could restore Ken's hearing. Being nerve-deaf, Ken of course remained deaf as a post, and the only result was that when he smiled only half of his mouth turned up, so that his smile was crooked.

In *Lessons in Laughter*, the reader will find such timeless themes of the deaf experience as the deaf man who is valued by his beloved mostly as an object of study, who turns his deafness to advantage on the job, who tries to pass as a hearing man, who is exploited by unethical hearing people, who resists transformation into what he is not, whose deafness disqualifies him from someone's love, who comes to see he is a member of a linguistic and cultural minority—but one different from all others.

There is much more to this engaging work, however, than solely a lesson in deaf culture. Self-portraits, painted or written, are an appealing genre, for they not only satisfy our curiosity about the artist and his times but, like halls of mirrors and rollercoaster loops, they titillate our sense of relativity; they play with the contextual frame in which perception occurs. When, in addition, they convey a fresh vision of the human condition, their appeal transcends their time and place.

Lessons in Laughter is such a book. On one level it is about the richly textured life of someone who has traveled widely and reflected deeply. On another level, it is an exploration of the story as a form and of storytelling as an activity. It is an autobiography constructed of vignettes. This is exactly right; as a history is more than a record of a social past, an autobiography is more than a record of a personal past. It is a construction, an art form.

The life of a storyteller is naturally composed of stories of all kinds—in sign language, in mime and visual vernacular, and in English, with both direct and indirect discourse. There are stories about the theater, where stories are performed on the stage, and there are multiply-embedded stories. For example, Bragg tells the story of an acquaintance telling a story in which a teenager goes to the library and happens on a biography of Bragg. The teenager finds the story of how Bragg cofounded the National Theatre of the Deaf so engaging that he attends one of their plays. There he meets Bragg and has him autograph his own biography. The acquaintance who tells this story proves to have been that very youth.

Lessons in Laughter is a coming to terms with one's self, and it takes place in the setting of the theater, where art is created and the stage is a metaphor for life itself. We learn the story behind the National Theatre of the Deaf, and behind the Russian mime theater to cite two examples. We learn how the artist constructs his story, with a colorful palette, projecting himself onto the subjects treated, addressing enduring human issues, including yearning, suffering, and death.

The fundamental reason that Bragg's life story appeals to a broad audience is that it engages the universal issues of the human condition clothed in the particular of relations between hearing and deaf people and among deaf people themselves. *Lessons in Laughter* is a cry of outrage at the crimes of the intolerant: the unwillingness of hearing people to allow deaf people self-determination; the recasting of deaf people's difference as deviance; the fraud perpetrated by hearing people who claim to normalize deaf people; and the refusal of hearing society to acknowledge deaf language and culture. Every deaf person, and every hearing person in the professions serving the deaf, will laugh and cry and rage—and reflect—while reading these stories. So will anyone, hearing or deaf, who has suffered the oppression of minorities by majorities.

These stories will cast their spell on a wider audience, however, for the deaf people in them battle bravely with life—to make peace with a dead relative, to care for a loved one in the hospital, to search for a profession compatible with one's identity, or to win the love of a beautiful woman and the respect of a coworker. Bernard Bragg's autobiography reveals that, beyond the uniqueness of the deaf experience, lies our common humanity, including the universal love of a good story.

Harlan Lane

Authors' Note

Although the incidents retold in this narrative are authentic, the names of a few of the characters and places have been changed in the interest of confidentiality. One person in particular, Dorothy S. Miles, asked that her real name be used.

Also, a word on the translation. The rhythm, syntax, and grammar of American Sign Language differ drastically from those of English. Therefore, any verbatim translation from American Sign Language to English often results in awkward, stilted language. In reality, a signer's story is a work of art, sparkling with witticisms and the most subtle nuances of expression. That is why we choose a free rather than literal translation of dialogue in this book. Of course, not all the dialogue is translated from sign language. Some deaf people are bilingual and use English almost as readily as they sign.

Lessons in Laughter

CHAPTER ONE

The Stage Is Set

A s I was checking into the Warwick Hotel in New York City in the fall of 1978, I glanced sideways and noticed that Sally Struthers was waiting to sign the register too. Behind her stood Jeff Bravin, and he was surrounded by the television crew who had just arrived from Hollywood. We waved at each other. The crowd around the registration desk was growing.

I had to concentrate on the registration card. It asked the day's date. I looked up at the clerk, and he said September 20. I could lipread that clearly.

September 20? I couldn't believe it—I had completely lost track of time. My birthday was only seven days away. As I went up to my room and began to unpack I pondered how to celebrate my fiftieth birthday, half a century of my life. I was in New York to begin shooting the TV film *And Your Name Is Jonah* for CBS and it would certainly take more than a week. I wouldn't be able to return home to Maryland, so how then was I to celebrate my birthday in a city that had become a stranger to me? I contemplated the scenery from my window, the skyscrapers and the traffic below. And then I thought of Windows on the World—that would be the perfect place!

After the first day of shooting I took a taxi to the World Trade Center and, once there, the elevator to the 104th floor. I entered Windows on the World and told the maitre d' I wanted a reservation for eight o'clock on September 27, then I asked him to show me around the place so I could pick the table. I strode around the huge room and finally stopped at a table with the view I wanted. "This is the table I want," I wrote the maitre d'. He wrote back, "I can't promise but I will do my best." After I ordered a birthday cake we smiled graciously at each other and I left.

The week of filming passed quickly. I had invited a few close friends to celebrate my birthday with me, and on the evening of September 27 we met in the lobby of the World Trade Center and took the escalator up. When we reached the restaurant I anxiously gestured to the maitre d', asking if the table I had chosen was available. He nodded yes. My elation was so obvious that my friends looked at me questioningly. One even asked me outright why I was so happy about getting that particular table.

I answered, "Wait, let's have our drinks first."

Our table was next to a window that looked out on a panorama of the East River and Brooklyn. The drinks were brought and I raised a toast. "You asked why this table is so important to me," I began, pointing at the panorama of multicolored lights below. "Look at the Brooklyn Bridge." Measuring in the air with my thumb and index finger a short distance from the farther end of the bridge, I added, "Do you see that red light behind it? Near it is Jewish Hospital, where I was born fifty years ago today."

They laughed and thought it a wonderful idea to celebrate one's birthday in this fashion. We had a delicious meal, after which the waiter brought out a cake decorated with the inscription, "Thanks, My Friends." They just loved it.

My associations with that window were much more complex and personal. While we ate dessert, I told my friends one of my parents' favorite stories. On their honeymoon my parents stayed in an inn in the Poconos, already then, in 1928, a popular spot for newlyweds. They loved their room, the view from the window, and above all, the cozy interior and large white bed. The morning after their first night at the inn, they went down to the dining room for breakfast. The other guests were chatting and hardly gave them a glance. My parents began to sign zestfully about their experiences the previous night. But suddenly they sensed a stiffening of the atmosphere. Glancing around they noticed that the other guests were either frowning and raising their eyebrows at them or trying to keep from laughing as they whispered to each other and cast meaningful glances at my parents. Mother blushed in confusion while Father grew increasingly annoyed. Finally he got up to find the manager. "What's the matter? Why are the others making fun of us?" he wrote down.

The manager stammered, "Oh, I'm so sorry, sir. I can't explain, but it is a tradition of this inn. Perhaps it would be best if you go up to your room and have a look under the bed. I'm sure you'll understand."

Mystified, my father hastened upstairs. What he saw under the bed was a large, shiny, brass cowbell. "You might say," I told my friends, "that I was conceived into a world that literally pealed with sound." They all laughed in agreement.

I sat back and thought further on the ironies of the window. Here we were, celebrating my birthday in a restaurant called Windows on the World at a time when a historic film, *And Your Name Is Jonah*, providing the first authentic window on the world of deafness, was being produced. The film's protagonist, a young deaf boy, is placed in a mental hospital because his deafness is mistakenly diagnosed as mental retardation. Three years of his life are thus wasted before the mistake is rectified and he is freed. Another part of his life is wasted on essentially fruitless efforts to teach him to speak and lipread. He suffers all these ordeals as a deaf person living in a hearing world that consistently misunderstands him. The film offered a fairly accurate depiction of my own life and the lives of countless other deaf people living in a world made for the hearing, except that we were spared Jonah's experience in a mental institution.

I had spent two years of my life giving encouragement and advice about deafness to Michael Bortman, the man who scripted the film. At times he was overwhelmed by the crushing burden of deafness, to which I had served as his window, but he persisted and finished his teleplay.

And now I was facing a more literal window, one showing the scenery of my childhood, a window opening on a baby born without benefit of hearing, born to parents also without benefit of hearing, born into a world that the baby did not know would always belong to people who could hear, a world that would always remain soundless.

I grew up in a signing environment. My parents, of course, always signed to each other and to me. My Aunt Marion and Uncle Clyde, who lived in the same building as we did, were deaf, too. And so were their friends and the friends of my parents who came to visit us. My five cousins, who also lived in the same apartment building, though hearing, always either signed or gestured to me. This was my world and I could not conceive of the existence of any other.

One day, when I was two and one-half years old, I realized there was a much greater, hearing world around me. This awareness came when my mother, for the sheer pleasure of testing how smart I was, sent me downstairs to the neighborhood candy store, two doors away, to buy a pack of Chesterfields for her. Clutching a half-dollar coin and a note for the store proprietor in my grubby little hands, I descended the stairs and entered the store. I gave the coin and the note to the proprietor and he looked at me and started to move his mouth. He did not sign at all, and I became visibly disconcerted by the strange movements of his mouth under his heavy mustache, so much so that he noticed my confusion and smiled. He read the note, gave me the cigarettes and the change and kept moving his mouth at me as I retreated outside. I slowly climbed the stairs to the fifth floor, where my mother greeted me with a big smile and a hug, proud of my accomplishment.

It was thus that I made the discovery of my deafness, all by myself. I suppose that it is different for hearing children of deaf parents. At an early age they learn to mouth their words clearly in order to be understood by their deaf father and mother, and they eagerly absorb through their ears, from the radio and television, and from the conversations of people around them, knowledge about the world they live in. To me, all this knowledge was shut off, and only meager echoes of it reached me through the window of my signing parents and relatives, a window that showed only a small segment of the surrounding reality, yet was my lifeline to it.

The candy store trip was my first direct realization that there existed another class of people, the hearing, the ones who ruled this world. I did not question this difference; it just was there. I thought deafness was a way of life and never linked it with sickness, defectiveness, or a handicapped condition. I thought, and I still do, that my deafness is just part of who I am.

I remained in that blessed state of innocence until I was about four, when I learned that, without the privilege of hearing, I was truly different. I used to play on the sidewalk of our street block. Mother had trained me never to cross the street and felt sufficiently sure of my safety to leave me alone outside.

One afternoon I saw a group of children hitting a ball with a broomstick. I tried to join them, but they kept moving their mouths at me and finally waved me away. This was the first time my deafness became a barrier to me, although at the time I still did not realize what that meant. The only thing I knew was that other children didn't want to play with me. Dejected, I climbed the stairs to my home and complained to Mother that the kids would not let me play with them. I also asked her why they were moving their mouths instead of signing as we did. She signed, "We are deaf and they are hearing. They speak words. We sign words. Go out. Play with them."

I do not remember how, but I conceived the idea of going back outside with a crate containing all my toys. I dumped them on the pavement and, one by one, the kids abandoned their game, trotted over, and began to play with my toys while I supervised to make sure they would handle the toys properly and not appropriate them.

Their attitude toward me changed. I was now their good friend. My Machiavellian maneuver worked. When dinnertime came and Mother appeared to call me home, I grabbed my toys from the other children, replaced them in my crate, and proudly carried it back home.

That is an incident I only vaguely remember. Mother told me about it much later, and my older cousins have also reminded me of it.

One memory that is much stronger is of the first time I observed a quarrel between my parents. My father was slicing the air with wide, angry signs, while my mother stood calmly like a rock buffeted by a storm. Finally he left in a huff. I asked her what they had been fighting about, but she signed that it was nothing and everything was fine. Then she started to play with me and tell me some stories.

This was the first but not the last scene of its kind that I witnessed. Another incident that sticks in my memory is when, after a violent argument, my mother removed the wedding band from her finger and threw it at a living room wall. On seeing this, Father left, slamming the door behind him. Mother too left the room. I was alone. I looked for the wedding band, found it, and hung it on the light switch. Later that evening, as I tossed in my bed, I noticed light streaming from under the door. I peeked through the keyhole and saw my parents signing to each other, no longer furiously but calmly. Relieved that they had made up, I was finally able to sleep in peace. The next morning, when I noticed Mother frantically searching for something under the table and everywhere else in the living room, I took the wedding band off the electric switch and handed it to her. She looked at me softly and thanked me with her eyes.

As a child, it frightened me when I saw my parents argue. Fortunately, these spats never went beyond verbal violence. My father never struck my mother. He never struck me either, in my childhood. Even so I always secretly took my mother's side. The problem was that I was never sure of how I stood with Father. With Mother I could always be sure, but Father was habitually cool and distant toward me, so much that I often felt sad. When I was disobedient, it sufficed for Mother to call Father for help and, when he directed his piercing, beetle-browed gaze at me, I would at once submit. Seen from the vantage point of an adult, I realize he was quite good at making me feel bad and was inept at making me feel good.

These angry scenes between my parents always disturbed me. One day I realized that my father's latest absence was unduly long. When I asked Mother about it, she told me that he was out of town looking for work and would soon come back. However, he did not.

After my father abandoned us we moved to Aunt Lena's home. She and her husband Joe, who was fifteen years older than she, were both deaf and they were very good to us. On days when school was closed Aunt Lena would take me to her stockbroker's and patiently try to explain to me what the figures on the ticker meant. Of course, I did not understand the intricacies of the stock market, but what mattered was that she communicated with me in a language, sign language, that I understood. She would also sign stories to me and, when I was at school, write me letters. Every Sunday, before I left for school, she would cook a chicken dinner for me.

Following an absence of nearly two and a half years, my father came back to my mother. At the time we were living in Aunt Lena's apartment on

Riverside Drive. At first, Mother did not want to take him back, but he kept trying to make her change her mind, promising that he would change. He was so persistent that she finally decided in his favor.

Aunt Lena was firmly opposed to the reconciliation. She argued that Father was not to be trusted, that because he had left Mother for such a long time, he was bound to do so again. And indeed, even before his absence of two years, he had often stayed away from home, especially after scenes with Mother. He would go by himself to see his deaf friends or visit the Union League Club of the Deaf where, with his superbly expressive signs, he was very popular as a great conversationalist. Despite Aunt Lena's misgivings, my parents reconciled. When Father went to Aunt Lena's apartment to remove our belongings, she refused to surrender them. She thought him a no-good who would only cause further grief to my mother. He left, but the following day he returned with a policeman, thus forcing Aunt Lena to surrender our things.

For years afterward Father and Aunt Lena remained cool to each other; it was only in their old age that they, by tacit agreement, again were on speaking, though not warm, terms.

> *At the time this all happened, I was not sure that I understood it. But, this could be why "Goldilocks and the Three Bears" was my favorite of all the fairy tales my parents signed to me. The three bears, Mama, Papa, and Baby bear, symbolized my family, and Goldilocks represented misfortune and ill fate that brought discord into our home, between my parents, and ultimately caused our dispersal.*

Everyday, I saw my cousins, bearing satchels with books, leave in the morning and come back in the afternoon, and I wondered at the regularity of their going and coming. When I asked Mother about it, she explained that school was a place where one learned to read, write, add, and subtract. I asked Mother why I could not go to school too, but she said I was too young, being only four, and had to wait until I was five. But I was already excited about going to school, and so Mother taught me the fingerspelling alphabet and, despite being deaf herself, tried to teach me to pronounce letters of the alphabet by showing me how to mouth them. Even so, I kept pestering her about school, continually asking when I could start attending it. To appease me, she taught me how to read the calendar and then showed me each day how many months and weeks and days remained until I would be five.

One morning some time after my fifth birthday, she acted particularly solemn. She dressed me from head to toe in my best clothes and led me to the subway. I wondered where we were going, but she looked so serious that I did not have the courage to ask her. So instead, I started counting the lights in the subway tunnel. For a change I also studied the pictures in the advertisements, which I could not read.

Finally we emerged at 164th Street in Manhattan and reached a massive, red-brick building with barred windows. We climbed the outside staircase and found ourselves first in a big lobby and then in what looked like a waiting room.

Mother sat silently with her hands folded while I stared at the pea-green walls. Suddenly, a tall thin woman with her hair combed into a bun appeared in the doorway. She was wearing a blue dress with a white collar, and a large bunch of keys hung from her belt. Her face scared me, it was so blank and thin-lipped.

Mother got up and nodded to the woman. The woman nodded back and signed to me, "Come with me."

I shook my head despairingly, looking at Mother and clinging to her skirt. "What? Why?" But she kneeled to bring her face to my level and signed, "Please go with her. This is school. Here you'll learn to read and write. I want you to be smart."

"No!" I protested. "I want to stay with you." Seeing the look of determination on her face, I begged her, "Please. Please."

"No. You will stay here all week. I will see you Friday." She kissed me quickly and left before I could catch her.

I wanted to run after her, but the blue-uniformed woman grabbed my wrist and held it firmly. I put up a struggle, but she was stronger. I could only watch as my mother glanced back at me and walked away.

Once Mother vanished, the woman started to drag me out of the room. I screamed and kicked, until I finally gave in and let myself be pulled along the long hallway without resisting. I followed her into the unknown world called school. She led me to a bathroom, where she roughly undressed me and started to scrub my body with a hard brush. When I resisted, she scrubbed harder so that I yowled with pain. Once again I gave in and then she became a little gentle. Still, all her movements were rough, and she treated me as if I were an object, a thing to be washed.

She toweled me dry with the same rough, indifferent movements and made me dress in the school uniform. Then she led me to a large, empty room with gray, peeling walls. She pointed to a bench near a window and told me to wait there.

From the window I could see a handful of children at play in a desolate-looking paved schoolyard. I walked to another window and saw the Hudson River and the George Washington Bridge. I pressed my brow against the windowpane, feeling alone and abandoned in this bleak and nightmarish new world and wondered why Mother had left me so abruptly.

I felt tears trickling down my cheeks as I stared at the gray walls. Suddenly the door opened and two boys my age rushed in. They were laughing and pummeling each other until they noticed me and froze. One of them pointed at me and signed, "New boy!"

As I stared uncertainly, the boy who had pointed at me left the room, leaving me alone with the other boy. He eyed me without saying or signing anything and stayed close to the door at the other end of the long room. He seemed as uncomfortable as I, and this added to the strangeness of the moment.

Then the door opened again and a horde of boys poured in, led by the boy who had pointed at me. They ranged in age from five to eight, my age group. They approached and surrounded me. I noticed that they all wore the same uniform as I—a blue shirt, gray knickers, black stockings, and black high-topped shoes. I also noticed that they were signing the same phrase, "New boy!" as they jostled each other to get closer to me. There was intense curiosity on their faces. My fear was gone, and in its place I felt amazement and wonder that they also were deaf. The feeling of estrangement with the world that I had experienced ever since my encounter with the candy-store proprietor had dissolved and I was stepping onto the shore of a world that was my own, the world to which I rightfully belonged and whose landscape was as familiar to me as a recurring dream. Here I did not have to share my toys in order to win the friendship of strangers living in another dimension. I felt a little safe now. I was no longer completely alone.

The boy who had brought in the others stationed himself directly in front of me and signed, "Home where?"

I did not know how to answer. After all, I was only five. I only pointed helplessly at the window and the world beyond it.

The boy, whose name, I learned later, was Stanley, signed again, "You new boy?"

I signed back, "Yes. Mother brought me here, but she left." And as I said that, I again felt abandoned and started to cry.

Stanley signed, "Yes, my mom brought me here too. Deaf school here."

"I want to go home!" I signed, sobbing.

But Stanley answered soberly, ignoring my tears, "No. We don't go home except sometimes on weekends. Here school, we play, make friends, all deaf."

Before I could answer, the woman who had brought me in appeared as if by magic, but then such sudden apparitions are familiar to the deaf, who cannot hear the sounds of doors opening or footsteps approaching. Towering above the crowd of little boys, who transferred their gaze to her, she signed to me, "What is your name?" She apparently wanted to see if I could spell my own name. When I fingerspelled, "Bernard," she turned to the boys and asked them, "What shall his name sign be?"

I looked on uncomprehendingly. "Name sign" was a new sign to me. Only later did I realize that in a school for the deaf everyone had a name sign. The boys looked at each other and tried out different combinations of name signs starting with the fingerspelled letter *B*. They placed the *B* on the cheek, on the chin, on the chest, and on the arm, but none of the signs satisfied the woman, until finally Stanley placed the handshape *B* on his brow. She liked it and nodded.

Once a person has a name sign, it is used throughout his or her school career. Sometimes it stays with the person forever, sometimes it changes when the person begins working. I was B-on-the-brow until high school.

The boys signed B-on-the-brow while pointing at me and began to introduce themselves to me. Each had a different name sign, sometimes connected to the initial letter of his name and sometimes relating to his physical appearance, or both. One boy had a scar on his cheek, and therefore his name sign was made by running a finger down the cheek. Another's name sign was made by placing a crooked finger in front of his nose, because he had a large, hooked nose. Still another's name sign was indicated by drumming the fingertips on a cheek because he had a round face. Stanley's own name sign was S-on-the-chin, and the woman's was R-on-the-left-shoulder because her name was Radulic.

Miss Radulic made the signs for eating and lining up, and the boys automatically lined up according to height. She took my hand and placed me between Stanley, who was just a mite taller than I, and Daniel, who was just a mite smaller but whose influence on my later life proved greater.

We marched single file down a long corridor until we arrived at open double doors that revealed a huge dining room bustling with hundreds of older boys and girls taking their places at tables seating ten each. We little ones sat down at five long tables, also ten to a table. When everyone was seated, lights flashed to catch our attention and a man in a black uniform at one end of the hall motioned us to rise while he signed grace.

Stanley sat down next to me. He assumed the role of my guide and protector and showed me how to help myself from the trays of bread and butter and the bowl of spaghetti and how to pass them on to my neighbor, Daniel. He also explained to me that our group was called by the fingerspelled sign *BK*, which meant Boys' Kindergarten, and that the man in the black uniform was the head supervisor.

I was overwhelmed by all these new sights, especially by the sight of my table neighbors, who signed with such zest and animation. They elbowed each other, roared with laughter, and made a mess with their food. In retrospect, I think they must have been very noisy as well, but that is only an educated guess.

I noticed that Stanley's signs were more fluid and clearer than those of the other boys at my table. By contrast, Daniel signed diffidently and awkwardly. Even though I was the new boy, he and others, too, seemed to look up to me, perhaps because of my signing skill—this was a new sensation for me. Later, I realized that deaf children of deaf parents usually have better signing skills. At the time I was quite content, feeling that I was among my equals.

When we filed back to the playroom, it was still light. I followed Daniel and the other kids to the playground and watched them kick a ball. Before I knew it, it was bedtime, and Radulic escorted us upstairs to the fourth floor, where we entered a large, high-ceilinged room that contained forty beds. Radulic led me by the hand to an empty bed and signed, "This is your bed. You sleep here." She gave me a nightshirt that reached down to my knees, showed me where to hang my towel and toothbrush, and left me. At the door, she switched the lights off and on to catch everybody's attention and signed, "Go to sleep!" before turning the lights off for the night.

I was exhausted by the avalanche of new experiences and almost instantly fell asleep. But some time deep in the night I awoke. Alone in the darkness, with only a small nightlight shining far off near the door of this vast dormitory, I began to miss my familiar room at home and my mother, and I started to cry.

Suddenly, I saw the beam of a flashlight coming through the opening door. An indistinct figure directed the light at my face, which blinded me, so I closed my eyes, only to open them again and watch the beam approach me. I closed my eyes to show that I was sleeping, but it kept shining on my face. Finally, I opened my eyes and found the night watchman staring down at me. He had a kind face and he offered me a piece of hard candy. I took it. He patted my head and left.

As I unwrapped the candy and sucked it in my mouth, I wondered how he knew that I was crying and not asleep. At home, when I was alone in my room and cried, my mother and father never came to see what was wrong, but here somebody came and unerringly identified me among the sleepers as the source of the weeping. Thus I gained another insight into the nature of deafness. The sound of my crying must have alerted the watchman, as it could not have alerted my parents for the simple reason that they were deaf themselves. This realization that my parents were deaf, too, strengthened my feeling of solidarity with the new deaf world I was in and made my longing for my mother more bearable. I was among my own kind.

I was five years old and the country was in the middle of the Great Depression. After my father left us, he wandered all over the country, often as a hobo, taking on whatever jobs he could get. He finally returned when I was six and ill with mastoiditis. He visited me in the hospital and began to court my mother until finally she was too exhausted to resist and took him back. She later told me that she had done it for my sake, so I could have a home.

Uprooted from my home, I soon adapted myself to my new surroundings. The other children in my kindergarten class used a mixture of signs, gestures, and mime resembling a series of film frames with cuts, long shots, and close-ups, quite dramatic. They did not just use language—they acted it out. One reason they did so was that most of them had hearing parents and knew little about sign language. At school, however, they began to pick up new signs from the deaf children of deaf parents, and this greatly expanded their language skills and made social beings of these lonely little children who until then had no one to communicate with and no way of communicating.

To me, being with my deaf peers became the familiar part. The unfamiliar part, which made me even more conscious of my deafness, of my being different, was the emphasis placed at that school on speech and lipreading. After being given a battery of hearing and other tests, I was placed in the first grade.

Wearing earphones and heavy old-fashioned hearing aids in chest-borne harnesses, we must have looked like extraterrestrial aliens. One after another, the teacher would summon us to sit facing her and then try to teach us to pronounce letters of the alphabet with the aid of flashcards and popping balloons that simulated plosive sounds. When my turn came, she pointed to letters on the blackboard and said something to me. I heard only indistinct noise in my earphones—hearing aids did not help me then nor do they now—but I knew what she expected me to do and pronounced the first few letters as well as I could, remembering the coaching my mother had given me.

The teacher looked surprised and excited. She left the classroom only to reappear with another teacher, to whom she said, "Look, Bernard can talk." They watched me as I uttered the next few letters, and they clapped and said "Bravo." Then the other teacher left.

I had gone from *A* through *J*. Now it was time to pronounce *K*. I did, and the teacher frowned. "No! Repeat." I repeated. "Wrong," she said and beckoned at me to approach and sit down at her desk. "Again!" Again I uttered *K*, and again she frowned. She inserted a finger into my mouth and tried to push my tongue back against the palate. I started to gag and choke. She became frustrated and tried another tack: she raised her left arm horizontally and placed her right arm under it so that her right hand, simulating the tongue, struck repeatedly from below the end of her left elbow, simulating the palate. I got the idea and positioned the tip of my tongue under my palate. But the sounds I made still left her dissatisfied. She made me sit down in front of a mirror in a corner and practice on my own while she went to work with the other children.

I practiced in front of the mirror until the end of the class, but nothing came of it. Next day the teacher again sat me down in front of the mirror and bade me keep practicing. This went on for days, until suddenly she jumped up and exclaimed, "Yes. You almost got it. Repeat!" I repeated, and finally got it—or at least she had made me think so. She left the classroom for a minute and returned with the principal; then she asked me to demonstrate my newly gained skill. Apparently I pronounced *K* to their satisfaction because they beamed, clapped their hands, and patted me on the shoulder.

From then on I practiced saying *K* in my bed every night until I fell asleep. I practiced uttering this one letter of the alphabet as earnestly as if my life depended on it.

Then came Open House day. The auditorium was filled with parents and other visitors and a dozen of us kids sat on the dais, with our teacher in front of us. She made a speech to the audience, but none of us on the stage knew what she talked about. When she finished, she summoned us one by one and made us recite something to the audience. From my seat on the extreme right I could lipread parts of the teacher's instructions to the other children, and I gathered that they had to do with the recitation of nursery rhymes. Every time a child finished "performing," the entire audience applauded. I stared at this mass of faces and clapping hands, and far in the back I discerned my mother's face.

Finally, the teacher pointed at me. I felt surprised, not knowing what she wanted of me. She beckoned to me and, obediently, I got up and walked to the center of the stage, facing her. She said something that I did not understand at all, and I helplessly gestured as if to ask, "What do you want me to do?"

She smiled and made that all too familiar gesture of one arm hitting the other from below. I panicked, conscious that the eyes of the entire audience, my very first audience, were directed at me, and I signed, "I forgot."

She smiled, "No. You can do it. Come on, Bernard."

I glanced at the audience. Everyone was leaning forward in suspense. I realized that I was keeping them waiting. I looked at Mother. There was an expression of wonder on her face, as if she wanted to know what her little Bernard would do next. I wetted my lips and then swallowed to clear my parched throat. I opened my mouth, positioned the back of my tongue on my palate, and made an explosive sound, just once.

The audience looked bewildered and there was no applause, but the teacher patted me on the shoulder and said, "Come on! Give Bernard a big hand! He has worked very hard to make this one sound. And he made it!"

People clapped perfunctorily. The teacher told me to bow. I bowed, one hand on my stomach and the other behind my back. As I straightened up, I glanced at Mother and saw from the expression on her face that she did not understand what was happening.

Let me now make a jump in time. One Friday when I was sixteen and came home from school for the weekend, my parents and I were sitting at the dining room table, chatting over coffee. Among the other experiences we shared I suddenly remembered the *K* incident. For some reason, I asked my mother if she remembered my first performance before an audience. She said she did remember me on stage but did not know why. I told her the reason, and she clapped a hand over her mouth and signed, "I've a confession to make. When you were little and I taught you how to pronounce letters of the alphabet, I skipped *K* because I did not know how to pronounce it myself."

"Oh," I signed, "so that's why I had so much trouble with that letter. Let me teach it to you now." I started the "arm over arm" demonstration, but Mother laughingly shooed me off, "No, no. Please don't—I don't want to."

I persisted until she finally gave in. And I did succeed in teaching her how to say that *K*. From then on, Mother could go to a restaurant and order a cup of coffee and make herself understood.

That is the funny part, but the sad part is that such an enormous amount of time was and still is being spent on teaching deaf children how to speak and lipread. Most of these children never learn to speak and lipread adequately, and their speech remains harsh and unaccented to the ear of the hearing. Most of that time could have been spent more profitably on teaching them to read and write well. That is one reason why many deaf children are less literate than their hearing counterparts. And if they go to oral schools, they become handicapped in other ways as well because, being forbidden to use sign language, they lose the opportunity to broaden their linguistic knowledge. Fortunately for me, my school was not strictly an oral school.

After our "speech lesson" my mother indeed ordered that "cup of coffee" by voice but not often, because whenever she did it, others stared at her, struck by the unusual quality of her speech. My teaching her how to say K was like the blind leading the blind, like teaching French when one has never heard a French word. But stranger situations occur when the hearing lead the deaf. The teacher who was so excited about my uttering the letters of the alphabet was deceiving me; to this day my speech is somewhat unintelligible. Even now this deceit is still widely practiced among speech and lipreading teachers, who, being used to their pupils' pronunciation, unwittingly encourage them to believe that, once they graduate and go out into the hearing world, their speech can be understood. I just cannot tell whether it is deliberate deceit or self-delusion brought on by belief in oralism, a particularly dogmatic faith developed by doctrinaires to whom any deaf child who cannot learn to speak and lipread (meaning an overwhelming majority of deaf children) must necessarily be an academic failure and, therefore, fit only for menial jobs.

This realization became concrete for me much later when I was a grown man and I had a disheartening experience that I can now laugh at.

My teachers had made me feel proud of my speech. Now and then hearing people whom I met would ask me questions about it, as if it were one of my most important accomplishments; "How did you learn to speak?" "Was it difficult?" "Can you hear some?" and so on. The upshot was that I got the impression that my speech was something I could brag about. And I was not unjustifiably proud. After all, I had suffered through all those years of speech lessons at school, with everyone—teachers, girlfriends, kids with whom I played on the street, cousins, aunts—correcting my speech all the time. I always tried to be a good sport and retain my positive attitude. In particular, I had thought I could do pretty well when talking to just one person at a time.

Then one day I had a humbling experience. On a visit to California I was picked up at the airport by three friends from college days. On the way to Riverside, we decided to stop for lunch at a restaurant just off the freeway.

We entered the restaurant and found we had to wait in a long line. No problem, we had time. The hostess, with pad and pencil in hand, went from one person to another in the line asking their names. When she finally approached us, and asked how many, I replied four. Then she asked my name, and I said "Bragg," just as I had been taught to pronounce it over the years.

She did not get it. "What?" I repeated a bit louder, "Bragg." She cupped her ear and said, "Can't hear you." I growled, "Bragg." People in the line turned their heads to look at me. I blushed a little. Damn it, I thought, I was probably shouting.

"Sorry," was all she said, shaking her head.

I decided to break the impasse by pronouncing distinctly each letter in my name, "B-R-A-G-G." She wrote down each letter, then she showed me the pad.

Incredulously, I saw that she had written down, "P-O-I-C." My companions, leaning over my shoulder, also read it. They burst out laughing. I looked at them, and deadpanned, "Do I really speak that badly?" They tried to stifle their laughter. One demurred, "Well, there's lots of noise here for one thing."

Let me note here that all three of my friends were hard-of-hearing. I was the only stone-deaf person among them, or deaf as a post as the saying goes.

Anyhow, I said soberly, "That's kind of you." Then another friend chimed in, pokerfaced, "You know, *G* sounds like *C*."

"Thanks so very much," I exaggerated.

During all this conversation the hostess kept waiting. Finally, pointing to the paper with "P-O-I-C" in her hand, she asked me if that was my correct name. Half-smiling, I said, "Oh, yes, that's right."

Then I told my companions, tongue in cheek, "That's quite an eye opener for me. Just think of all those years I kept trying to improve my speech."

They laughed, as I had wanted them to. The hostess came back, looked at the pad in her hand and mouthed broadly, "Mr. POIC."

I quickly raised my hand, grinning, "That's me."

My constant, enforced, and ultimately fruitless efforts to learn how to speak and lipread were not the only bane of my existence at the New York School for the Deaf (NYSD), or Fanwood, as we called it, after Fanny's Woods, the name of the estate the school occupied on 164th Street. Even after the school was moved in 1938 to White Plains, New York, we continued to call it Fanwood. The NYSD modeled itself after a military school, so the pupils and the teachers and administrators all wore uniforms. A military school is always more or less authoritarian, and mine contained some teachers who tried to decide for us, the deaf, whether what we did was right or wrong rather than whether it was acceptable or normal behavior for children our age. They drummed into us the virtues of being "normal," of being "just like the hearing." They tried to force us to be, rather than to become what we are. Fortunately, there were some exceptions; otherwise, I would not have such fond memories of NYSD.

Mr. Ryder, our fifth-grade teacher, wanted us to believe we were far too young to decide what came naturally to us, and what was not to be questioned. After all, we were deaf and we did not know any better. We believed him because we were living in an isolated world. There were ten of us in his class, twelve- and thirteen-year-old boys.

Mr. Ryder was rather small, very slender, in his mid-forties. The balding spot on his head was surrounded by a horseshoe of fine-spun reddish hair. His close-cropped mustache was equally silky and reddish, and even his teeth had something silky about them. He wore a close-fitting black military uniform, a shirt with a stiff white collar, and a black tie. Crossed-rifle ornaments and the metal insignia "NYSD" were fastened on his lapels. He obviously took special pains to acquire a spit-and-polish military look, but, as I realize now, to an impartial observer and also to such sharp observers as children, his efforts could not disguise his habitual air of a fussy, aging schoolmaster. He was strict and demanding like a martinet, but at the same time he was neurotically squeamish—a fatal combination. He was a man who would become furious over the slightest noises we made (which we, of course, made unconsciously), such as scraping the floor with our feet, tapping pencils or drumming fingers on our desks, stamping on the floor, and writing on the blackboard with chalk in such a way as to make a nerve-racking scraping noise.

Above all, Mr. Ryder could not tolerate the sound of our laughter. He must have had a mania about it. Being deaf, we had no idea how our laughter sounded. We thought it came naturally to us and was not something we had to learn. But Mr. Ryder did his best to disabuse us of that notion. Anyway, I did not realize at the time that laughter is man's best invention.

Whenever one of us laughed, Mr. Ryder would glare at the culprit and shout in sign, "Stop laughing!" Or he would say, "If only you could hear yourself laugh, you'd be nauseated. It makes hearing people think you are animals like cows and pigs." We did not know what "nauseated" meant, but with the cunning of the ignorant, we guessed it must be something unpleasant.

Mr. Ryder always picked on one boy in particular, Sam. I gather the sound of Sam's laughter must have been especially braying or harsh. He tried to suppress it because Mr. Ryder looked daggers at him. One morning Mr. Ryder, on entering the classroom, announced he was going to teach us how to laugh the proper way. Personally, I felt puzzled by the notion that laughter could be taught. He asked us to rise, place our hands on our ribs, open our mouths and, without making a sound, let air in and out while shaking our rib cage and feeling that shaking with our hands. Then we had to put our hands down and say "aaah," "aaah," "aaah," again and again.

Mr. Ryder patted a student's head approvingly, as if petting a kitten, if the "aaah" came from his chest and not from his head. After a while, he asked us to place our hands on our ribs again and, while letting air in and out in short spurts, to say "aaaaaahhhhhhh."

We must have looked ridiculous, but Mr. Ryder praised us for the "beautiful, proper, natural" way our laughter sounded. He congratulated all of us, except Sam, and told us hearing people would never guess we were deaf. He ordered Sam to sit in the back, all by himself, isolated from us, simply because he had failed the lesson in laughter.

Years later, while in the company of a hearing friend, I met Sam. We chatted over old times and had some laughs. After Sam left, my hearing friend told me that he found Sam somewhat strange because whenever he laughed, no sound came from him.

My schoolmates and I grew up in a world where we dared not question the decisions of hearing people. But there came a time when I dared to challenge their decisions and the power they were exercising over us.

Marvin ran toward me, gesturing for me to stop the hand press I was working on. I pushed the stop rod and asked him what had happened.

"Know what? Your name is in the *Fanwood Journal*."

I was surprised. "Which page?"

"The front page. It's being printed now."

"Really? I'll sneak a look at it. Hope Mr. Renner won't catch me."

I left my machine and, crouching so that I would not be seen, crept past the booth enclosing Mr. Renner's office. It helped that I was only fourteen years old and not very tall.

I approached the big printing press on which the monthly school newspaper was being printed. I grabbed a copy off the press and looked at the first page. And indeed, in the center there was a paragraph announcing the results of the Stanford Achievement Tests (SAT). But my expectations turned to shock as I saw that I had ranked third. This simply could not be. A month ago it had been announced in class that I had scored the highest among the three boys who took the SAT. The shock turned to horror; this was merely a school newspaper, but to me it was as important as *The New York Times*. It was read not only by the students and teachers at Fanwood but also by about five hundred parents, including mine, and alumni. To me, that readership was the entire outside world.

Third-ranked! I couldn't believe it. I drew back and asked Marvin to stop the press. He signed with one hand, while carrying a stack of newspapers with the other, "Are you crazy? Can't do it. Go see Mr. Renner."

I rushed to Mr. Renner's office. "Mr. Renner! I'm sorry to interrupt you, but you've got to stop the printing press."

"Why? What's the matter?"

"Stop the press, please. A terrible mistake has been made."

He got up. "What's wrong?" He looked scared.

I showed him the front page, pointing at the offending paragraph. "The names are in the wrong order. The highest scorer on that test was me."

His face grew cold. "How dare you leave your workstation and sneak away; why are you nosing into other people's business?"

I signed haltingly, "I was told my name was on the front page. Naturally, out of curiosity, I went to see it. I can't understand how this mistake could have happened. Could you please stop the printing and investigate before the paper is distributed?"

"Go back to your machine and work. Mind your own business! I received this copy from Mr. Ryder's office."

"I can't imagine a mistake like that. The proper order for this year was me first, then Peter and Rick."

"If you don't go back to work at once, I'll send you to the principal's office."

I gave up and walked back in the blackest of moods. I worked on the hand press, feeding and removing the papers mechanically until lunch break, when, instead of going to the dining hall from the print shop, I ran to the Academic Building to see my social studies teacher, Mrs. Nies, who was still in her classroom correcting some papers. She looked up and saw me. Her stern face, with its carved features, was softened by eyes and mouth that radiated kindness and compassion and by being wreathed in curly white locks. When I told her what had happened, she said she knew I was the top-ranker and was sure this was a mistake or an oversight on Mr. Ryder's part. She then suggested that I see him directly about it. I thanked her and said, "That's what I thought, but I wanted to check with you first."

Her comment was entirely in keeping with her nature. "Trust yourself. Trust your own judgment."

I ran to the dining hall, where the dormitory supervisor stopped me and said I would be punished for my lateness by an hour's rifle drill at four o'clock. A fat lot did I care. I ate my lunch in silence, gulping down the standard fare of meatloaf, peas, and mashed potatoes, and then it was time to go to the Academic Building for my afternoon classes. When I entered the building I went first to Mr. Ryder's office, but he was not in, so I proceeded to my social studies class. The class started but my mind was not on it. I sat there and tried to figure out how to approach Mr. Ryder.

All of a sudden, the door opened and Mr. Ryder came in. We all stood up. Smiling he said, "Please be seated," and, stepping softly like a dapper cat, he approached Mrs. Nies and started to discuss something with her privately. It did not take long, and he turned around and started to leave. As he opened the door, I stood up, my heart pounding, and called out to him, "Mr. Ryder, excuse me."

He looked slightly surprised. "Yes, Bernard. What do you want?"

My mouth was dry. My throat hurt. I could not speak. So I signed, or rather stuttered in sign, shaking with emotion, "I only want you to know that there's a mistake in the school newspaper being printed today."

His eyes narrowed. "What mistake?"

"A mistake in the ranking of SAT scores. My name is listed third, but it should be first."

He said flatly, "That's not a mistake."

I was shocked. "But could you please explain?"

There was a half-smile on his face. "No. I can't. That's my business." And saying this, he closed the door behind him.

Everyone in the class was staring at me. Mrs. Nies told me to sit down and directed the class to continue. But my mind was not on the subject. I was dazed and upset as I ruminated over Mr. Ryder's mysterious answer. When class was dismissed, I approached Mrs. Nies and asked, "Did I understand Mr. Ryder right? Did he really say it was his business? I think that's as much my business as his."

She waited before answering, "Yes, Bernard, I know."

"What should I do? I can't let him get away with it. I don't know anymore whether it was a mistake or not, but I feel he owes me an explanation."

"Maybe you can—," she began.

"Do what? Ask Mr. Ryder again?"

"I don't know, but you must figure out for yourself what to do. Possibly I could help you but I'd much rather you helped yourself."

Never before had her simple wisdom and sweetness struck me with such impact. Just being with her softened my hurt. Not for long, though. Finally, I asked, "But how? Nobody will listen to me. Not Mr. Renner, not Mr. Ryder." And I added, all the while knowing how unjust I was to her, "Not even you. Perhaps I should go straight to Superintendent Bradford?" Her smile told me that was the decision she had expected me to make.

It was nearly four o'clock. I ran to the superintendent's office, but he was not in. I had to do the rifle drill, so I went to the storeroom to pick up a dummy rifle and walked my paces back and forth on the parapet facing the grand staircase fronting the driveway, thinking all the while of the letter I was going to write Superintendent Bradford. As soon as it was five o'clock, I proceeded to the dormitory and asked a supervisor for permission to use his typewriter.

I typed the letter with my index finger, erasing error after error all the while. When it was finally done to my satisfaction, I ran with it to the superintendent's office and slid it under the door. Then it was back to the dormitory and an evening during which I largely kept to myself.

That night was one of my worst. I could hardly sleep; I kept repeating in my mind Mr. Ryder's words. The following morning I went to the Vocational Building and worked at my hand press, watching expressionlessly as Marvin picked up a stack of school newspapers from the big printing press. The slowness of the press belied its size, for it was an old-fashioned machine that took more than a day to print a mere thousand copies of a four-page school newspaper.

Suddenly, the door to the print shop opened. Superintendent Bradford hurried in, with a sheet of paper in hand, and went straight to Mr. Renner's office. I could see them huddle together. After a while, Superintendent Bradford left and Mr. Renner rushed to Marvin and ordered, "Stop! Stop the press!"

Marvin pushed the stop button and the press came to a halt. Then Mr. Renner picked up Marvin's stack, carried it outside, and dumped it into a big trash can. He then sent another boy to the linotype with some copy to set. Soon the boy came back with a linotype slug, and Mr. Renner placed it in the matrix, which he reinserted in the press bed. He pushed the start button and the giant ponderously came alive. When the first new issue of the newspaper appeared, Mr. Renner stopped the press, picked up the copy, proofread it, and then told Marvin to go ahead with the printing.

After Mr. Renner returned to his office, I sneaked past his office and peeked at the freshly printed page; there, on the front page, my name was listed first. Noon came. I stepped out of the Vocational Building and saw Superintendent Bradford hurrying to his car. He noticed me and stopped, beckoning to me. "Bernard, I postponed my flight this morning so I could attend to the business connected with your letter. I talked with Mr. Ryder. That was just a mistake which has now been corrected. Are you satisfied now?"

I was dumbfounded; I could not answer. I stared at him until, finally, he continued. "Mr. Ryder used a three-year average to determine the scores. That can't be done because the SAT only measures your progress over a year."

The realization struck me that that was how Peter got to be top-ranked! He was Mr. Ryder's pet. However, I kept this to myself and replied, "Thank you very much."

"I only did what was right. Bye, Bernard."

I watched him leave, and, even though I should have been feeling happy, I felt dejected, now that the enormity of the injustice done me sank in.

Years passed and I became a teacher myself. One year I attended a convention of teachers of the deaf in Vancouver, Washington, joyously meeting old friends and making new ones. Among the familiar faces one stood out—Mr. Ryder, grayer now but as nattily dressed as ever, still wearing the same squeamish expression. I noticed him first and was not particularly anxious to greet him. He came to me, however, shook my hand, and ultimately asked me to have a drink with him at the hotel bar.

We ordered drinks. He remarked, "Look where you are now, and rightly so. You were my star pupil." He raised his glass, "To good old Fanwood." We clinked glasses and drank.

I never met Mr. Ryder again, but I was told that he was dismissed from his post as principal when it was discovered that he lacked a master's degree. He then moved to Los Angeles, where he taught at a small oral school until he died.

But I loved my school, despite the presence of such unsavory types as Mr. Ryder, who are bound to crop up in any institutional setting. It was my own world, where I could mix with other deaf children and lead that normal social life which I could not experience fully among my hearing peers in New York City.

Besides, people like Ryder are counterbalanced by people like Bob Panara. One day, in the fall of my junior year at the NYSD, a new face appeared like a thunderbolt and changed my life.

The door opened and the new teacher walked in. We rushed to our seats, staring at him with astonishment. He was a tall, black-haired, strikingly good looking young man and he wore a trim suit and tie. He approached the teacher's desk and sat down behind it. "My name is Robert Panara, and I'm a graduate of Gallaudet College," he signed. From Gallaudet? That meant he was deaf like us! He asked us to introduce ourselves, and then he described the subjects he would go over with us in our two-year college preparatory class—composition, grammar, literature, and algebra.

We drank in with our eyes everything he signed. Using body language and facial expressions, he signed confidently and unerringly, showing us that he was someone to be reckoned with and that he loved to teach. In contrast to the choppy, abrupt, and often homemade signs we normally used among ourselves, his signs were a miracle of vividness and eloquence. Most of the other teachers in our experience mangled their signing and kept their faces wooden. They also used language that was way above our heads, building a communication barrier between us. Mr. Panara established immediate rapport with us because he was one of our own and could communicate with us in our own language, sign language.

But above all, what electrified and enthralled us about Mr. Panara was his very embodiment of a living, breathing revelation of the potential of sign language. Before we met him we had never realized that this, our native language, could be such a powerful vehicle for expressing the richest and subtlest feelings and conveying nuances of meaning as sophisticated as those of the most articulate English speakers and writers.

His approach was simple but effective. Some days he would devote an entire hour to explaining a single stanza of a poem, illustrating in sign the meaning of each word and phrase with unusual clarity, providing as it were a graphic and visual interpretation of the poem. Moreover, he demonstrated to us the meaning of rhythm and meter by tapping his feet and drawing sculptures in the air with his hands.

On other days he would describe to us the plots of plays by Shakespeare, Aeschylus, or Eugene O'Neill, and of books by such authors as Hawthorne and Dumas, providing capsule descriptions of the principal characters. His technique was not so much to describe as to enact. When discussing that part of the plot of *Cyrano de Bergerac* in which the hero duels with the marquis who taunted him for his long nose, for example, Mr. Panara would parry and thrust with an imaginary rapier.

He caught and held our attention not just because of the lucidity of his signing but because of his evident love and enthusiasm for literature. At the same time he taught us something about English, until then a strange second language to us native signers, by interpreting in sign not just the overall meaning but every individual word in lines of poetry or quotations from plays, thus making them finally come alive for us.

I always entered his class with eager anticipation. My classmates, too, clearly enjoyed Mr. Panara's dramatic way of teaching. To see him was, for me, to experience a continuous journey of discovery.

By this stage in my school career, I had developed a reputation for being an expressive signer. To be sure, till then my experience was mostly confined to rendering psalms and hymns in sign. At one of our weekly Jewish Bible classes, Meyer Lief, the deaf lay teacher, singled me out to sign the Twenty-third Psalm; and at the memorial services for Alice Judge, the school librarian, I was asked to sign the hymn, "Abide with me, Lord / Fast falls the evening tide. . . ." And more recently I had had the shaky experience of signing a poem to four hundred people at one of the Union League Club of the Deaf's monthly literary evenings. My father was supposed to give a rendition of Poe's "The Cask of Amontillado," but at the last minute he fell ill and I was asked to replace him. That was a moment I will never forget. There I stood on the dais with that big crowd facing me, and I froze for what seemed an endless moment. I saw people start signing to each other questioningly, and this finally spurred me into action. I received a standing ovation that night. To this day, old-timers whom I meet now and then enjoy reminding me of that unforgettable moment when I stood there frozen with fright.

At any rate, when Mr. Panara decided to produce a Christmas play, he picked me to codirect it with him as well as to act in it. The play was *A Christmas Carol* by Charles Dickens, and I played Scrooge.

One consequence of that experience was that Mr. Panara and I became good friends. Now and then he invited me to eat out with him. For the first time in my life I felt accepted as a deaf adult. Just as heady was the experience of writing stories with his help. I felt as if I had been sleeping all my life until he appeared to wake me up. Above all, he gave wings to those acting and directing talents that I had inherited from my father.

My father was the only deaf child in his family; all his brothers and sisters were literate young people with serious interests in the arts. One younger sister, Lenn, became a Shakespearean authority. Another older half-sister, Kate, took my father along to the opera and ballet as soon as he was old enough. Deaf though he was, he developed an appreciation for them by taking in these artistic experiences through his eyes.

One of my earliest theater memories is of going with my mother to see a play that Father produced, directed, and acted in at the local deaf club. The play was called *Auf Wiedersehen*, and my father starred in it as the father of a grown son and daughter whose escape from Germany was almost foiled. The villain, a Nazi officer who was a classmate of these young people, lets them leave Germany for the sake of old times but refuses to let the father leave. At the end, the father shoots himself.

The whole play was done in dramatic sign language. Melodramatic as it was, it left me enthralled and filled with admiration for my father, whose powerful and moving signing dominated the entire performance. He raged, wept, and was tortured by anguish, and the whole audience was swept up in his emotions. In the final act, alone on the stage, he looked at his children's photographs with inexpressible grief, then turned and walked away with shoulders hunched. The curtain descended. Suddenly, we felt the noise of a gunshot; it was such a mighty blast that, even though deaf, the audience was jolted by fright. The play was a roaring success among the deaf, like the other plays in which my father acted. It is a pity that at the time, the 1940s, the hearing world was not yet ready to appreciate signed plays because my father would have become a great actor.

If my fate as an actor was more fortunate than my father's, it was largely because Mr. Panara was the first to encourage what was and is best in me.

A comet like Mr. Panara could not blaze long over our school. After a couple of years he moved on to a fitter place—he was offered a teaching post at Gallaudet College. Gallaudet had cropped up frequently in my conversations with Mr. Panara. To us deaf, then and now, Gallaudet University in Washington, D.C., the world's only liberal arts university for deaf students, is our Athens and Harvard combined. Every ambitious deaf schoolchild dreams of taking and passing the entrance examinations to Gallaudet. I too dreamed of it, and Mr. Panara encouraged me to pursue my dreams.

I brought my face close to the shower nozzle, surrendering myself to the delicious sensation of the spray. This was my last night at Fanwood after thirteen years. In the fall I would be entering Gallaudet. I was looking forward toward a carefree summer, free of the constant supervision by dormitory counselors, free of having to march in a file from the dormitory to the classrooms and the dining hall, free of punishment drills with the dummy rifle and white gloves. Oh, sweet freedom!

My mood was abruptly spoiled when, through clouds of steam I beheld a maliciously scowling face. It was Silver, the same Daniel Silver I had met on my first day at the NYSD, and with whom I had grown up ever since. I rubbed my eyes and looked again. He looked all wrong. The message he had signed to me looked all wrong too. Had he really signed that he was going to kill me? Was I in my right mind? Was he kidding? I had never before seen such a savage snarl on his face. I asked him to repeat.

Chopping the air violently with his hands, he signed, "You saw me all right."

I noticed another naked figure in the shower room. Through the cloud of steam I discerned the face and torso of Michelangelo's David supported unsteadily on two bony polio-ravaged shanks. It was Goldblum. It seems my eyes had been closed a long time and I had not seen either of them enter. I asked Goldblum, "Did you see what he said?"

"Yes."

I glanced at Silver, but his face bore such a forbidding expression that I asked Goldblum instead, "Is he serious or kidding?"

Goldblum was obviously as perplexed as I and anxious to smooth things over. He signed earnestly, "I'm sure he is joking."

Silver lashed out at him and told him to, "Get lost!" Then, face to face with me, he snapped, "I meant what I said."

This was getting scary, and I still did not know why he had made his threat. With a forced bravado I signed to him, "Okay, what are you waiting for? Why not go ahead and kill me now?"

"Not now, I'll wait."

"Why wait? Why bother telling me now?"

"I just want you to know that now."

I tried the ironic approach. "If you say you'll kill me, could you at least tell me when? What date? And perhaps you could also tell me how?"

He burst out, "I'll tell you when. I'll wait until you reach the pinnacle of success. I know you will go far. Then your life will be all the more precious to you."

"Oh, I see. And then you'll expect me to grovel and cringe. Isn't that what you mean?"

"You got it! But I haven't yet decided how to finish your life."

Goldblum broke in. "Hold it! What's wrong with you two? You're acting as if you're in some play."

But he shrank back on his two spindly legs when Silver turned violently against him and signed with broad gestures as if trying to assault him, "You stay out!"

"I don't get it," Goldblum persisted, his courage returning. "You two have been pals for years. Why are you enemies all of a sudden?" Addressing me, he asked, "What have you done to make him that furious?"

"Search me," I answered. "I have no idea what's come over him." I turned to Silver and asked, "If you've got something against me, let's have it out. Tell me what it is." I waited, but the only response I got was a menacing smile on his face.

Neither Goldblum's famous powers of persuasion, which even then made him a leader of the deaf, nor my reasonableness made any impact on Silver. He laughed sardonically. "That would be the easy way out for you. No way. Finished! I won't discuss it! Period! You saw what I said!" He slashed the air with his hands so close to my face that I drew back in self-defense.

Enjoying my reaction, he scornfully turned toward his shower nozzle. Goldblum hobbled back to his nozzle. I adjusted the spray of my own nozzle to cold, hoping it would wash away what seemed a bad dream. But I could not regain my previous mood of exhilaration. I turned off the shower, toweled myself dry, and walked out, ignoring Silver and Goldblum.

Back in my room I could not sleep. I sat down on the windowsill and looked at the starlit night, trying to figure out the mystery of how I could have offended Silver. We were such good friends, and now this! I reviewed the history of our friendship. Not only was he almost my double as far as build, hair, and features, but he was also my frequent companion. We complemented each other; I excelled in the drama club and in classroom work, had passed the entrance examinations to Gallaudet, and was a cadet captain. Silver excelled in sports and was among the school's best basketball players, but he felt insecure about his English and often relied on me to write love letters for him. Still, we never were in love with the same girl, so this could not be the source of the conflict. Besides, my writing his love letters seemed only to satisfy some kind of vanity in him because he knew how to handle women, a knowledge which we all envied. I thought we were pretty well matched.

I hoped his anger, whatever the source, would fade in time and we would be friends again. I resolved not to be bothered by his threat. As for that "pinnacle of success" in my life that he said he was waiting for, I would have a long way to go if I ever hoped to reach it, since the world in the early 1950s was closed to the deaf. Printing and teaching were just about the only trade and profession open to us. So how could Silver decide that I would go far? What did he mean then? Perhaps he was upset because I was chosen to give the valedictory address at tomorrow's graduation? If not that, what then?

I gnawed on these troubling questions until sleep shut my eyes. In the morning I put on my uniform—blue shirt, black tie, gray coat with the four stripes of a cadet captain on each sleeve, gray trousers with a black stripe running down each side, and a hat with a shiny black leather visor. Just like the uniforms at West Point.

The auditorium was full. I delivered my valedictory address with confidence. I had worked on it for a month with the help of my English teacher, Miss Heney, and it was full of the usual expressions—"face the future," "thank you," and "good-bye." From time to time I looked at the audience. My parents, aunt, and uncle were there. In the front row sat my teachers, some of whom I had worshiped for their genuine dedication. Behind me on the stage were the unspeakable Mr. Ryder, and now faceless and nameless notables.

One sentence in my address seemed particularly fitting to me. I looked at Silver, who was sitting among the other graduates in the second row, arms folded on his chest, eyes fixed on me with clinical curiosity, and I emphatically signed directly to him, "Those who experience blows and frustrations in life can benefit from them. Adversity makes them better men." I thought it a perfect message for Silver and I looked into his eyes as if to say, "Mark it well." But he did not stir and eyed me insolently.

I finished my address. Then the superintendent gave his little spiel of uplifting farewell to the graduating class and handed out the diplomas. There was a concluding prayer and the ceremony was over. We cadets got up and marched out of the auditorium and around the campus common. Then we approached the flagpole. I faced my company, Company B, and signed, "Present arms!" Twirling their rifles like batons, they executed this ritual with martial precision. Then I about-faced toward the flag, whipped the sword out of my scabbard, placed the hilt against my brow with a flourish in a final salute to the flag, about-faced again toward my troop, and, feeling moved by the finality of this moment, ending this stage in my life, I brought my hand upward to spell, "Dismissed!" The cadets broke up and scattered to greet their families and friends.

As I waited for my family, Silver approached me once more. I hoped he would explain his conduct and forget and forgive, but instead, he walked up to me and signed, "I know you meant those words for me. No way. I haven't changed my mind a bit. Remember it well."

I finally signed back, "I'm sorry our friendship has to end like this."

He shrugged, "I am not," and he turned and left.

I was taken aback by the quality of his signing. As it had been the day before, his signing was that of a man with fire in his belly. He gestured rapidly, breathing heavily, like one whose patience is at end; his chin was thrust forward, his teeth were bared in unnatural laughter, and his eyes glinted with fury. This was a complete change from the old Silver, the good sport and cheery signer. I found this metamorphosis even more disquieting than his threats.

I was soon surrounded by my parents, relatives, friends, and teachers. They embraced and kissed me and shook my hand. But I could not enjoy my graduation and newfound freedom. I tasted ashes in my mouth.

Once inside my uncle's car, I turned to take a last look at the school buildings from the rear window. They grew smaller and smaller, like things of the past, receding in memory. But to me the terrible threat that loomed over me in that blue June sky grew in magnitude.

It kept hovering at the edge of my consciousness during my first three years at Gallaudet, years that flew at times and dragged at others. I threw myself into activities at Gallaudet—studying, rehearsing in plays, being with friends, joining a fraternity, but the awareness of Silver's threat never left me entirely, and at times it made me feel like a marked man, one singled out for a peculiar fate.

Silver had disappeared after graduation. I found his sudden disappearance disturbing. The world of the deaf is a small one, where everyone knows what everyone else is doing, yet whenever I asked mutual friends and acquaintances from New York about him, they could give me no answer. I would have felt better, I would have had peace of mind, if I had known that he had found some stable job, gotten married, and had children, or even if I had just known where he was. But he had simply vanished without a trace.

Then he reappeared, unexpectedly yet expectedly, at the end of these three years. I was sitting in my room in College Hall, typing out a column for the *Buff and Blue*, Gallaudet's student newspaper, when I felt forceful knocking at the door.

I got up, opened the door, and saw a freshman, who informed me, "A couple of guys want to see you downstairs."

"Who? Why don't they come up? Why call me out?"

But he answered, "I don't know. They said they're from New York."

It took only a moment for me to bound down the staircase and emerge outside. When I saw who was waiting for me I froze. It was Silver. I recognized him instantly, although since I last had seen him his face had acquired a beefy color, the color of a man who spends his life outdoors, and his hairline had receded a bit. His face remained impassive as he looked at me. I was stricken with a sudden dread but managed to hide it.

I recognized his companion too. He was Roggins, the school bully at Fanwood. Unlike Silver, he smiled at me, but his was the crafty, thick-lipped smile of a mugger ready to browbeat and rob any passerby he deemed harmless.

Yet to me, Silver's stony face looked more menacing. For an awkward moment I wondered what to say, and finally I signed hello to them.

Without any preliminaries, as if he had seen me only yesterday, Silver signed matter-of-factly, "Could I talk with you?"

I decided to take it lightly. "Sure, come up to my room."

They followed me up the stairs. Once inside my room, their eyes took in its interior—the double-tiered bunks, the four desks and chairs, the book-cases. When they faced me again, I invited them to sit down.

Silver began jokingly, "So when are you going to become a professor?"

"What do you mean?"

"I asked because you have a talent for lectures. I didn't forget your graduation-day 'lecture,'" he said with a smirk. Then he chortled, "Too bad it fell on deaf ears. Real deaf ears."

Roggins laughed uproariously as if on cue, like a hyena, displaying a mouthful of hyena-like teeth. I alone did not laugh.

After a pregnant pause Silver looked at Roggins. "Could I talk with Bragg in private?"

Roggins answered, "I'll wait outside." He saluted me and left. It was an insolent salute, but then, everything about him was insolent and threatening.

I was alone with Silver. I felt like cursing myself for my stupidity. Could it be that it was all prearranged, with Roggins serving as a lookout? How could I be so dumb and make the whole thing easier for them? If I were to try to escape, Silver might shoot me in the back, and outside there was Roggins ready to grab me. I'd rather face Silver and perhaps persuade him to drop the gun—if he had one.

Unlike three years ago, he was no longer signing like a man possessed, about to commit a desperate act. Now his signs were measured and supremely confident. I was watching him as if hypnotized, but the detached observer in me recorded certain details that made him look outlandish. If he was my double, he was its coarsened and weathered version. He wore sideburns that were much too long and had a ducktail haircut. His face looked bloated and petulant, and he wore expensive but mismatched casual clothes—a striped shirt and plaid trousers.

Strangely, once Roggins had left, the self-assured look on his face slowly gave way to a look of hesitancy. He now signed in broken sentences, as if not knowing how to say what he wanted to say, "I came here—well, I guess you know—I thought you might. . ."

I could see that my worst fears were not going to be realized. The more he hesitated, the less apprehensive I felt. I decided to help him and nodded, signing, "Yes, sure. Go on. Maybe you want to talk about the same thing that we once discussed."

"Yes . . . . That's why I came here. Let me tell you what has happened since we last saw each other."

He smiled, for the first time, a wistful smile that softened his features. He told me that, after his graduation, he lived with his parents, with whom he could not get along. They had refused to learn sign language, and this made communication with them almost impossible. Only his sister was close to him and had learned sign language for his sake, but the summer we graduated she got married and moved out. He spent every day that summer going to Coney Island because he disliked work intensely; he especially hated to be bossed around.

One day, as he lay on his beach towel, observing the bathers at the seashore, he noticed a woman a few feet away from him who wore a bathing suit, sunglasses, and a garden hat, and who was reading a book. Next to her on her blanket lay a sleeping man. Something about her gripped his attention. He could not describe the attraction he felt for her—all he knew was that he could not tear his eyes off her. As he watched, she put the book down and extracted a pack of cigarettes from her handbag. She put a cigarette in her mouth and rummaged in the handbag for matches but apparently could not find them. She looked up and, seeing that his eyes were fixed on her, smiled and said something. Like most deaf people, he could not lipread her. But again, like most deaf people, he could guess the obvious. He got up, walked toward her, struck a match, and lighted her cigarette. She puffed at it and started talking to him very fast.

He said slowly, in the flat and barely distinct voice of the deaf, "Wait. Not so fast. I'm deaf," and pointed at his ear.

She laughed. "I don't believe you. You heard me when I asked you for a match." He did not actually lipread her, but he could see an amiable skepticism writ large on her face.

He tried to describe to her in words and pantomime how he could see for himself that she was looking for matches in her handbag—no words were needed to grasp that. She understood. They carried on a conversation largely based on gestures. They communicated. The man next to her was her husband. He slept soundly throughout their initial meeting.

Before long, they became lovers. Afterward, Silver continued, they met whenever they had a chance to be together. Doris was one of those people who take to sign language like a swan to water, and soon she became fluent in it. She could even read his signs in darkness, in bed, by feeling his hands move—as he signed this last phrase, his gestures became sinuous and erotic and he looked at me searchingly to see what effect this had produced on me.

Once they could communicate, they held many frank conversations. But as time went on—and their relationship lasted some two years—their conversations became more and more like those between a psychiatrist and her patient. After all, Doris was a psychiatry major. She had come from Canada in order to enroll at the medical school of Columbia University.

In the end, he began to suspect that he was to her not so much a lover as a patient whom she needed for her own professional learning and satisfaction. His suspicions grew as she kept asking him about his childhood experiences, about his school, his teachers, friends, and enemies. The more he told her, the more probing were her questions. Finally, he could not stand it anymore and belligerently accused her of prying into his private life. "What the hell am I to you?" he asked, "Your patient or your lover? I won't let you analyze me like I was some guinea pig."

She smiled painfully and signed, "That's not true. I love you dearly. I want to know you better. I want to know who you are inside. I can tell that way deep down you are unhappy. You are troubled. Believe me, I need you as much as you need me. Won't you let me help you to know yourself better?"

She pleaded with such sincerity and conviction that Silver opened himself up to her more and more. She entered his world, his greatly different deaf world. She entered his mind, just as he had entered her body, thus gaining double gratification, as he put it in picturesque signs, sculpturing in the air images of the penetration of a lurking selfhood and of obelisks, rings, and jets of ecstasy in a multicolored universe.

One day he showed her, at her request, his photograph album. She looked at it attentively, asking him to identify all the people in the photographs. When she saw me in one of the photographs, and after he had fingerspelled my name to her, she said to him, "You and Bragg look so much alike, you could be mistaken for brothers." He said nothing. She asked him to pronounce my name, a request which he found strange because, after she had learned to sign, he relied on signs and fingerspelling alone to communicate with her, but he acceded to her request. His response evoked a secretive smile on her lips. He grew suspicious. Did she know something? But he just did not feel like finding out.

Yet, when it was time for her to go home to Canada, they had a long talk, and he finally admitted to her his deep-seated feelings of resentment toward me, his feeling that life was unbearable until my existence could be blotted out from the face of the earth. He told her of his dreams of killing me in various ways—by knife, by gun, by axe, by rope. He resented my being ahead of him in everything except sports, especially because we were so much like brothers. When he signed that last phrase, he smiled shyly at me.

He had resented especially my having passed and his having failed the entrance examination to Gallaudet.

Anyhow, once he had admitted to Doris the motives behind his hatred of me and his urge to kill me, she told him that it was in reality an urge to kill himself, an urge to change places with me, a projection of himself onto me, because he was rejecting himself. So, to sum it all up, he concluded, she finally made him learn about himself and how to come to terms with himself and regain his self-esteem.

He stopped and looked at me inquiringly. I wondered at both the strangeness of his tale and the ease with which he used Freudian terms, an ease that looked doubly strange in the signing hands of a deaf man who had no college education. Obviously he had learned a lot from Doris. I felt grateful to that unknown woman for rescuing him from his obsession and for obviating the menace that had for so long been hanging over me. At the same time, the psychological jargon he was using so facilely seemed to prove the truth of his story. Still, what did that woman mean when she said that she needed him as much as he needed her, since she abandoned him after two years? Did he perhaps invent her declaration to salvage his vanity before me? Did he perhaps want to believe it himself because, as his actions showed, he had only a tenuous toehold on reality? And was it not in reality a kind of case history to her, a case history with sex thrown in, an unusual instance of transference? Might not the very glibness with which he had reeled off those terms indicate that he was "cured" only superficially? And what about her husband? Silver had never mentioned him again.

So many loose ends about this tale, I thought. I did not feel like asking him these questions because I was already deeply involved with him against my will, and personal questions would only compound my involvement. But, there was one question that cried out for an explanation.

"One thing I don't understand," I signed. "Why did she ask you to pronounce my name?"

It was obvious that he had been waiting for me to ask. Calmly and deliberately he answered, "'Bwaakk,' 'Bwaggg.' She told me those were the sounds I often made in my sleep."

I felt a chill down my spine. These nocturnal groans reflected the intensity of his obsession with even more terrifying impact than his talk of guns, knives, axes, and rope. But my terror was tempered by a feeling of relief now that he seemed to have gotten over his fixation, as he would probably term it. I made a clumsy attempt at a joke, "And they say that the deaf don't talk in their sleep. Ha!" We laughed and he, entering into the spirit of jollity, joshed back, "Except that they pronounce words in their sleep differently each time, because they never hear them."

"Say, were you in New York all that time? You vanished like a stone in a pond. I asked many deaf people about you, but no one knew what had happened to you."

He answered, "I wandered all over America after Doris left me. I told you I hated to be bossed. And since, being deaf, I did not know how to establish my own business, I decided the only way to remain independent was to become a peddler of manual alphabet cards. Since the world had screwed me, I told myself, I was going to screw the world. Of course, this meant I had to avoid the deaf world because so many deaf people hate peddlers like poison; after all, peddlers spoil their image before the hearing, who come to identify all deaf people with beggars and underworld characters."

Watching me closely, he added, "But that was not the only reason why I withdrew from the deaf world; I wanted you to be beside yourself with uncertainty and worry, not knowing where I was. I always knew where to find you."

I was staggered. He stopped and waited. My worst suspicions were confirmed—he was indeed capable of such demonic deviousness. What in God's name did I do to deserve this treatment? The punishment of living three years in fear simply did not fit my crime, whatever it was. Or it could be that I was merely an instrument serving his perverse self-realization. But why me? I felt seized by violent indignation. At that moment I had never loathed anyone more than this man.

Still, I did not respond. To respond would betray my feelings. But he could tell exactly what I was feeling. He hesitated, then added, "There is something else I have kept so far from you—my dependent emotional attachment to you, which prevented me from being an autonomous and self-reliant individual."

He had been signing these phrases woodenly, as if from memory. Next, however, he started to bring out each sign with strenuous effort, as if attempting to relieve himself of an enormous burden. "You see, I also admitted to Doris that what broke the camel's back was not those entrance examinations but the knowledge that we were going to go our separate ways, my feeling of not having you anymore at my side, of being lost without you."

"But now," and as he signed this, his expression became beseeching, "my anger at you and my hatred of you have dissolved. I see you again as the friend you were. And I only hope you feel the same, that you feel toward me the friendship that you had felt for a long time before that evening in the shower room." He stopped, then signed haltingly, "Forgive me."

As I looked at this man, this terrifying bogeyman who turned out to be only a bedsheet flapping in a breeze, and who now sat with his head and shoulders submissively bent, my detestation turned to pity for a suffering human being who was begging me to release him from his torment. I forgot all my doubts about his being "cured" and was flooded with gladness that he could admit it all so frankly to me, that the long nightmare was over not only for me but also for him.

I shook my head. "I have nothing to forgive you for." I looked at my watch and added, "Come, let's go get something to eat. It's on me."

But he answered regretfully, "I wish I could, but I promised Roggins to drive back to New York with him today after I talked with you."

So we parted, shaking hands.

Silver has since rejoined the deaf community and is now more or less happily married. At his wife's insistence, he gave up alphabet-card peddling and terminated his association with Roggins, so as not to embarrass her before the deaf community. He found a job as a shipping clerk, and now has a paunch and a well-groomed graying mustache. His pink complexion is offset by his brown eyes which twinkle genially; only sometimes their gaze contracts to a needlelike sharpness. I meet him now and then, but never by design, when I am in New York, and then we exchange small talk, as if the shower scene and its aftermath had never taken place.

CHAPTER TWO

The Rehearsal

Theater is in my blood. The pleasure I felt about being admitted to Gallaudet College was doubled by what I knew from Mr. Panara's tales about its theater and about Professor Hughes, the drama teacher. Once I entered Gallaudet I would finally be able to act in classical theater instead of in the farces and melodramas familiar to me from my father's theater company. That was such an alluring prospect to me that when the Drama Club at Gallaudet was about to audition for its annual major play, Ferenc Molnar's Liliom, *I presented myself. Ever since Mr. Panara had told to us about that play, I had wanted to be able to perform Molnar in sign. Now I had the chance to do so, even though I was a lowly prep, a member of the preparatory class, set up because most new students at Gallaudet lacked the credentials to enter the freshman class at once.*

Wearing the short-visored buff-and-blue cap embroidered with the word "RAT," as behooved a preparatory student, I introduced myself to Fred Collins, the president of the Drama Club, and told him I wanted to play the leading part in *Liliom*. He looked me up and down as I explained to him about my theatrical experience, about my father being the manager and director of an amateur deaf theater group in New York. "Never heard of it," he answered, "But maybe you are right for the role. I'll let you know."

And he did let me know, a couple of days later, but not with the answer I expected. Fred told me that Professor Hughes said the rules barred preparatory students from acting in a major play. My hopes were dashed. The world collapsed around me. At least that was how I felt at the time. As I walked across the hallway, Professor Hughes stopped me. "Are you Bernard Bragg?" he asked. When I nodded, he continued, "Yes, yes, Fred told me. Your turn will come." And when I answered affirmatively, he added, "Don't lose heart. There's always the future," and left me.

This was the first time I had talked with him, and I thought it very gracious of him to say that. The impression he produced on me has stayed with me to this day. Professor Hughes was very short, not more than five feet tall, and he wore his white hair parted in the middle, in the old-fashioned way. He had a certain proud dignity that was accentuated by his penetrating eyes; his reserved and erect bearing, like that of a Spanish grandee; his habit of always wearing a flower in his lapel; and his habit of signing without moving his lips. I have often reflected on his refusal to move his lips when signing. He belonged to the old school of signers, who believed that mouthing words would impair the beauty of natural sign language and impede its natural flow. Perhaps that also was why his name sign was H-on-lips, placed at right angles on the lips as if to suggest silence.

His mode of signing was a revelation to me. Where Panara used "total communication," a combination of signing with speaking, resulting in a cultured, literary, "Englished," sign language, Hughes's signing hewed to the different, natural structure and syntax of sign language, always concise and graceful, conveying the subtlest nuances with astounding precision. To watch him sign was to observe a high priest solemnly conjure spirits with incantatory gestures. I thought it an honor and a privilege to observe such greatness. In addition, Professor Hughes was the best director and acting coach I ever met in my life—and I have met quite a few.

At that point, however, I had to bide my time until I could benefit from his teaching. When spring came, some of Hughes's students were charged with producing and directing one-act plays that were open to anyone, so I eagerly signed up for one of these plays, "In the Days of Daze," a farce using King Arthur's Round Table, in which the actors were allowed to improvise. I played Sir Lancelot and made the most of my role by using and elaborating on the tricks I had learned from watching vaudeville and my father's acting troupe. My props were a cape, a sword, and a wig. On stage, I wrapped myself in my cape so impetuously that its folds struck my face. When I removed my sword from the scabbard, the hilt detached itself from the blade. My wig was so loose that its fringe blinded me and I staggered in circles until I landed on Lady Guinevere's lap. Based on the audience's reactions, I must have been very funny. That was also when I first began to develop my talent as an improvisator. I was anxious to know Professor Hughes's reaction to my performance, so I stole a glance at him now and then. Whenever we made eye contact he would nod his head as if to tell me to go on.

My next opportunity to perform came in the fall of my freshman year. When I returned to Gallaudet after summer break, I became a pledge of Kappa Gamma fraternity, at the time the only fraternity at Gallaudet. One of the high points, or rather hijinks, of my pledgeship was a play I had to improvise at extremely short notice. One night, as we pledges stood submissively in the fraternity's secret den, nicknamed the Torture Chamber, Kamoos Kolson, the probation leader, brusquely announced to us that we had just two days to select, rehearse, and produce a twenty-minute play for presentation to the entire student body. To enhance the effect of this announcement, he ordered that we be blindfolded and marched out of the fraternity shrine.

Later that night, we held a meeting and I was unanimously chosen the play director. I calmed my fellow pledges, "Relax. You won't have to act. Just stand in the wings and do what I tell you."

"What about a script?" they asked nervously. "Don't worry, I've got it in my head. You won't have to say anything. It'll be a 'Who done it?' I'll tell the story of a murder in a mansion. While I tell it I'll ask each of you to appear and I'll introduce you as the murdered man, the butler, the lawyer, the victim's older brother, and so on," I reassured them. "All each of you has to do is assume the pose of the butler, the lawyer, and so on."

It took me just one evening to rehearse them for their roles. When the evening of the second day approached, we were ready.

Here I should mention that fraternity tradition called for the Grand Rajah of Kappa Gamma to stamp resoundingly on the floor with his foot in the middle of the twenty-minute play, rise, and walk out of Chapel Hall, followed by all the brethren. This would surprise those on the stage and leave them dangling.

It was not seven o'clock yet, but Chapel Hall was already full with a curious audience composed of our fellow students and some teachers. Only the first row was empty, by tradition. Punctually at seven the door opened and the brethren of Kappa Gamma marched in, led by the Grand Rajah. It was an impressive sight, which we pledges watched from behind the stage curtain. The brethren were wearing hooded blue robes with skulls embroidered on their chests, their faces grim, their hands hidden in the wide sleeves of their robes, as they marched slowly and majestically to their seats in the front row and, in unison, sat down.

The curtain opened to reveal me standing on a stage whose only prop was a fireplace with an antique clock standing on the mantle.

For this role I wore a dark suit and tie and I addressed the audience in the manner of the folksy stage manager in Thornton Wilder's *Our Town*.

"Tonight you will witness a murder investigation in a mansion in New England."

I turned my back to the audience and approached the fireplace, picked up the antique clock and set its hands at twenty minutes to twelve, for all to see, declaring, "You will know the murderer by the time this clock strikes midnight."

Then I summoned my fellow pledges from the wings and introduced each character in turn. The pledge playing the dead man simply lay down on stage and remained motionless. The pledge playing the butler adopted an officious pose. The others, playing their respective roles as the police chief, the lawyer, the older brother, the younger brother, and so on, stood in the poses in which I had coached them.

The minute hand of the clock approached ten minutes to midnight. I launched into an explanation of the background of the crime—the will in which the dead man left all his estate to his youngest brother. I glanced at the clock: it was now exactly ten minutes to midnight but still the Grand Rajah did not stamp on the floor, and the Blue Brotherhood, as they called themselves, did not rise and march out. I just could not believe my luck. I started to discuss the motives of the murderer. It could be the youngest brother, because he needed the money urgently to pay a gambling debt. Or it could be a jealous older brother. Or it might be the butler, who nursed a long-held grudge against the victim.

From time to time I glanced at the clock. It showed seven minutes to midnight, then five. Still, the brethren did not rise and depart. I saw that I had mesmerized them by my tale. The closer the minute hand of the clock crept toward twelve, the more frenzied my signs were and the more excited I became as I speculated suggestively about the killer's motives. I again grabbed the antique clock, this time turning it around so that the audience could not see its face, and exclaimed in sign, "Soon now, lights will be out, and then you will know who the murderer is!"

On cue, the lights went out. The curtain descended. When the lights reappeared, the audience saw a large sign clipped to the curtain, announcing in large letters, "TO BE CONTINUED NEXT YEAR."

The audience applauded wildly. The Grand Rajah finally awoke from his daze and, stamping his foot feebly on the floor, arose, along with the entire Blue Brotherhood. They marched out in double file with as much dignity as they could muster, while the audience laughed and screamed.

We pledges, behind the curtain, whooped with joy and pummeled each other's backs like a winning football team. Our euphoria did not last long. That night, in the Torture Chamber, was the worst of our pledgeship. Every pledge except me got a double portion of whacks on his backside—I got a triple one.

Incidentally, that year's congregation of pledges still holds the honor of being the only one ever to have disrupted the fraternity's "walkout" tradition.

Later that winter Professor Hughes picked Molière's *The Miser* as the major play for the year. We of the Drama Club, of which by then I was a full-fledged member, met in Chapel Hall to be assigned our roles. Hughes began with the role of Harpagon. Looking at me, he signed, "You'll take this role."

I thus became apprentice to a wizard. He was superb at analyzing character and motivation and conjuring sign language into a sparkling fountain of Molièrean wit. I hung on his every word, or rather his every sign. His suggestions never rang a false note. Whenever I developed a new interpretation, a new sign, a new movement, I looked at Hughes for approval, so much so that a fellow actor asked me irritably why I was always glancing at Hughes.

Most often Hughes agreed with my interpretation, and sometimes even smiled slightly in surprise at it, as, for example, the time I blew up at the actor playing a servant and turned away from him only to turn my head once more and peer suspiciously at him from under lowered eyebrows. When Hughes did not like something, he would call me over. I would approach, sit down on the edge of the proscenium, and he would ask, "How do you feel? How do you react?" as if I were Harpagon himself. "You suspect everyone. Feel it. Feel that way."

And I did. I made myself look very small, walked with doddering steps, and shook my fingers when signing. I also wore a white wig and craned my neck up at everyone because of my temporary "short stature." One unintended result was that, when we gave a performance of *The Miser* for the deaf community in Akron, Ohio, I learned that quite a few people in the audience thought it was Hughes, not I, who played Harpagon, and, when the curtain went down and the lights came up, the audience was surprised to see the real Hughes sitting among them.

Apparently the audiences loved Molière, and so the following year the Drama Club staged *The Bourgeois Gentleman* and the year after that, *Tartuffe*. Each time Professor Hughes picked me to play the leading role. Each time I went to the Library of Congress to do research on how famous actors had interpreted these roles in the past before developing my own interpretation.

As my self-confidence grew, I looked for Hughes's approval less and less. At my graduation in 1952 he shook my hand silently and withdrew only to return and declare, as if overcoming his reserve with difficulty, "I'll miss you." After I moved to California we kept in touch. At that time, in 1954 and 1955, there simply were no opportunities for deaf actors. Though I minored in drama at San Francisco State University, I had no hopes of ever achieving anything more on the hearing stage than acting as a spear carrier. Even so, like my father and Professor Hughes, I had a dream—the dream of performing for all audiences, not just for deaf audiences, Luckily, I was "discovered" by Marcel

Marceau, who invited me to join him in Paris. That was the beginning of my professional career in theater.

It was too late to share this thrilling news with Hughes; by then he was dead. He had made the perfect stage exit; on the annual Awards Day he had been in Chapel Hall where he was presented with a copy of the *Tower Clock Yearbook*, which was dedicated to him that year. With that copy in hand, he was walking down the steps when he suddenly clutched his breast, keeled over, and tumbled down the steps, dead of a heart attack. Dying, he released the yearbook from his grasp. As it happened, that year the color chosen for the cover of the yearbook was black.

At Gallaudet, as in Shangri-La, time seemed suspended. Before I knew it, my preparatory year was almost over and the college was about to close for the summer. I became worried about finding a summer job. There were opportunities as a hotel dishwasher or as an errand boy at a print shop. But each time I was too late—somebody else had snapped the job up.

Since I had to vacate the dormitory anyhow, I decided to go back home. Immediately after I returned to my parents' home in the Bronx, I started to read the Help Wanted pages of newspapers. One advertisement caught my eye.

"Dishwashers wanted for a summer camp in the Berkshires." The Berkshires! This ad caught my fancy because part of my childhood had been spent on my grandfather's farm in Sharon, Connecticut, and I love nature. That was also a time in my life when I had developed a craving to write poetry. Nature, poetry, the Berkshires. I tore off the ad and took the subway to Manhattan.

The address given was that of a tall building across the street from the 42nd Street Public Library. I walked in and took the elevator. I was optimistic. There was no reason why they should reject me, I figured. When I stepped out of the elevator and entered the office, I saw a few other college types waiting to be interviewed. I was fourth in line. The secretary saw me carrying the ad in my hand and said something which I figured to mean an invitation to sit down and wait, which I did.

The other three guys left the room, one after another, at intervals of five to ten minutes, exiting through a brown-paneled door. I was next. The secretary looked at me and said something. This was it, I thought, I thanked her and knocked at the brown-paneled door and went inside.

I saw a smallish man whose wavy silver hair belied his youthful complexion. He apparently sized me up quickly and I was to his liking. He motioned for me to sit down and started talking. He talked nonstop and very quickly. I was stuck since I could not lipread him and did not know how to stop him. Finally, he closed his mouth, as if after asking a question.

It was my turn to speak. I said in a low voice, trying to enunciate as clearly as I could, "I'm sorry, I can't hear."

"You can't hear?"

"That's right. I'm deaf."

He contemplated my answer for a while, then smilingly pointed at the other door in his office, "Go this way, please."

I thanked him and opened the door, thinking I was going to fill out an application, and was stunned to find myself in the hallway.

I took the elevator down. My spirits were down, too. In the lobby, the elevator opened and a crowd of people pushed past me to get in, without even waiting for me to get out first.

I crossed the lobby and found myself in the hot, humid, and sunny street. People were scurrying by, jostling me while I just stood there. I looked up at the tall building, trying to locate the windows of the room that the silver-haired man had so unceremoniously tricked me into leaving, and I wondered how many more times in my life I would meet with the same fate because of my deafness. Was my life to be like this from now on? Was I to slink away with my tail between my legs, a reject, without fighting back? No! I decided to insist at least on my right to receive an explanation.

I took out a pad and a pen and wrote, "I can't understand why you treated me in this manner. I could understand it if the job involved hearing, like using the phone, but you simply made me leave without any explanation. I would appreciate your giving me a specific and rational explanation for not hiring me as a dishwasher."

Bearing the paper in my hand, I turned back and rode the elevator up again. There were about ten people in the anteroom. The secretary shook her head and put up a hand in protest. I brushed past her, knocked at the brown-paneled door, and entered.

The silver-haired man was startled to see me. He got up and pointed threateningly toward the same hallway door. Intimidated as I felt. I would not give up. I placed my note on his desk and pointed at it for him to read, but he would not read it; instead he picked it up and handed it back to me. I again placed it on his desk and burst out, "Read it. I won't leave until you read it."

He flinched, seeming to understand my speech. He picked up the paper, sat down, and read it while I stood trembling with anger and determination, my chest heaving as I watched him.

He laid the paper down, took his black-rimmed glasses off, looked thoughtfully at me and motioned for me to sit down.

At that moment I felt like leaving, but I sat down. I knew that what I had written him was sensible and any person in his right mind could not very well disagree with it. He asked me if I could lipread, and when I said, "A little bit," he asked how I communicated with people. "By writing," I spoke and gestured. He wrote down his reply for me. "I'm concerned how you will get along with other workers in the camp kitchen." I wrote him back, "We'll write to each other, and also I can teach them sign language, mime, gestures. No problem. Give me a chance to prove myself. Besides, being deaf, I don't talk on the job." He looked up at me with a smile and hired me.

The Berkshires never looked lovelier or more majestic. Every morning I got up at dawn and wrote poetry while the mists hung on the mountaintops. Then I went to the kitchen, with its steamy heat and piles of dishes to be washed and put on shelves after they had been dumped on the counter by the waiters hurrying in from the dining room.

And so it continued for two months. It was a good life. During the morning and afternoon breaks I ran to the lake and glided slowly through the blue water, under the blue skies and white clouds. At noon and in the evening, it was back to the kitchen and the sweaty toil. Later in the evening I joined the other staffers in a hut, a so-called social hall, especially set aside for us, where we played games and some of us strummed guitars. On weekends there was singing and dancing in that social hall. I usually jitterbugged with a student from Vassar, and I helped organize a series of Saturday evening skits in which I did my bit as a mime.

I suppose that my talents as an entertainer had helped dispel whatever fears and misgivings my hearing fellow workers had. I became an accepted member of the staff and taught quite a few people to sign, especially those working with me in the kitchen.

One morning the assistant camp director showed up in the kitchen and asked for volunteers to help pull weeds from cornfields and gather hay from the meadows and transport it to the camp barn. I saw my chance to get out of the kitchen for the next two or three days and raised my hand, pointing to myself. He took down my name and left. The boy next to me signed, "You'll be sorry. It's a hell of a job. You don't know what you are letting yourself in for." But I answered him, extending my arm rapturously, "How can you compare outside work, close to nature, with this sweltering kitchen and these rubber gloves." He signed back, "Good luck. Hope you'll come back in one piece."

My spirits thus dampened, I showed up at the cornfield the next morning and started to pull out the weeds by hand. By noon my back, arms, and hands all ached from continual bending, pulling, and straightening up.

The second day I continued this backbreaking work. The third day, they moved us to the hayfield. When I and the other four laborers arrived, we were met by Charley, the foreman, and his teenage son, who drove a tractor pulling a gigantic hay wagon around the field.

Under his blond crew-cut thatch Charley had a square-jawed face, and his body was broad-shouldered and muscular. When he started to talk to me, one of the laborers told him of my deafnesss. He scowled and gestured commandingly at me to pick up a pitchfork from the hay wagon, whereupon he leaped onto the wagon and climbed to the top of the pile of hay. He then began to rake the pile together as the rest of us threw pitchforkfuls of hay onto it.

By midmorning I had quite a few blisters on my hand. It was my own fault because I had forgotten to bring along my work gloves. One of the laborers noticed it too and, before I could stop him, shouted to Charley. "What?" he clearly mouthed in reply, thrusting his jaw interrogatively. I showed him the blisters. He grinned maliciously and put his finger in his mouth and began to suck it, pointing at me and miming a baby drinking from a milk bottle.

I said nothing but inwardly boiled with rage. I took out a handkerchief, tied it around my hand, and kept pitching the hay under the scorching sun. Charley remained straddled atop the pile of hay and shouted commands like a frenetic demigod.

Noon finally arrived. We ate our lunches, brought from the camp, across the road at a picnic table. I drank and ate with frantic haste; then, aching all over, napped in the shade.

When I awoke, all the laborers had gone. I glanced at a clock through the window of a nearby hut. I was fifteen minutes late. I ran as quickly as I could to my hut to get a pair of work gloves, then grabbed the pitchfork on the way back and rushed to the hayfield.

Charley stood on his pile of hay, arms akimbo. I gestured to him that I was sorry to have overslept, but he placed the thumbs of his outspread hands at his ears, waggled his hands, and then, with his tongue out, balled up his fist and pumped his arm in that universal if not peculiarly Italian obscene gesture. My first impulse was to drop the pitchfork and respond to him in kind, but I recalled the silver-haired man and how he had wondered whether I would get along with others. I bowed my head and started to pitch hay. The same laborer who had been worried about my blister, an elderly man, showed me sympathy. The others just laughed.

The crew continued shoving hay onto the wagon. Suddenly it became dark. I looked up and saw lowering black clouds scud across the horizon. Charley became frantic and urged us to hurry, hurry, and get the hay to the barn before the rain came. We pitched faster and faster. Finally, we were done.

Near the barn Charley excused his son and two of the laborers, retaining me and a burly man in a cowboy hat. Gesturing, he ordered me to climb to the loft and redistribute the hay there.

Flying missiles of hay struck me as Charley and the burly farmhand pitched them upward into the loft from the hay wagon outside. They pitched them in faster than I could redistribute them in the corners of the loft. The hay bounced off my body as I caught it in my pitchfork and redirected it. The air was full of dust and chaff so that I began to sneeze and feel as though I were suffocating. I caught Charley grinning as he shoved the hay upward directly at me. I gritted my teeth and worked even faster. Soon the loft began to be filled up and I kept climbing above the rising mass of hay.

It was now as dark as at twilight, although it was still afternoon. The two men looked up at me and saw me kneeling, panting with exhaustion and coughing. The farmhand said something to Charley as if telling him to let me go. Charley gestured to me to come down and swap places with him, as there was still some hay left in the wagon. I jumped onto the wagon and he climbed into the loft with the agility of an athlete.

By the time I landed in the wagon, Charley was already in the loft receiving the first shower of hay from the burly farmhand. This was my chance. With newfound energy I began to pitch hay at Charley faster and faster, harder and harder. All my anger, my frustration, my personal antipathy toward Charley, suddenly were released. It became a battle between us two alone.

I was the victor in this contest. Charley was now up to his neck in hay. He swayed and tottered. He extended one arm and gestured, "Help!"

I reached up and, supporting him by the arm, helped him jump down onto the wagon, on which he collapsed in complete exhaustion. At the same time the skies finally opened and a heavy rain began to fall. Charley and the farmhand jumped off the wagon and ran to take shelter under the barn's eaves.

But I leapt down in the opposite direction and, swaying from sheer exhaustion, walked away in the pouring rain, some of which I drank in through my open mouth. I fell onto the ground and lay spread-eagled, letting the rain cleanse and refresh me. After a while, I got up.

On the way back to the camp I had to pass the barn. Charley and the farmhand were talking. When Charley saw me, he looked at me with a calm unusual for him and beckoned to me. I wondered what would happen next. His hand went into a breast pocket and came out with a pack of cigarettes, which he held out to me.

Hiding my surprise, I nonchalantly took out a cigarette. He struck a large kitchen match against his trousers and lighted the cigarette for me. As I watched him, still wary of what he was going to do next, he raised his large hand and rested it on my shoulder. We looked at each other gravely. He nodded, and I nodded back.

I walked down the field toward the camp. The air was fresh and brisk. The sky began to clear up and the sun reappeared. I could still feel that hand resting on my shoulder.

When I returned to the Gallaudet campus in the fall I met a new foreign deaf student, Maurice Black, from Israel. At the time foreign students were still a rarity at Gallaudet, but even now that their number is nearing one hundred, none of them equals Maurice, whose impact on our campus was so shattering that to this day he remains a Gallaudet legend.

Our eyes were riveted on the blackboard. It was covered entirely with wiry lines of sentences in a neat and tiny handwriting that analyzed in clear, perceptive language the characters in Chaucer's *Canterbury Tales*. We had never before read such a brilliant critique of Chaucer's masterpiece. To be sure, it was over our heads, but we could tell it was an original, intellectual tour de force.

Our teacher, Dr. Powrie Vaux Doctor, or "Doc," as he was known on the campus, was just as awestruck. Apparently Doc got more than he asked for when he told Maurice to write his answer on the blackboard, since the young man did not know enough sign language to answer in sign. We could see disbelief and respect in Doc's gaze.

It was yet another surprise sprung on us by Maurice in the two weeks since the semester had started at Gallaudet. He had only recently set foot on American soil, having arrived from the fledgling state of Israel, and his arrival here had set the whole community abuzz. We had an authentic genius in our midst. He knew the answer to everything, and, as he demonstrated, he knew everything that was being taught at Gallaudet. He dazzled the teachers and baffled the administrators, who did not know where to place him. In the first week of classes he complained that, while still in Israel, he had already completed the whole syllabus, including English, chemistry, and physics. He was given tests and passed them all with perfect scores. He was obviously in the wrong place, and indeed he only stayed the year with us. But while he was at Gallaudet, the administration decided to give him an indefinite status, halfway between that of a junior and senior. And that was how he ended up in our Western Literature class, being taught by Doc.

Maurice finished writing on the blackboard, put down the chalk, worn to a stub, and walked to his seat in the back row. "Walked" is an understatement; he did not so much walk as shuffle, his head habitually bent and his shoulders hunched, with the ever-present grimacing smile. We stared at what he had written. We could not understand half of it, but we could see he had gotten it all together, producing a masterful and incisive study of Chaucer's characters. In the process he had preempted Doc's own lecture because the hour was almost up.

Doc sat motionless. Then his pink face broke out into the convulsive and disconcerting laughter that was his trademark. "Bravo!" he signed, and he clapped his hands. We all joined him in applauding Maurice.

When the class was over, I caught up with Maurice to introduce myself. I shook his hand vigorously, but he responded limply and his hand felt cold and clammy. He was about twenty-five years old, short, slightly built, with jet-black straight hair and a chalky white complexion as if he had never seen the sun, which was strange considering that he was from sun-scorched Israel. It was the complexion of a man who had spent his life among books. His white shirt was buttoned all the way up, but he wore no tie. He had on a dark brown coat and unpressed pants of the same color and scuffed black shoes.

Just as the administrators did not know how to place him academically, we students did not know where to place him in our community. For the plain fact was that he did not belong to our world; in fact, he belonged even less than did other foreign students in our midst. Sooner or later they adapted, but he alone stood out. Just as his intellect amazed us, his appearance and way of talking mystified and amused us. We did not know what to make of him—and he did not know what to make of us. In two weeks he became the sensation of the campus.

He was as curious about us as we were about him. He tried his best to make friends, but the trouble was he didn't know how. He was an anomaly to us, a savant transplanted to a strange continent peopled by a strange tribe, trying to make himself understood by aborigines who thought his attire, his language, and the manner in which he expressed himself irresistibly comical. The language he used, with its rich, rolling, long words, would have been at home with Dr. Samuel Johnson but not with our sports-loving and fun-loving college crowd. Instead of signing, he fingerspelled every word, which we thought a tiresome practice.

He was interested in women, too, and tried to approach them, but he did it in the worst possible way as far as they were concerned. During his first week on the campus, for example, he approached Gloria, a beautiful young woman and asked her outright, "Do you think that there is a similarity between Kierkegaard's and Nietzsche's concepts of repetition?"

It was his way of trying to make friends with Gloria. He asked this question without the trace of a smile, fingerspelling every word. He was clearly in dead earnest. He thought he was flattering Gloria by showing how highly he thought of her intellect. But he might as well have been talking Chinese to her. She of course looked at him as if he were a circus freak and, with a forced smile, hastily excused herself, leaving him mystified and saddened.

Being an optimist, he tried again, this time with Evelyn. On the way out of the cafeteria he caught up with her and asked her, again without any preliminaries, "Beauteous lady, would you accord me the ineffable pleasure of sharing with me a delectable repast on the morrow?"

This was Greek to Evelyn, but with her feminine instinct she divined the gist of his request. Amused as she was by the ornate language of this oddly dressed man, she pointed to a fraternity pin on her dress and explained to him that she already had a boyfriend. They parted smiling, with Maurice bowing in the European manner. His attempts to make friends with other students on the campus began and ended in a similar way. He would try to make their acquaintance by asking them their opinions on philosophical, cultural, literary, and even political issues. It was clear that he was floundering wildly, that this fountain of knowledge was completely ignorant of the mysteries of small talk.

But what respect he forfeited by his conduct he won back by his astounding fireworks of erudition. It was clear to everyone that he outshone the professors themselves; that, in short, he was a genius, an authentic genius, the likes of whom had never been encountered before at Gallaudet.

I offered my friendship to this visitor from another world. I asked him to play chess with me, and he beat me in ten moves. I asked for a second game, and he beat me in eight moves. When I asked for a third game, he smilingly refused. All the same, he took a liking to me, and I became his lifeline, so to speak, to this new world. He started to visit me in my room quite often and seemed willing, up to a point, to answer questions about himself. It turned out that his family was of Lithuanian extraction. In Lithuania his name was Mordechai Szwarc, but here in America he used the name Maurice Black. His grandfather was the Gaon of Vilna, who, as he patiently explained in amazement at my ignorance, was both a spiritual leader and a man as famous to pious Jews for the splendor of his mind as Einstein is to the secular world. Maurice, in turn, asked me questions that reflected his eagerness to be part of the social life at the college and win new friends.

One evening, after I had sufficiently won his confidence, he came in looking depressed and told me that he simply could not make friends. I protested that it was not true. He had me and a few other friends too.

He said, "Yes, but the female students shun me as if I were a leper or something in that category."

I asked, "Can I talk openly with you?"

"Most assuredly."

"That's fine. I like your spirit. First of all, say 'girls' instead of 'female students.'"

"Yes, and?"

"Second, unbutton your collar, or wear a tie. That's the way a cool cat looks in America. I'll let you have one of my ties."

"Thank you. And tertio?"

"What's 'tertio'?"

"Third, in Latin."

"Why didn't you say so in the first place? Speak plain English. Third, pick up your feet when you walk. Straighten your shoulders."

I showed him how to do it. He copied me, very clumsily. I let it go for the present and continued:

"Stop using ten-dollar words like holism and paraphenomenology."

"But then what should I discourse about?"

"Fourth, 'talk,' not 'discourse.' Use plain English." Still, I was stumped by his question, and finally I said, "Anything except politics and intellectual issues."

"Yes, but then what's left?"

"The weather or what interests the students."

"But what interests them?"

"Sports. Talk about sports. And jokes. Make jokes. About sex, too."

He was shocked. "You mean it? You're pleased to be jesting!"

I said, "Sure, I mean it. Students here like it. They're no different from students at colleges elsewhere in this country. And get involved in social activities, in the Student Body Government."

"Yes, I shall endeavor to do so. I don't know how to express my gratitude to you."

"Let's go have a training exercise now," I said, and led him out into the hallway, where I availed myself of my military-school training by having him march back and forth the length of the hallway in the correct straight posture, chin up and feet stepping briskly up and down rather than shuffling.

After a while I was more or less satisfied and bade him goodnight. He said, "I am extremely appreciative of your efforts."

"Any time," I waved my hand nonchalantly. He turned around and walked away, shuffling again, but after a few steps he glanced back at me, stopped as if remembering what he had learned, straightened his shoulders, and picked up his feet.

Still, as I watched him walk away, I had my doubts. I shook my head, without much hope. I did not expect him to change overnight. I sighed and went to bed, too tired to finish my homework.

The very next evening, as I was in my room trying to catch up with my homework, he burst in, wearing the tie I had given him and looking as if he had just made a great discovery.

He said, "You won't believe this, but I've already found the magic words."

"What are you talking about?"

"Magic words for winning friends."

"You mean you've already won new friends?"

"I've already won quite a few tonight."

"What are these magic words?"

"Go to hell."

He fingerspelled them with a straight face, but with obvious relish. I stared at him, unsure whether he was in his right mind.

"Come on, you're not going to tell me that these are magic words for winning friends."

He smiled and said, "I'm not kidding. 'Go to hell' in my country, Israel, is a strong insult, but here after supper I saw a student tell another, 'Go to hell.' I braced myself to witness a fistfight, but no, nothing of the kind. To my amazement, the other student roared with laughter, clapped the insulter on the shoulder and walked out with him, their arms around each other's shoulders. When I went to the Reading Room and saw Mark Wait reading a newspaper, I tapped his shoulder. I wanted to test the effect of those words on him. So I fingerspelled to him very slowly and carefully, 'Go to hell.' Imagine my surprise when he burst into laughter and shook my hand. I still couldn't believe what was happening, so I accosted a few other students, and each time the same thing happened: the student would laugh, shake my hand, or feign a swipe at my chin in the spirit of jollity and clap me on the shoulder."

I stood looking at him, not knowing whether he actually believed this was a magic phrase. Each time he had said "Go to hell" he spelled out the words slowly and with an intent and expectant expression on his face. Immediately afterward he would break out into his grimacing smile. At any rate, I thought, he was catching on.

But was he catching on? I have no way of knowing, because the following year Maurice Black transferred to the University of Michigan, where he remained until he got his Ph.D. in aeronautical sciences. The last I heard, he was leading a team of aircraft designers in Israel.

There is no better social life for deaf people anywhere in the world than at Gallaudet College. Elsewhere they meet in large numbers only periodically, on weekends or occasional weekday evenings, at clubs for the deaf, at outings, at basketball tournaments, or on weekly bowling nights. At Gallaudet they are together from morning till night, sharing the unique pleasure of living in a place where they are the majority and hearing people are the outsiders; where their own language, sign language, is the dominant language and which hearing people are expected to learn if they are to be accepted by the community. At Gallaudet the students revel in their rich social life as if wanting to make up for years of isolation and storing up the experience of normality before they emerge into the hearing world and become the outsiders.

That rich social life also includes romance, of course, and to me this evokes the memory of a very special romance.

We laughed, Ken and I, having discovered we had another thing in common. He was a senior and I was a freshman, but nearly from the first day of my arrival on the campus of Gallaudet College we just naturally fell in together. He and I both came from New York City, and while I was still at the New York School for the Deaf in White Plains, he had already become well known to the pupils there—any deaf person who becomes a Gallaudet student is automatically a legendary hero to deaf children. And now I found that he had previously gone steady for a while with the same girl I did.

My hero turned out to be human, all too human. Far from being patronizing, he treated me as an equal and introduced me to the mysteries of campus life. It was he who taught me to drink beer and coffee and go out late at night instead of going to bed early.

In fact, it was late one night when we were at Wrigley's, an all-night spot off campus where hamburgers and coffee were of doubtful quality but prices were low, when we discovered we had both dated the same girl. We were as usual discussing the three P's—philosophy, poetry, and people. At one point he mentioned Wendy, a sophomore he used to date. I perked up and said I had gone out with her for a year before I entered Gallaudet. We laughed and congratulated each other on our good taste. Ken asked why I had stopped going with her. I answered that she had become serious about me much too soon, just as I was starting to sow my wild oats. So she left me for a hearing guy who worked in her parents' grocery store. When I asked Ken why he had given up on her himself, he said that he kind of liked her but was too shy to become serious about her.

I responded, "You shy? Are you kidding? I've seen you go out with other girls, laughing and joking."

"I'm only shy when I become serious about a girl."

"What do you mean?"

He got up and looked at himself in the mirror on the wall facing our booth. He asked, "What do you see?"

My eyes followed his and I said, "You and me."

He signed, "Be honest."

It was easy to guess what he meant. The left side of his face was partially paralyzed, owing to an operation done on his ear when he was six by a so-called medical doctor who thought he could restore Ken's hearing. Being nerve-deaf, Ken of course remained deaf as a post, and the only result was that when he smiled only half of his mouth turned up, so that his smile was crooked and one eye remained unblinking. The overall effect, however, was not that of a sneer, because his gentle and pleasing personality shone through.

His comment was a shock to me because he was not the kind of person to indulge in self-pity. I said, "You know perfectly well that many people, girls included, like you for what you are, not that you look that bad. Wise up, old man. This isn't like you. Something is bothering you?"

He answered, "Yes, it is a girl. But let's not talk about it."

So we walked to the campus, said good night, and parted for our rooms. I fell asleep as soon as my head hit the pillow, probably because I had drunk too much beer. I was awakened at eight by Red, a scrawny, fellow frosh, who hammered the metal-shod bottom of my door with an iron bar until the noise, loud enough to wake stone-deaf people like me, finally caused me to open my eyes. For this daily service I helped him with his homework. I had to cram for a test at ten, then go to classes, then rehearse with the Drama Club for hours afterward. This was typical of my days, so I did not see Ken for some time.

All the same, I was curious to know who he meant. I had noticed that he was beginning to go out with Mildred, one of the prettiest, most fun-loving students on the campus. She had recently broken up with a guy she had been dating for two years, and currently she was unattached.

That was in late April. I did not pay much attention to them, because of the final-exam fever before the college closed for the summer. Just before it closed, however, Ken admitted to me the depth of his feeling for Mildred. I asked him how she felt about him.

"Seems she likes me more than I dare believe—and probably more than she cares to admit."

"That sounds good. Looks like you're not that shy, after all."

Ken and I spent the summer back in the Bronx, where my family had moved from Brooklyn. We used to meet on weekends on the boardwalk at Coney Island near Nathan's Hot Dogs, where many deaf people congregated. Then we would go off for a swim. During one of those swims Ken mentioned to me offhandedly that he was corresponding with Mildred in California. I had the impression that things were going well between them.

When the fall came and we returned to Washington, Ken entered American University to study for a master's degree in English. Mildred became a senior and I was in my sophomore year.

Though he now lived off campus, Ken visited Gallaudet often, and each time he did, he would pick up Mildred at her dormitory, Fowler Hall. Still, there was a difference between them and other couples: I never saw them hold hands.

The mystery was compounded when one day in late September Ken showed up in my room. We chatted, swapped jokes, roared with laughter. It was just like old times. Suddenly, his face became serious and he signed, "I've a favor to ask of you."

"Sure. Anything for a pal."

"But this won't be an easy one."

"For a good friend like you nothing would be too hard."

His expression still intense, he signed, "I want you to take Mildred out to Carol Sparks' birthday party at Bonat's."

Bonat's was a popular French restaurant at the time. His request was odd, but I signed, "That's easy. But why me, not you? Are you cramming for an exam or something?"

"No, but that's what I'll tell her."

"I don't get it."

"I only want to test her."

"Test her for what?"

"This is strictly between us. Okay?"

"Of course."

"It is a long story. You see, we have been going out for almost five months, and every time I bring her back to Fowler Hall and want to kiss her good night, she turns her face aside and offers her cheek for me to kiss."

He paused, then continued, "I had thought at first that it was because she wasn't sure of me, but through our summer correspondence I got the feeling that she more than just liked me. I thought things would change in the fall when she came back to Gallaudet, but no dice—same old story. Still the cheek, not the lips. I don't know what to think. Hell! Could it be that she can see no farther than my disfigured face? Then why does she go out with me? I just can't understand it, and it torments me."

I asked, "So exactly what do you want me to do? Shall I ask her why she won't kiss you? Shall I find out for you?"

"No, no! I don't want you to discuss this with her at all. All I want is for you to take her to the birthday party and then, when you take her back to Fowler Hall, I want you to kiss her fully on the lips, if she permits it."

I felt uneasy. Now I understood what he meant by saying that this would not be an easy favor. Inwardly I felt disturbed by his wanting to make me a part of this scheme, which was becoming too complicated for my liking. At the same time, the intensity of his feeling moved me. I asked, "So you want to see how she'll react? Accept or reject my kiss?"

"Yes. I can't stand it any longer. Help me. I must find out where I stand with her. I know this is deceitful, but I just can't bring myself to talk it over with her. Will you help me?"

I was at a loss as to what to say. I blurted out, "I can't do it. I don't want to. Why can't you ask her yourself?"

"I'm not sure if she'd be honest with me. For a friend you find this favor so hard?"

I didn't answer.

His face hardened and he asked, "Yes or no?"

"I'll hate myself. . . . Damn it! I'll do it for you."

The night of Carol's birthday party came. Mildred had accepted Ken's suggestion that I be her escort because she thought he had to study for an exam on Monday. Just as I was leaving my room to pick her up, Ken came in. He complimented me on my new tie and asked if he could stay in my room until I returned. I told him it would be a long wait.

"I've waited long enough already. Remember, kiss her good night when you bring her back to Fowler Hall. Watch her reaction."

I felt uncomfortable. There was nothing gentle about him now and he terrified me. His face was thinner and his red-rimmed eyes glowed. I wanted to back out.

He read my face and, despite himself, smiled crookedly.

"Don't worry. I won't do anything foolish. But I must know the truth. You promised. You must keep your word."

"Fine," I said reluctantly and ventured out to Fowler Hall. On arriving, I sent someone upstairs to get Mildred while I joined the crowd of Carol's friends, about a dozen couples. Shortly afterward, Mildred tripped down the stairs on her high heels, her dark mane flowing; she was tall, almost as tall as Ken, with a dimpled face and a sensuous mouth. She was laughing. As everyone looked on, she signed to me, "Hi! Tonight you're my substitute boyfriend." That made me feel all the more guilty about the trick I was to play on her.

Our crowd rode in a trolley to Bonat's in Northwest Washington. We arrived before Carol. Half an hour later, Carol herself, a majestic blond beauty who was the campus queen strode in with her boyfriend, Jim, at her side. Jim was both an honor student and the captain of the varsity football team. She looked surprised and delighted when she saw the birthday cake, the candles, the balloons, and the applause by the dozen or so couples who had prepared this surprise for her in a private room of the restaurant. She smiled through happy tears as a friend photographed her while Jim, who had helped plan the surprise party, stood smilingly by.

Ours was a colorful group; the prettiest young women and the most athletic and sociable young men were gathered at Bonat's that evening. We chatted, laughed, and joked. We drank beer and wine, and we danced.

After dinner, and after Carol blew out the candles on the birthday cake, she opened our gifts, oohed and aahed over them, and kissed each of us. We all danced again. Mildred and I danced well together. We had a grand time and I was able to keep from thinking about my mission.

Finally, the party was over. We went out into the street where I hailed a cab to take us back to the campus. Now the gaiety was gone and I felt tense. I was hoping that she would refuse my kiss.

As Mildred and I reached the door of Fowler Hall, she signed, "Thank you for a wonderful evening," grasping the door handle. I had to act fast. I said "That was fun." I brought my face close to hers, making sure that she would have barely enough time to decide whether to let me kiss her on the lips. She did not move. I kissed her on the lips for two or three seconds before she drew her face away. She looked surprised. She smiled oddly, turned around, and entered Fowler Hall.

Stunned, I stood for a moment in silence, then walked slowly toward College Hall, feeling sick at the pending confrontation with Ken. I braced myself as I entered my room. Ken was sitting in an armchair facing the door, a rapt yet desperate expression on his face. Closing the door behind me, I faced him, but I kept silent because I did not know what to say. Never before had I felt so helpless.

He looked at me, and he knew. His gaze became blank. Finally he broke the silence—that silence which to the deaf is stillness of movement.

"She let you kiss her?"

"Yes."

"On the lips?"

"Yes."

He rose heavily and reached for the door. "I'm going home now. Thanks for the favor."

As he closed the door behind him, I panicked and rushed after him. He was slowly walking down the stairs, leaning on the banister. I slowed down and followed him. He left College Hall and approached his car. As he got in, I opened the door on the passenger side and got in, too.

He turned his unseeing stare at me. His eyes focused and he sensed my concern. He said, "Leave me alone."

"Are you sure?"

He made an abrupt series of staccato gestures, "I'm fine. Go back to your room."

"No, we haven't finished talking about it."

"We have. You told me enough."

"Well, you see, she didn't have a chance to turn her face away. I kissed her too fast."

"That may be so, but the point is, she let you kiss her. I tried for five months and nothing happened. She let you kiss her on your very first date. You are handsome and obviously she goes after good looks."

"Bullshit. But okay, fine. What are you going to do about it?"

"Nothing. I just wish I were dead. Life means nothing to me without Mildred. She's the love of my life. I wish the earth would sink under me."

Now I became more concerned than ever, for in the back of my mind I kept thinking of the cyanide. The rooming house where Ken lived contained another deaf roomer, Wolstein, a graduate chemistry major burdened by a peculiar brand of gallows humor who liked to boast to all comers—except the landlady—that he kept samples of deadly cyanide in his room. He had brandished them at me the last time I had visited Ken. His door was never locked, and it was easy for anyone to enter his room. I remembered the interest with which Ken had watched Wolstein exhibit his samples to me. So now I signed, "Let me go and stay with you overnight."

"I know what you are thinking. Don't worry. I won't do anything to myself. She doesn't deserve it."

"Now you know what she's like. So forget her. There are plenty of other women out there."

"Yeah. She can go to hell for all I care."

"That's the spirit. Now you're waking up."

"Let me go now. I'm exhausted."

"Can I trust you?"

"Don't worry, I'll be all right."

"Are you going to talk to her?"

"Yes."

"Tell her the truth, but be gentle with her," I advised.

"She has to explain to me why she led me on."

"But first find out why she let me kiss her but not you."

He turned the ignition on. I stopped him. "Wait! You know I've always looked up to you. Let me continue to look up to you. Good night."

He smiled and nodded, then he stepped on the pedal and drove off. I watched as the red glow of the taillights of his car receded in the darkness.

The next day, in the late afternoon, Ken walked into my room. He looked pale and shaken. He had dark circles under his eyes and his hands trembled.

I jumped up and asked, "What happened? You're white as a sheet."

Staring at me, he said, "She loves me."

"What! Did you say she loves you?"

"Yes, she loves me. She loves me. She told me so, and I believe her."

Then he began to tell me what had happened. He had picked her up that morning and taken her to his apartment. She had noticed at once that there was something strange about him and had bombarded him with questions, to which his only answer was that he was exhausted after cramming for the test. Once they arrived at his place, he made her take off her coat and sit down. He described to her the stratagem he had used with my help, and suddenly he dropped his understated manner of signing and exclaimed with large angry gestures, "You let Bernard kiss you fully on the lips. I've been trying to do that for five months, and every time, you offer your cheek instead!"

She became ashen-faced and tried to interrupt him, but he shouted, "Let me finish!" and screamed in gestures. "Yes, I used Bernard to test you! What kind of person are you? Couldn't you see farther than my face?"

She cried and begged, "No, that's not true! Let me explain." But he refused to let her talk and shouted, "I'm not finished! How could you be so cheap and make sport of my deep and true feeling for you?"

She got up, screaming, "Not true! Not true!" and seized him by his shirt front, but he pushed her away and she fell on the bed. She frantically implored him, "Ken, Ken, let me talk. Are you finished? Let me talk!"

He sneered, "Go ahead. Talk! What have you to tell me? Nothing but lies. You're full of deceit. Do I have to listen to your lies?"

Tears streaming down her face, she signed, "Hear me out. At least hear me out."

"Hear? I'm deaf." After this feeble attempt at cynicism, he stopped uncertainly and was silent. She began to reproach him. "You destroyed it all. You ruined my plans. Why did you do that awful, base thing to me? If only you knew the truth, the real reason why I didn't let you kiss me on the lips."

He signed rudely, "Okay, spill it out. And tell me why you let Bernard kiss you on the lips but not me. What is it?"

Her manner became firm and angry. "Okay, I'm going to spill it out. Damn it! Damn you!"

She explained that when the college had closed for the summer, and she and Ken began to write to each other, she started to realize how much she loved him. "Couldn't you read between the lines?" she asked him. "But you were only leading me on," he answered.

"If that's true, why should I be doing that? Leading you on for what?"

"Why don't you say it? If you love me, say it. Do you love me? Or, damn it, are you still playing with me?"

She sobbed, "I was going to tell you, but you spoiled it all."

"What do you mean? Are you feeling guilty because of what happened last night? More lies!"

"Oh, no! Damn it! I'm not finished. Listen to me, please, please."

"I'm listening."

"Bernard took me by surprise. I was not expecting him to kiss me. He knows I'm your girl. He means nothing to me. So it was a frame-up! How deceitful of you—and of him too!"

"Look, that was the only way I could find out where I stand with you."

"Why didn't you just ask me yourself?"

He grew confused and was at a loss for an answer.

"Finally you are listening, let me tell you what really happened."

When she came back to Gallaudet for the fall, Mildred confided in her roommate Carol that she loved Ken and wanted to give him a very special present for his birthday, which was November 25th. But since she came from a poor family and had very little money, she thought that the most precious gift she could give Ken would be her first real kiss and the declaration of her love for him. She had asked Carol to arrange the birthday party for Ken at his place. "And now you ruined it!" she burst out.

Ken was shocked. Disbelievingly, he said, "You invented this story just now."

"No, no! That's God's truth!" She beat on his chest with her fists. "If you don't believe anything I say, I'm going to prove it to you."

"Go ahead."

Mildred embraced him tightly and kissed him fully on the lips. He lost his balance and fell to the floor, and she fell on top of him. Once on the floor she kept trying to kiss him with a wild intensity while he twisted his face away from hers, this way and that. Her kisses landed on his cheeks, nose, eyes, ears, and neck.

Her very physical presence, the touch of her body, and above all her evident desperation finally washed away the rage and suffering in Ken and he began to respond to her. They both cried and kissed, as their intertwined bodies rolled on the floor until they reached a wall. Each new kiss was longer and longer as the undertow of passion drained them of all strength to resist and they surrendered to the profound and ecstatic happiness of union between two people who love one another.

When it was over, their bodies resting in a welter of cast-off clothes, they smiled and gazed into each other's faces, which still glistened from their tears.

Ken stopped signing and sat quietly. The combination of poetic restraint and candor with which he had signed his story to me was inexpressibly moving. The light from the window was falling on him. I saw how tired he looked, yet how his eyes shone with a new luster.

I watched him for a while and then said, "Strange how this turned out in the end."

He got up, put on his coat, and approached me, stretching out his hand. We shook hands, smiling broadly.

At the door he stopped, turned around, and faced me. "Oh yes, I almost forgot. Mildred wants you to know that she is going to even the score with you one of these days."

What I am going to narrate next is an occurrence that puzzles me to this day. Did the Reverend Mr. Fortune fall into the very trap against which he warned? If there ever was a time warp, as science-fiction fans call it, this was it, and I and some two hundred other people were witnesses to it.

I cannot forget a lecture one Sunday evening in the early 1950s and the upheaval that it produced. Sometimes, too, I wonder what it had meant to the lecturer who had been indirectly responsible for the uproar, and whether he had ever been told the truth about it.

In that pretelevision era signed oratory was still an art. The orators were prized by all deaf communities for their "golden hands"—for the classical, mellifluous, and dramatic manner in which they transformed a speech into a feast for the eye and mind. Their delivery in sign was a joy to behold, and their spellbound audiences savored every rhetorical device, every nuance of sign language, every grand gesture, just as much as the ancient Greeks and Romans must have relished listening to speeches by Demosthenes and Cicero.

Every Sunday evening at seven o'clock the auditorium of Chapel Hall at Gallaudet College was crowded with an eager audience. Distinguished preachers, lecturers, professors, and visitors from different parts of the country would come and deliver thrilling speeches. Nearly all these speakers were accomplished signers; the rare exceptions were assigned topnotch sign language interpreters such as Mary Benson, a rapid-fire signer and martinet dean of women, or Edward Scouten, a loving, dedicated professor. Both were renowned for their precise word-for-word interpretation in sign.

On this unforgettable evening I arrived in Chapel Hall anticipating an enjoyable time. Although it was not yet seven, the auditorium was completely filled. The front row was occupied by the faculty, and the rows immediately behind it by "Normals," hearing students at the Normal School, where they trained as teachers of the deaf. Many of these Normals were foreigners. We ordinary college students sat behind the Normals.

It was a cold November night, but inside it was comfortably warm. We were facing a man in clerical clothes—a black suit, a black shirt with a white clerical collar—who looked so handsome, so picture-perfect, with his wavy graying hair, that he seemed more like an actor playing the part of a preacher than a real preacher. His name was Fortune, if I recall correctly, and he was a Baptist minister from some southern state, Georgia or South Carolina. Although he could hear, his parents were deaf, and he was such a superb and charismatic signer that he did not need an interpreter. When he began to deliver his speech, I paid close attention. At this point I must confess that the reason for my intense interest was not so much the desire to be inspired by the Reverend Mr. Fortune's wisdom and reasoning; by his explication of the meaning of life, of religion, and of man's relationship to God; or by his utterance of profound philosophical truths; no, my real reason was to revel in watching the oratory of a master signer.

I was not disappointed. Every sign that he formed with his hands was so true, so exact, so masterful, so emotion-laden. He looked at us lovingly, and he signed lovingly. In short, he had us in the palm of his hand, an expression which surely should be more than figurative.

He talked of how important it is to a man of God to share the word of God with others, and how important it is not to digress from the Holy Scriptures or indulge in personal philosophizing. Belief in the word of God, he said, was paramount. This is what makes the man of God confident and credible. Otherwise, he, the man of God, becomes confused. The important thing is to reach out and touch people.

After signing for some time in this vein, the Reverend Mr. Fortune stopped, watched us, smiled with the confident smile of the master orator, and said he had a story for us to illustrate his point.

I sat up excitedly, as did many others. The story was about a preacher who tried to digress and philosophize instead of following the word of God. One Sunday morning the preacher rambled on in this way, introducing various personal digressions and extraneous remarks. Now and then the preacher would look at his audience, and each time he would be upset at the sight of an old man sitting in the front pew who kept shaking his head as if to admonish the preacher. This sight made the preacher more and more nervous and confused. He lost the thread of his thoughts, stammered, and finally stopped altogether, forgetting what to say next. He tried to save the situation by ending his sermon and asking the congregation to rise in a concluding prayer, which they did, though surprised by the sudden brevity of his sermon.

After the prayer, the preacher, still angry and upset, walked over to one of the older parishioners and asked her, "Who's that old man? I never saw him before. Why does he keep interrupting me?"

The woman said, "Oh sorry!" and, placing her hand on the preacher's arm, she added, "What a shame he upset you. He's spastic, he has some kind of palsy."

We all burst out laughing. I could see the shoulders of the Normals in the row ahead of me shake with laughter, and as I looked around, I saw that my fellow students too wore broad grins on their faces. A few braver ones among us even clapped their hands.

The Reverend Mr. Fortune surveyed us with the practiced smile of the star lecturer, clearly enjoying the effect he had planned in advance. Then he predictably began to expand on the anecdote as a way of illustrating the need for the man of God to remain true to the word of God without letting himself be distracted.

Some three minutes passed. The Reverend Mr. Fortune continued signing. Suddenly I noticed that the shoulders of the Normals in front of me were shaking as if from laughter. I was mystified because I had not observed that the preacher had said anything funny. Perhaps I had missed something? But no, I glanced at my fellow deaf students and did not see any of them laughing. They were giving each other puzzled looks. Had we deaf missed something?

We no longer watched the lecturer; instead our gaze fastened on the shaking shoulders of the Normals in front of us. What was so funny? I did not know, but something about those shaking shoulders and the Normals' attempts to stifle their laughter by clamping their hands over their mouths infected me, and I began to laugh too.

Then the other deaf students started to laugh. We stared at each other, not knowing why we laughed, but we kept laughing. The merriment spread like wild fire. We laughed to the point of hysteria.

The Reverend Mr. Fortune saw us laughing and he became increasingly nervous and confused in his delivery. He began to stammer. It was obvious that he had lost the thread of his thoughts. He finally came to a stop: he signed to us to rise and he closed with a prayer.

We rose and, while he was praying, we had trouble stifling our laughter. Right after he signed *amen*, the Reverend Mr. Fortune snatched his Bible from the pulpit with shaking hands and strode off the platform, in his haste almost falling off the steps. At the same time, the college president, Dr. Elstad, ran up the steps to the platform and bawled us out. In effect, he told us that he was appalled by our behavior, by us who supposedly were "the cream of the crop" of deaf students from all over the country. He then hurried backstage, apparently to catch up with and placate the preacher.

We were crushed by Dr. Elstad's harangue. We stared at each other, not understanding what had come over us just a while ago. Then someone asked the Normal students just what had happened, just why they had laughed so.

They all spoke up at almost the same time, saying that it was one person who had started the gale of laughter some three minutes after the Reverend Mr. Fortune had told the anecdote about the preacher. That person laughed so hard and so infectiously that the other Normals could not resist joining in.

Professor Scouten took it upon himself to identify the culprit, who turned out to be a female Normal from Siam (now Thailand). When Scouten asked why she had started laughing, she looked frightened and kept saying, "I'm sorry, please."

Scouten then asked her, "Please tell me what you did."

What happened—the Siamese woman said—was that, while the Reverend Mr. Fortune was narrating the preacher anecdote, she listened attentively to every word he uttered and tried to translate them for herself into Siamese, since her English was not very good. When the preacher concluded his anecdote with the word *spastic*, she was surprised to hear everyone break into laughter. She alone had not laughed, simply because she had not known the meaning of the word *spastic*. She kept saying to herself, *spastic*, over and over, trying to figure out what it meant. Finally, unable to wait any longer, she nudged her neighbor for the whispered answer. Once she understood and linked the word to the anecdote, she started laughing helplessly, despite her efforts to hold back her laughter.

She laughed a little too late. She laughed, I think, spastically.

I thus learned at Gallaudet that things are not always what they seem and, as my next experience shows, appearances should not be taken for granted. Ever since I have been haunted by the moving secret of a young woman who looked hardly likely to have any secrets.

I could hardly wait for the train to arrive in Washington. I wanted to get there before all the young women I liked would be grabbed up for the Junior Prom. I had lost a week because of my mother's illness, but I was glad she was recovering.

I paid the cabbie and, with suitcase in hand, I bounded up the steps of College Hall. In those days—the early 1950s—the upper floors of College Hall were used as the men's dormitory; on the first floor were classrooms. On the second floor, where I lived, I had to pass the open doors to the Reading Room on the way to my room. There was a sheet of paper posted on one of these doors, and that made me stop and put down my suitcase. The paper listed the names of women students and, as was then the custom at Gallaudet, men would place their names opposite the names of the women who had agreed to be their partners for the Junior Prom, two weeks away.

At the same time, inside the Reading Room I saw my old pals Jack, Mark, and Bill, lolling in armchairs. They were not reading anything; "Reading Room" was a misnomer for that large airy lounge where students congregated to gossip, swap scuttlebutt, and watch television.

When I went to check the list on the door I saw that somebody else had already scrawled his name opposite the name of my favorite girl. I scanned the list for more names, but all the other women I liked already had dates. My friends knew what I was looking for and laughed as I turned around and faced them. They gestured, "Too late," "You're stuck," and as I sheepishly nodded, Jack said, "Why don't you ask Ruth Greenfield?"

Ruth was quiet and nondescript; the only time people noticed her was when she bumped into them, which she often did. She had tunnel vision, meaning that her peripheral vision was pretty bad. Consequently, she had developed a wide gait and could not help jostling people she passed.

The guys looked at me to see how I would react. A spirit of challenge rose within me. I looked at the trio and said, "Perhaps that's not a bad idea. I'll think about it. So long, old boys." I picked up my suitcase from the landing and sauntered toward my room.

Later the same day I left for Fowler Hall, which at that time was the women's dormitory. Once inside, I asked a young woman who was passing by to go and get Ruth, and she climbed the stairs to the third floor while I waited. A moment later she came down and told me that Ruth had trouble believing that I wanted to see her; she thought she was being kidded, but finally she was persuaded. Then I saw Ruth with her wavering gait descend the stairs slowly, leaning on the rail. Her round eyes regarded me timidly. "Hello, Ruth!" I said and shook her hand. "Let's sit down." We walked to the first-floor lounge and sat down. Then I asked, "May I have the pleasure of inviting you to be my partner at the Junior Prom?"

She was flabbergasted and made me repeat my words, as if she could not believe them. Then she protested that she did not have an evening gown. I suggested that maybe she could wear a party dress. But Ruth, showing a surprising firmness, objected, saying that she was going to get herself a gown.

"Fine," I answered. "Let me know the color so I can get a matching corsage for you."

During the two weeks before the Junior Prom I told no one that Ruth was going to be my partner, for I was brewing a plan, which for the time being would remain a secret. The only communication I had from Ruth in the meantime, during a fleeting encounter in a hallway between classes, was that the color of her satin gown would be sky blue.

On prom night I showered, shaved, applied cologne to my face, and with the corsage box in hand, walked in the gathering night toward Fowler Hall, where the men were picking up their partners. I asked that Ruth be called, and shortly afterward she came down to the lounge. She was all dolled up, her hair in ringlets, light makeup on her face. She looked lively and radiant. I helped her pin the yellow corsage on her satin gown because her fingers were trembling from excitement. Then we left for Ole Jim, one of the oldest buildings on campus that was now a wrestling gym on weekdays and a dance hall on weekends.

On arriving, Ruth was, like all other young women, handed a dance card at the door. We went up to the second floor where the dance was being held. I signed my name on Ruth's card and then, excusing myself, went to look for Jack, Mark, and Bill. I collared them, so to speak, one after another, and made them sign their names on Ruth's card, one after another. No one objected, but they did not look amused. Then the lights dimmed, leaving the revolving, glittering, multifaceted globes on the ceiling cascading multicolored lights onto the dancers and the garlanded walls. The band started to play. I had the first dance with Ruth. She stepped on my toes constantly during that first dance, but, by the time we finished the second and third dances, she had become perceptibly less nervous and more confident as I held her firmly and guided her across the floor.

A musician on the platform lifted a sign with a large number four, indicating the fourth dance. I told Ruth to wait a moment and raced to Jack, who was chatting at another corner of the dance floor with his partner, Flora, my favorite redhead. I reminded him it was his turn to dance with Ruth. Good sport that he was, he moved toward Ruth; as the band started playing, my arm encircled Flora's waist. We danced the fox-trot. Our feet moved rhythmically in tune with the vibrations of the beat that we felt with our chests and by picking up visual cues from other dancers. I glanced at Ruth and Jack; now and then she raised her half-intimidated, half-happy eyes to look at him as they were dancing. When the next dance started, I snagged Bill, leading him like an ox on a rope toward Ruth; then I danced with his date. For the following dance I corralled Mark. Ruth still looked happy. She clearly did not guess what was happening.

When it was time for a break, the lights went on and the musicians laid down their instruments and left. The crowded dance floor emptied as the couples emerged from the garlanded door of Ole Jim into the darkness of the April evening.

I left the building with Ruth. We walked across the silent campus toward Hendrix's, a then popular restaurant several blocks away. I felt there had been a change in Ruth. She smiled a lot and her arm rested in mine snugly. We did not talk much because it was not easy to read each other's signs in the semi-darkness. Once we entered Hendrix's, though, she became more talkative. Over coffee and dessert, she started to share surprising confidences with me. She told me about her dreams for the future, when she would be independent and living on her own, "but of course with a white cane." I was not sure I had understood her signs, and I asked her to repeat. She said, "A white cane and, if I can afford it, a seeing-eye dog."

I still was not sure what she meant and thought she was joking. I said, "You aren't that blind."

"Oh, no. But I'll be fully blind in about sixteen months. The doctor told me." Ruth told me that a year ago she had learned from her physician that she was going to become completely blind and there was nothing medicine could do to prevent it. She described how she spent many hours walking in her room with a blindfold on so that she would be familiar with its layout once she had lost her sight, and she added that she was learning to read and type braille.

She seemed to look forward to that menacing future, not with anxiety but rather with quiet courage. She talked about it very candidly, sharing her feelings and plans with me, but not to get my sympathy. She simply seemed to want me to know about it as if it were something ordinary and usual.

I was so intrigued by her conversation that I forgot the time. When the waiter hovered near our table, I looked at my watch and signed to Ruth, "Time to go back to Ole Jim."

I danced with her a few times and then we swapped partners again. I could see she was having a wonderful time. She was all smiles in that glittering dream world of Ole Jim. Her last few dances were again with me.

Suddenly the lights went on. It was over. I glanced at my watch: it was ten minutes to curfew. In those days the female students had to be back in Fowler Hall by 1:00 A.M. on prom night, on pain of sanctions. Prom night was a big concession, every other night they had to sign in by ten.

We walked to Fowler Hall. When we reached the door and stopped, Ruth turned around to face me. She signed, "It was the best evening ever in my life.

Thank you."

I nodded my head, not knowing how to reply.

"It was my first dance and, I'm afraid, my last," she said. "But I'll always remember it as long as I live. Good night."

I kissed her, and then she walked into Fowler Hall. As I stared after her receding figure, I saw that her shuffle was now modulated to a gait that had something enticing and feminine in its swaying awkwardness. She had bloomed. I walked back to College Hall. As I entered the Reading Room, the inseparable trio were already there. Bill exclaimed, "Here comes the ladies' man!"

"And the stealer of dance partners." This came from Jack, who added, "You made us dance with Ruth so that you could dance with our dates. Clever of you."

Then I told them Ruth's story. I concluded, "Be happy you danced with her." I stretched, yawned, and signed, "Time for bed."

Once in my room, I turned the lights off. The shutters were closed tightly. I lay in my bed. My eyes remained open, yet I saw nothing—just total darkness along with my own familiar silence.

The summer following my junior year, I worked as a cocktail glass washer at Hotel Washington in Bretton Woods, New Hampshire. Shortly after my arrival there I began dating a waitress, Carol, who was also a college student, and who could hear. It was my first experience in a serious "mixed" relationship.

I had been attracted to Carol immediately, but we did not start getting close until the day she found me lying on a hill slope reading a book of poetry. She asked me what I was reading, and we soon discovered we shared a love of poetry. Carol asked me to teach her sign language. From then on we not only saw each other daily at the hotel restaurant but went out together frequently, especially to a nearby swimming hole.

In three months she learned to communicate with me remarkably well in sign, and our intimacy grew. Toward the end of summer, after Carol left for Boston and Simmons College, my parents stopped by to visit me. They worried on discovering that I was going with a hearing girl and argued that it would not work. They said I would pay the usual price of feeling excluded, standing there like a stick of furniture while my future hearing wife would chat with other hearing people. "For companionship and good communication, it is better to marry your own kind," my mother claimed, and my father nodded approvingly.

I listened without comment. It was good to see my parents again. We had dinner together and I accompanied them to their room at an inn. There, suddenly, the atmosphere turned dismal. They got into a heated argument; Father wanted to drive on to Maine but Mother, a stay-at-home, insisted on returning to New York and responded with a calm obstinacy to my father's increasingly heated signing. At last he grew so frustrated that he declared he would drive to Maine by himself and stormed out of the room, leaving us alone. He would return after cooling off, we knew. But Mother at once changed the subject and reverted to the issue of my going steady with a hearing girl. "Mixed marriages never work," she declared with such conviction that I commented, "You seem to talk from your own experience."

"Yes, that is true," she answered. Perhaps trying to forget the unpleasant scene with Father, she launched into reminiscences of her youth. Among the New York deaf community she had been known as one of the fabulous three Stoloff sisters—Lena, Marion, and herself, Jennie. She was gay, pleasure-loving, and fond of a hearing man, Peter, who reciprocated her feelings. Then along came my father, who had been in love with her ever since they had gone to the same school, the Lexington School for the Deaf, and whom she had always kept at arm's distance. He had to absent himself for long periods, traveling from one city to another, but during his absences he used to write her poems and letters declaring his feelings for her. She enjoyed receiving and reading those poems and letters and, despite her attachment to Peter, they made her curious to see Father again. Once he sent her a simulated pearl necklace along with a letter saying that he would arrive at Grand Central on such and such a day and he asked her to meet him there.

She decided to go, wearing the pearl necklace, and met him as he stepped off his coach wearing a camel's-hair coat and a snap-brim hat. Even then, and always afterward, he was a dapper dresser. They went to a restaurant where, because of a prior engagement that my mother could not break, Peter was waiting to meet them. Once there, my future parents began to chat fluently and with gusto in sign language while Peter, who knew only the basics of sign, looked on uncomprehendingly. At the same time, he began to understand a basic truth; after the meal, and before dessert was served, he stood up, excused himself, signing to my mother, "I'll see you soon." She asked when, and he replied, "Perhaps next week."

"Did you see him again?" I asked.

"No. He never came back."

"Do you still miss him?"

Her face became wistful. "Yes."

"What would it be like if you had married Peter?"

She laughed. "I would not have you."

I commented that sometimes a choice must be made between love and ease of communication. "Did you really love Peter?" I asked. "I was very fond of him," she answered. "Perhaps it was a summer romance." The door opened and Father walked in, as cool as if he had just returned from a stroll, signing to Mother, "Let's go back home to New York." We all drove off in Father's Packard and soon afterward I returned to Gallaudet. Carol and I kept up correspondence for some time, but it gradually died away.

Midway in my senior year a kind of fever seized me and my classmates as we began to worry about getting a job after graduation. At that time just about the only profession open to deaf college graduates was teaching—at schools for the deaf, of course—and for this very reason there was intense competition among us for the best teaching jobs. We took courses in education and did some practice teaching at the nearby Kendall School for the Deaf, but above all we hoped to get favorable references from the most influential man on the campus, more influential even than the college president Dr. Elstad—Dr. Powrie Vaux Doctor.

To me this problem caused special anxiety because all my job-hunting efforts are inextricably bound up with my uneasy relationship with my father, a relationship that came to a climax in Annapolis one day toward the end of my senior year.

As the bus lurched on its ride to Annapolis, I felt my breast pocket to make sure I still had the bomb I was going to explode in my father's face. I was carrying a letter that I expected to provide me with one of the most gratifying moments in my life, and it would complete my emancipation from home, from my father. I was going to meet him and my mother in Annapolis, where they were visiting friends.

On the long bus ride thoughts of my father prompted old memories to come alive. One evening when I was sixteen, my father began to question me about my future. I was congratulating him on his performance in a play and telling him of my dream of working full time in theater when he suddenly cut me short and called me a dreamer. He said I was not being practical, and that in this world, ruled by the hearing, the deaf cannot go far. Then he said, "You're sixteen already. It's time for you to start thinking about getting a job," he signed. He went on about how hard it was to get a good job and said that, since I had already learned a lot about printing under Mr. Renner at the print shop of the New York School for the Deaf, which had a good vocational department, next year I should quit school and get a job as a printer. "Know how many years it took me to get to where I am now?" In fact, it had taken him a long time. He had started out as a house painter and even bridge painter, then had gotten a job with the Works Progress Administration as an illustrator. Once the war started, deaf people found it easier to get jobs, and my father became an apprentice at a lithographic plant, where he advanced to a journeyman, joined the union, and finally began to earn a good living. Not that it improved his disposition much; he continued to be what he always was—beetlebrowed, irascible, and demanding.

Uneasy as I felt about his wish, I meant to obey it and become a printer because I wanted badly to please him. But it was in the fall of the same year that Mr. Panara came to the NYSD and awakened my literary and theatrical enthusiasms. Only then had I begun to dream of going to Gallaudet. For some time afterward I was torn between my feeling of duty toward my father and my desire to attend Gallaudet. Finally, about a year later, I rebelled against my father for the first time. I told him that I wanted to finish school at the NYSD and go on to Gallaudet and become a teacher.

He became furious and asked me if I knew how much it cost to go to Gallaudet and how low a salary teachers were receiving. But nothing he said could sway me. I told him there were state scholarships for Gallaudet students, and that a teacher's pay might be low but the prestige was high. He retorted, "What's prestige? You can't eat it. Teaching is a sissy's job; all you do is scribble on the blackboard." "Not true," I protested. "I want to teach because I know what it's like being deaf and trying to learn. I want to follow in Mr. Panara's footsteps." To strengthen my argument, I added, "He has confidence in me." This was a tactical mistake because it infuriated my father and he reproached me. "You follow that teacher instead of me—your own father."

"Yes," I signed. "You are my own father, but that doesn't mean I have to become what you are."

"What!" He rose and approached me threateningly. "Are you ashamed of me?"

"No," I protested. "I am proud of you, but I won't be happy working with machinery. I like to work with children. Please, don't make me quit school."

He sat down. "I don't give a damn. Fine, go ahead and stay in school, and enter Gallaudet. But you won't get a penny out of me."

"Fine. I'll work my way through college. But please understand. I've tried to follow you in everything. I always tried to please you. I want you to be proud of me. All I want from you is your consent to my pursuing my heart's desire."

"I don't give a damn. Follow your heart's desire for all I care." And with that he got up and walked away.

I went to my bedroom, uncertain what I should do. Should I abandon my plans in order to make my father happy? How could he be jealous of Mr. Panara or think I was ashamed of him? I wondered. I was still angry when the door opened and my mother walked in. She signed furtively, "Don't listen to your father. Decide for yourself, don't let him stop you. Don't worry. I'll help you out somehow."

I asked her why he felt like that, but she answered, "I don't know, but that does not matter. Please be strong. Do it for your own sake, not for his sake." Before she left the room, she asked me not to tell my father about our conversation.

So I stuck to my decision, and she did help me out. After I went to Gallaudet she sent me five dollars every week. My father knew about it, but he never said anything. My aunt Lena also helped out, sending me a check now and then to tide me over.

The bus made a sudden stop, jarring me out of my reminiscences. Soon I was caught up in my recent problems. In the winter of my senior year at Gallaudet, I began to worry about what I would do after graduation and, like the other seniors, started to think about writing job applications to schools for the deaf all over the United States.

But there was a serious obstacle, and its name was Doc. As editor-in-chief of *The American Annals of the Deaf*, Powrie Vaux Doctor had close personal contacts with superintendents of schools for the deaf throughout the nation. He was the man all seniors went to see when they wanted a job reference. Without Doc's stamp of approval no senior could hope to get a teaching job. To make matters worse, he was a man who practiced favoritism on a grand scale. If he liked you he helped you get ahead; if not, you were in his doghouse for life. As it happened, like Mr. Ryder, he favored those students whose speech and lipreading skills were the best. Since I was not among them, I knew I would be wasting my time to ask him for a reference.

But then there was Dean Irving S. Fusfeld. He was friendly toward me and not without a certain amount of clout himself, so one day I just walked into his office and asked him, "Is it true that Doc is the only person to ask for job references? Isn't there anyone else on the campus I can ask?"

"Yes, there is," he answered.

"And could that person be you, perhaps?"

He smiled, "I'd be happy to recommend you."

He asked me what school was my first choice; I told him the California School for the Deaf at Berkeley. He had the kind of face that shows no emotion, but there was a twinkle of surprise in his eyes when I mentioned that school. Not without reason, for the Berkeley school at that time had a reputation as the school with the most progressive system for educating deaf children. The school philosophy supported the use of sign language in instruction as well as in extracurricular activities, such as sports and the school's literary society. Moreover, it paid the highest salaries to teachers, and it had never, so far, hired any deaf teacher who didn't have at least several years of teaching experience. One had either to have a lot of chutzpah or be very ambitious to apply for a job there. After a while, Dean Fusfeld asked, "What is your second choice?" I said it was my alma mater, the New York School for the Deaf, and added that, just to be sure, I would be sending job applications to some fifteen other schools as well. He reflected, then responded, "Yes. You can add the following phrase in your letters to these schools: 'Dr. Fusfeld will be happy to write you as a personal matter.' Please bring me a list of all the schools you will write to."

When I got back to my room I started typing the letters of application. It took me all week to finish typing all seventeen letters, but I finally completed them all, placed stamps on them, and mailed them off, not before giving Dr. Fusfeld the list he had asked for. Then I waited, as did my fellow seniors, in an atmosphere of anxiety and anticipation.

At that time it was a custom for the head senior to pick up the mail for his classmates and distribute it to them. Our head senior was Alexander, a tall, rangy, and very amiable guy. Each morning he would locate each of us seniors—this was no problem since Gallaudet was then a small college with an enrollment of 250—and hand us our mail. In the late winter and in the spring of our senior year, we were particularly anxious to get our mail, hoping that it would include a letter of job acceptance from some school for the deaf. To see Alexander in the morning was like being pumped full of adrenalin, although the anticipation most often gave way to disappointment. I too became party to these shifts in mood.

A week passed. Nothing. Another week. Still no word. Then one morning I saw Ted Martin distributing the mail instead of Alexander. This gave me a jolt, for I considered Martin unreliable. He was a special favorite of Doc, which didn't surprise us because he had been deafened at fourteen and his speech was perfect. He was one of those deaf persons who enjoy passing for a hearing person—and almost succeed. But I also had a specific reason for my anxiety; a few weeks previously Martin had asked me which schools I intended to apply to for a job, and when I named Berkeley among others, he signed that I was a dreamer. When in reply I asked him what schools he himself was applying to, he also named Berkeley. I commented, "So I am a dreamer! What about you?" But he merely smiled and walked away.

When I saw Alexander later that day with Weber, a mutual friend, I protested to Alexander about letting Martin distribute the mail. He said he had not felt well that morning and, since Martin was his roommate, he had asked him this once to distribute the mail for him. But I told him I did not trust

Martin at all with such sensitive mail as replies to job applications. He pooh-poohed my fears, calling them unfounded, and said that he would continue to ask Martin to substitute for him now and then. Weber supported him. It was the two of them against me, and I admitted that I was probably wrong.

During the third week of waiting, I received a letter from the Montana School for the Deaf offering me a teaching job. This got me excited and I went to see Fusfeld. He read the letter and, looking at me impassively, counseled me to wait and not answer it yet. Then three days later I got an offer from another school, the West Virginia School for the Deaf. Again I went to Fusfeld, and again he advised me to wait.

So I waited and waited in almost unbearable anxiety. Days passed. One afternoon I was in my room reading a book when the door opened and Alexander and Weber entered, giving me a strange look. "Where do you keep your crystal ball?" Alexander signed. He proceeded to tell me that earlier that day he and Weber had to go shopping off campus, so he again asked Martin to distribute the mail for him. About fifteen minutes after he left Alexander realized that he had forgotten his money, so he and Weber returned to his room. The door was locked, so he unlocked it. Martin was inside, and of course, being deaf, he had not heard the sound of the key being turned in the lock.

When Alexander opened the door he saw Martin steaming open an envelope over a teakettle on a hot plate. Nearby on the desk lay a pile of undistributed mail. "What are you doing?" he angrily challenged Martin, who stammered, "Oh well, you know. . . ." He did not finish his reply because Alexander, normally a very placid guy, slugged him in the jaw.

So now Alexander and Weber wanted to apologize to me for doubting my suspicions. Alexander added that he did not know what to do about Martin; he wondered whether he should inform the college authorities about Martin's tampering with United States mail and violation of privacy. Weber, however, advised him against it, saying, "Let it ride. That would ruin his future for good. You punished him enough." We agreed to keep the whole thing quiet.

From then on, hail, rain, or whatever, only Alexander distributed the mail. And not long afterward he said he had something for me. From the stack of envelopes in his hand he extracted one and waved it at me. "From California," he said.

My heart tightened, but I thought it was probably some advertisement. When I looked at the envelope, however, I saw that it was from the California School for the Deaf at Berkeley. I thanked Alexander and rushed up to my room. I closed the door and placed the envelope on my desk. Slowly I cut it open and extracted the sheet of paper and began to unfold it carefully, peeking at each succeeding line as it presented itself to my vision, like a poker player slowly moving down his palm so as to see what card he was dealt.

I arrived at the line, "I am happy to advise you that. . ." and closed my eyes, praying silently that it did not mean I was being offered a job only after I had earned several years of teaching experience at some other school. Then I read on, and I felt like jumping onto my desk and whooping with joy: I was hired for the coming September.

I showed the astonished Alexander and Weber the letter when they entered my room to ask about it. I had scored a big coup, and my friends congratulated me heartily. Weber exclaimed that it was a good thing Martin got caught before he steamed open that letter and flushed it down the toilet. Then Weber asked me to let him have "the honor and privilege," as he put it, of conveying the news about my good fortune to Martin. I did not refuse.

At dinner time Weber found Martin in the cafeteria sitting with his girlfriend at a table. "Mind if I sit down here?" Weber asked as he placed his tray on the table. Martin made an inviting gesture and, after Weber sat down, they talked for a while before Weber tackled the subject. "By the way," he asked, "did you know that Bragg got the job at Berkeley?"

Martin smiled, "You're kidding me. Very funny."

"No, I am serious. Bragg got the letter this morning."

"Impossible."

"How can you be so cocksure?"

"Doc hasn't told me yet."

"Oh really, does Doc always have to be told first?"

All trace of jollity left Martin's face. He hastily got up and excused himself, saying he was in a rush to leave.

When Weber told us this we laughed, knowing where he was in a rush to go.

The following day President Elstad summoned all seniors for a special meeting in Chapel Hall. When we arrived, he was standing on the platform. Doc was sitting in the front row and Dean Fusfeld in a back row.

President Elstad delivered a short and angry declaration to the effect that Doc was the only person responsible for job placement and job references, and that anybody who needed such help should come to Doc alone. I wondered why he was talking after the fact. This had never before been made clear or official. But I also knew the answer; Doc had so much power on the campus that even Elstad was afraid of upsetting him. I turned my head and glanced at Dean Fusfeld. He was listening thoughtfully, supporting his chin on a hand. Our eyes met and he nodded slightly for my benefit. He had had the temerity to challenge the mighty Doc.

The bus again came to an abrupt halt, which shattered my reverie. I looked through the window and realized I was back in the present. I was already in Annapolis. I felt my breast pocket once more to make sure that the letter was still there, that the letter with which I hoped to resolve my lifelong conflict with my father and be free at last of his domination, free to live a life of my own on the other side of the continent.

With anxious steps I proceeded to the printing shop where my friend Taras Denis was working. We had known each other since Fanwood. He had recently quit his teaching job because the salary was so low. With a wife and baby to support, Taras simply could not afford to remain a teacher. He found a printing job in Annapolis, earning twice as much. He was waiting for his union card with which he could find a job anywhere in the United States.

I walked into the printing shop and saw my father and Taras, who was resignedly bent over a linotype keyboard. As soon as my father saw me, he signed half-mockingly, "See what he did," pointing an admonishing finger at Taras and then at me. "He quit teaching, went back to printing, and now earns a decent salary. All the time you spent at Gallaudet was worth nothing. Take up printing before it is too late." His eyebrows bristled in a familiar expression of discontent as he looked at me triumphantly. What could I do but admit my big mistake, his expression seemed to say.

But it changed to puzzlement when in reply, now that my long-awaited chance had arrived, I declared, "I swear to God I'll never ever touch a linotype keyboard again so long as I live!"

Both my father and Taras looked awestruck. Their glances met as if they were asking each other whether I had gone mad. Savoring their reaction and my moment of truth, I took out the letter from my pocket and handed it with a flourish to my father. "What is it?" he asked suspiciously. When I made no reply, he opened it.

I watched my father intently. There was no expression on his face as he read the letter. Taras looked on over his shoulder after I had gestured at him to do so. When my father finished, he made no comment. In the meantime Taras got up and shook my hand, congratulating me on my good fortune. Still, my father said nothing. I waited anxiously, hoping that he would say something complimentary, admit that he was wrong, or at least say that he was proud of me. His silence seemed to last forever. Finally he took a deep breath and signed, "California." He smiled. "That's where I always wanted to move."

CHAPTER THREE

Tryouts

I wanted to be independent, but for some reason I just couldn't seem to get away from my father. He followed me to California one year after I had started teaching there, but even before then his shadow preceded me with the people I met there. His move was a blow to my dream of independence. I was disappointed, yet, in a way, my feelings about him were mixed because there were some things I liked about him—not just his talents as an actor and a painter, but also his gift at storytelling, especially at telling stories of the days of his youth in the West. And now, upon my arrival in California, I had a story of my own to tell about the West.

I traveled to California in style in the brand-new 1952 Dodge of Don Bullock, one of my classmates. He and I and three other college friends were traveling West together. The moment I sat down in the car, it took off. I stuck my head out the window to wave good-bye to Mother, Father, and Aunt Lena.

A new life was opening before me. The car left Manhattan and moved westward, ever westward. I recalled all the stories my father had told me about his own travels across America during the Depression. Now is my turn, I thought; now I will gather material for stories of my own.

It felt good to be sitting in a comfortable seat in a brand-new car that smelled new. It was a completely different experience than that of my father, who, while he had abandoned my mother and me for several years, had been riding the train as a hobo and hitching rides on horsedrawn carts, trucks, and old jalopies. He had eaten fried hash at campfires and peddled pins and needles in rain and snow across the continent, whereas my friends and I would stop now and then at highway restaurants; our trip was pure vacation. He had quit high school in order to look for work; I completed college and was now off to teach in golden California. He had slept in barns and flophouses; I would be sleeping in motels.

73

All the time we were driving West my father was constantly in my thoughts. His presence never left me as the car rolled past wheatfields and cornfields and across the mountains of the continent. When we stopped in Yellowstone Park and I got one of my classmates to photograph me in my new ten-gallon hat and cowboy boots, I thought of how my father may have been digging ditches on the other side of the road.

There was a golden sunset when we reached California. We continued to Santa Monica, the home of Don Bullock's parents, who invited me to stay with them for a while. It was July; school did not open until after Labor Day, and the whole summer belonged to me. I swam in the Pacific Ocean for the first time, and in my mind I saw my father swimming along with me. Whatever I did, wherever I went, I saw him constantly in my mind.

Then Bullock told me that I was invited to a pool party by some well-to-do deaf couple whom I had never heard of. "How did they hear of me?" I asked. "Because they know your father," he responded.

In the evening we drove to a California ranch house with a big kidney-shaped swimming pool. Some fifty people were already there. Bullock introduced me to the host, his wife, and the others. I was meeting these people for the first time, but some of them said they had heard of me. "How?" "You're Wolf Bragg's son."

There was plenty of food and drink. It was a real Hollywood-style pool party. And the people there looked Californian too: suntanned, healthy, wearing brightly colored leisure clothes.

After we ate and drank from a buffet table, the host, a tall, thin man with a foxy smile, asked me, "Would you like to see a porno movie?"

I was unprepared for this question and asked hesitatingly, "Here and now?"

He answered, "Oh, sure. Everybody's going to see it. Besides, your father is not around. You are over twenty-one," he added, grinning. "Are you worried because you're a teacher? But you are a grown-up. Nothing wrong with that."

I answered with bravado, "No, not at all. I'm pretty much my own man."

He nodded approvingly and then waved his hands to attract everybody's attention and signed, "Come, everybody to the garage. We'll be showing the dirty movie now."

Hiding my feelings of shock at his candor, I looked at the others to gauge their reaction, but no one seemed perturbed. At the same time I caught glances directed at me accompanied by a kind of chuckle. All this attention made me feel uneasy, but I decided to ignore it and attributed it to my being a teacher. Anyhow, there was no way for me to retreat. I followed the crowd.

Inside the large garage were folding seats arranged in rows, enough for the fifty of us. Somebody pulled down a screen, and somebody else turned off the lights. It was dark and uncomfortable and I asked myself, What am I doing in here? Suddenly, the screen came to life. I saw a gorgeous girl in a skimpy bathing suit walk down what looked like a theater runway and assume the characteristic poses of a fashion model. She wore a smile frozen on her face as she turned elegantly this way and that to display her bathing suit. She walked back to the stage, turned once more to face the unseen audience, and disappeared. Strange. Another girl appeared, wearing a bathing suit of a different design. She also struck fashion-model poses. She was followed by still another model. What a lame porno show, I thought. But my host, who was sitting next to me and apparently observing my reactions, nudged me and signed, "Wait, it's not over yet. The big surprise is coming."

"I can't wait," I answered.

All of a sudden somebody pushed up the garage door and two cars, their headlights blazing, slowly rolled inside. Men wearing epauletted and belted raincoats, apparently plainclothesmen, sprang out of the cars. One of the men, who wore a fedora hat and seemed to be the chief inspector, stationed himself in front of the screen, and started to bark out commands through clenched teeth. In response to these commands, the detectives began to tug and shove the viewers toward the garage walls.

Camera flashes began to pop. One blinded me. I tried to cover my face, but it was too late. The man who snapped my picture, who I assumed was a reporter, was busily writing something in a pocket notebook. I was horror-stricken: tomorrow my picture would appear in the newspapers. People at the Berkeley school would see it—good-bye to my teaching career. What school would employ a teacher caught in a porno film raid?

The chief inspector caught my attention again. It was impossible to read his lips, since he seemed to be speaking through clenched teeth. Then for some reason, my gaze began to focus on him more attentively. He had a remarkable face: a large nose, narrow-set eyes, and bushy eyebrows. The whole was not unhandsome. It was a face with character.

I stared at him, and he began to stare back at me. Why did he look so familiar to me? Then I remembered. When I was a little boy my father would tell me stories about Elmer Priester, the world's greatest deaf prankster, as he put it. And he had described Elmer's looks to me, too. The chief inspector's face matched Elmer's image in my mind. No, it could not be true. But really the resemblance was remarkable.

I looked at the other guests in the garage. Why were they all stealing glances at me? Why were their postures relaxed, and why did they appear amused?

My suspicions grew stronger. I was sure now. I slowly formed the hand-shape *e* and placed my hand on the cheek, this being the name sign for Elmer Priester. With my other hand I pointed at him. He froze. His mouth opened. Then he smiled, took his fedora off, and signed, "Yes. You got me!"

My eyes darted to both sides and I saw that everybody had burst out laughing. "How did you know it was me? We never met," the "chief inspector" signed.

"You were in many of my father's stories. He described to me your famous pranks, to say nothing about your famous profile."

My father had caught up with me again, but then the story about Elmer is mainly my own story, not his. Before I knew it, I began to have more stories to tell, by then without my father's presence in them.

I have many more stories about Elmer the Great, a legend among the deaf. Even today, deaf people who never met him continue to retell stories about his exploits. It is time for some of these stories to be immortalized in print as part of deaf culture.

All the people at the party surrounded me, clapping me on the shoulders and shaking my hand, while I smiled foolishly. Then the whole thing was forgotten. I had a drink with Elmer, who pumped me about the latest news of my father. We talked for a while, and then he excused himself saying he had to leave on some urgent business. The party was nearing its end, so I decided to sit down. I found a vacant deck chair at the poolside near a couple whom I had not noticed before, and we performed mutual introductions. Nick was short and thin and had a rather mournful look about him while his wife, Beth, also short, was plump and had a round, amiable face. They both were in their sixties.

I began the conversation by saying, "What a joke on me! I'll never live it down."

"No, no," Nick signed. "You outwitted Elmer by recognizing him and spoiling his joke. You are a hero and to be congratulated. Besides," he continued, "that was nothing compared with the jokes that Elmer has played on me and Beth."

"Tell me about them," I asked him.

He turned to Beth with a quizzical look, and she nodded and said, "Yes, go ahead, my dear."

So he launched into his narrative while I watched in fascination. A few years ago, he began, one Saturday evening at about nine o'clock he and Beth were sitting on the sofa discussing the illness of Beth's brother Jim in Oregon. That particular evening they had decided to stay home instead of going to the club of the deaf. Suddenly, the doorbell lights flashed. Nick opened the door and saw Elmer. In those days the TDD, a modem attachment that can turn any telephone into a miniature teletype, was not yet invented and so deaf people were unable to announce visits to each other beforehand. Although surprised by Elmer's appearance at this late hour, Nick invited him inside.

The moment Elmer planted himself down on the sofa the doorbell lights flashed again and when Nick opened the door he saw a uniformed Western Union messenger, who game him a telegram and a receipt to sign.

Nick returned to the living room and exclaimed, "Beth, a telegram!"

"Oh, my dear! I hope it's not bad news about my brother," she signed worriedly.

He tore open the envelope. He read the telegram, then, disbelievingly, read it again.

"What is it? For God's sake, tell me," Beth pleaded.

Looking thunderstruck he slowly signed to her and Elmer, "Irish Sweepstakes—$75,000."

Beth grabbed the telegram from him and read it. She clasped her hands on her chest. "Oh, you won $75,000."

"Yes, if I read it right." He took the telegram from Beth and showed it to Elmer. "Read it."

Elmer read it and said, "Congratulations! You won $75,000!"

With shaking hands, Nick took out his wallet and extracted from it a lottery ticket, then he looked at the telegram again. "Look, Beth, the number is the same! I can't believe my eyes. Look!"

She reeled as if almost fainting. "Whoopee! You did it!"

She grabbed him by the waist and they danced a kind of jig. She then hugged Elmer too.

Nick exclaimed, "I'm gonna buy a Cadillac!"

"I want a mink coat!" Beth added.

"You'll get it. What else?"

And they quickly jotted down a list of these and other things they wanted. In those days, the early 1950s, $75,000 seemed a fortune. After composing their list, Nick suggested they go to the club of the deaf and tell everyone. Beth agreed and signed, "That's wonderful. Let's go! Now we will know who our real friends are and who are not!"

What an odd remark! One is generally supposed to learn who one's friends are from calamity—not from sudden prosperity, I thought to myself.

Elmer drove them to the club. On the way, Nick asked him to stop at the Wells Fargo Building. Nick ran up to the bank and lovingly patted its wall, signing, "That's where my money will be." But Beth signed to him, "You old fool! Hurry back to the car. I can't wait to see those deaf faces turn green with envy when they hear of our good luck."

They arrived at the deaf club, where the usual Saturday night crowd was gathered. People were sitting at the bar and in booths, so Nick pounded on the bar and waved his hands to catch everybody's attention. "I won $75,000 on the Irish Sweepstakes! The drinks are on me!"

Word spread throughout the club on winged hands. Some people would not believe it; they laughed and accused Nick of kidding, so he got out the telegram and jubilantly shoved it in front of their noses.

He and Beth were mobbed by well-wishers. The bartender expertly filled and refilled glasses for everyone. Soon Nick was jovially waving his overflowing glass of beer in the air without spilling so much as a drop while lustily signing with his other hand about his good luck. Beth alternately sobbed and laughed like crazy as her friends looked on with admiration, feigned or not. The couple announced that as soon as the money was in the bank, they would withdraw it, and go on a spending spree.

When the club closed, Elmer drove them home.

As Beth went into the house, Elmer pulled Nick aside and said, "Wait. I have a confession to make. I should have told you earlier. The telegram was nothing but a hoax."

Nick signed, "You're out of your mind."

"No, no! It was only a joke."

"Now you're really joking. How can it be when the number on the telegram was the same as on my lottery ticket?"

"I know. I was with you when you bought that ticket, remember? I copied the number. Then I sent you the telegram myself."

"Bull. I don't believe you."

Elmer took out a copy of the telegram from his pocket and showed it to Nick.

Feeling as if a ton of bricks had just fallen on him, Nick said dejectedly, "So you did it." Then, his mood shifting to outrage, he asked, "But why?"

"Well, otherwise you'd never have experienced the most wonderful moments in your life. You did truly enjoy that excitement while it lasted, and it cost you nothing."

"Hey, wait," Nick signed. "But I spent fifty bucks on the drinks."

Elmer took out a slip of paper and, consulting it, said, "Your tab was exactly $48.55. Here, let me pay it." He elaborately wrote out a check, which he handed to Nick, saying, "That's the penalty I have to pay for enriching your life with a thrilling adventure."

"You sure have a weird sense of humor," Nick commented bitterly as he pocketed the check. "But what will I tell Beth? Do you realize what this will do to her?"

"She'll get over it, don't worry."

Beth came to the door and asked, "Still having your little chitchat? Come, dance with me." She pulled Nick toward the living room and tried to whirl him around, but he just stood there passively and let himself be pulled this way and that like a lifeless puppet.

"What's the matter? Don't stand there like a zombie," she ordered Nick. But he sat down, or rather wilted onto the sofa, and signed, "Sit down. I have something to tell you. Brace yourself."

Feeling alarmed, she sat down quickly and asked, "What's wrong? Is it your heart? Are you feeling ill? It can't be. Only last week Dr. D'Albora said you're as fit as a fiddle."

He answered, "Wait a moment. Nothing to do with my heart. My heart is as fine as ever, except that it's broken."

"Broken? What do you mean?"

"If I tell you, your heart will be broken also."

She sensed misfortune and looked at him and Elmer with fright in her eyes. Nick signed to Elmer, "You tell her yourself."

Patting Beth's hand reassuringly, Elmer told her what had happened, prefacing his narrative with, "As I told Nick, it was all a hoax."

At first she refused to believe it. Then she got up, signing, "Why? Why?" and ran into the bedroom, slamming the door behind her. After that, Beth refused to speak to Elmer for two weeks.

"Two weeks? That's all? You and Beth must be a remarkably forgiving couple," I commented.

"But that is not all," Nick continued. A year later they visited Beth's brother in Oregon. They had a wonderful time seeing the sights of Portland and environs when suddenly one afternoon they got a telegram from their real estate agent in Los Angeles notifying them that their house had burned down. Immediately, they cut short their vacation and flew home.

On the plane they wondered what, if any, of their belongings had been saved and figured out the insurance payment they would be receiving for the house. When they landed in Los Angeles, they took a taxi to the site of their burned house. On arriving, they were dumbfounded to see no trace of fire; their house was completely unscathed. When they unlocked the door, they saw Elmer inside sipping coffee and smiling innocently.

"So that was you?" they demanded.

"Guilty," he smiled innocently.

Beth started to choke him, but Nick pushed her away and asked, "Elmer, why did you do that to us? Why? Why?"

"Why? I felt lonesome for you."

Beth signed furiously, "I'll never forgive you." She ran to the bedroom and locked herself in.

"Was that the end of your friendship with Elmer?" I asked.

"Wait," Nick signed. "I'm not finished."

Months later, at ten o'clock one evening, as Nick and Beth were relaxing in their living room, the doorbell lights began to flash. Who could be there so late, they wondered. Nick opened the door and saw a young man he knew from the deaf club. "What's wrong," Nick asked. The youth nervously answered, "Sorry. Elmer had a heart attack. He was unconscious, so an ambulance picked him up. But he was dead on arrival at the hospital. I know how close he was to you, and that's why I came to tell you."

Nick and Beth were overcome by shock and grief. They hugged each other. But then she pushed him away and ran into the bedroom. He followed her, worried about her condition. When he entered he saw her standing on a chair. "What are you doing?" he asked. She told him, pointing at the trunk on the top of the wardrobe, that she was getting out her black dress so she could start mourning right away.

Just then the doorbell lights began to flash again. Were more deaf people coming to bring them their condolences? they wondered. Nick ran to the door. In walked Elmer in a hat and raincoat. Nick was stunned, thinking that he was seeing a ghost. Nick signed, "Oh, you sonofabitch."

"Why? Aren't you happy to see me?"

By then Nick had recovered from his surprise, and exploded, "But why did you have to play this awful stupid joke on us?"

"I just wanted to see how much you and Beth would miss me."

Nick slowly turned around and sat down heavily on the sofa. "Where is Beth?" Elmer asked. "In the bedroom," Nick answered. "She's looking for a black dress. Better hurry before she puts it on."

"That was real fast," Elmer commented. "So she cares for me that much. Well, that's nice." He then walked into the bedroom and calmly watched Beth, who was still standing on the chair. She noticed him from the corner of her eye and signed, "Oh, did you know that Elmer is dead?"

"Oh, yes," Elmer answered.

She did a doubletake and almost fell off the chair. "Elmer!"

"As you can see."

Nick signed, "Well, that's the end of the story."

"But what happened between you and Elmer after that?" I asked.

"We became friends again a month later."

I could not restrain my curiosity any longer and again asked, "How come you and Beth always forgive Elmer so readily?"

Nick looked baffled by my question and glanced helplessly at Beth. She extended her arm and grimaced as if waving away a pesky insect, crossed her cupped hands on her breast like a diva about to burst into an aria, and smiled angelically, "Oh, but really he is like a little boy to us. We love him."

I arrived in Berkeley fired with ambition to excel at my new profession. To be sure, I looked forward to my first class with some trepidation, but I believed that I was ready. Nothing could faze me, I thought. I was going to be another Mr. Panara, admired and looked up to by my deaf pupils, for whom I would open wide the gates to learning English.

The joke this time was on me.

By the end of my first week of teaching I already knew enough about my students' English skills to realize what a daunting challenge these pupils posed. Most of them were twelve years old, but their English was at second- or third-grade level. Unfortunately, this is not unusual for deaf children, to whom sign language is their native language and English a second language.

I myself had totally revised my concept of English after my encounter with Mr. Panara, who had opened my eyes to the glories of literate sign language even before linguists "discovered" American Sign Language (ASL) and demonstrated its value as a full-fledged language, as noble as Shakespeare's. Before Mr. Panara, I was made to feel ashamed of sign language by my teachers. I had been taught to regard it as evil, impure, a polluter of English, as something to be used on the sly with one's companions. I was not the only one to feel so; my mother used to practically order me to tear up her letters every time I was through reading them. She was simply ashamed of her poor English and always made sure I would not be contaminated by it. For many years, even in my adulthood, I would read her letters with my eyes closed to her language and, without thinking, tear them up and cast them away. I feel like a fool now for having done so. She wrote some lovely letters. She wrote from the heart.

I understood these deaf children so well, having been one myself. I knew what it was like to learn English by eye only, without benefit of hearing speech. And I resolved to apply what I had learned from Mr. Panara, to teach English with the aid of ASL, by translating into sign language the concepts of English grammar and syntax.

Now and then I would turn my back and write various grammatical rules on the blackboard. On one such occasion, however, as I turned around to face the class, I was astonished to see the children laughing and giggling.

"What's happening? Did I miss out on something?"

I scrutinized their faces, but they were deadpan. My gaze fastened on one boy, Larry, whose face looked the most innocent. In a flash I knew he had been making silly and perhaps derisive gestures behind my back. I pointed at him and exclaimed, "It was you!"

He was honest enough to answer, "Yes."

"Well, probably you don't realize it, but you're taking advantage of my deafness. We both are deaf. You know it's not fair. I can't hear you sign behind my back, so don't do that again. Now, all pay attention!"

Again I turned my back to write on the blackboard. From the corner of my eye I saw Larry jump up and make some signs. I turned quickly, pointing at him. "There you are again. That's the second time. Well, what should I do with you?"

"Okay, okay, I won't do it again."

I figured he was doing this on purpose to test my patience and see how angry I would get. "If you do it a third time, I'll have to punish you," I warned. "Is that clear?"

"Yes, yes," he nodded eagerly as if I was promising him a reward.

I continued the lesson; yet no sooner had I turned my back to write some examples than Larry was again up to his deviltry.

"Okay, you asked for it. Go stand in the corner."

He leapt up, smiling and happy, and sauntered to the corner. I stopped him. "You look so happy. What is so wonderful about standing in the corner?"

He answered, "I don't have to listen to you. Here in the corner I can dream."

I was flabbergasted. I had not been taught how to cope with this kind of situation during my practice teaching at Gallaudet. I decided to send him back to his seat. "I'll think up something to fix you later," I signed.

"Fine with me." He walked back and flopped onto his chair in a half-reclining position.

I distributed test papers to the children, and while they worked on them I walked around the room, wondering how to handle Larry. I now had a stronger feeling that he was testing me. If I failed with him, I would lose the respect of the entire class. I could not let him get away with this.

In the back of the room was a walk-in closet where the children hung their coats. In one corner I saw a separate, partitioned-off teacher's closet with a door of its own. I opened that door and peeked inside. It was a narrow space, six square feet at most. That was it! I smiled at the thought of shutting Larry in there, but of course I could not do that and risk his having to spend the rest of his life seeing psychiatrists.

So I closed the door and walked back into the classroom. Still, I was wondering what it would be like to be in that closet. As the children were still working, I returned and entered the small closet, closing the door behind me. Curiosity can make you do funny things.

I stood quietly for a moment. Yes, it was pitch-black inside. What did I expect anyway? And the air was stuffy, too. I smiled, thinking how funny it was, and heaven forbid anybody should know what I was doing now.

After about five seconds, I was ready to leave. I tried to turn the doorknob but it would not yield. My eyes widened as I realized I was locked in. I panicked and broke into a cold sweat. I raged at myself for having gotten into such a predicament. All kinds of thoughts raced through my mind: What will the children think of me when they find out; most of all, what will Larry say to me? What if my supervising teacher were to enter the room with the important visitors from Sacramento who were on the campus today? She would ask, "Where's Mr. Bragg?" The children would answer, "He's in the closet."

I then imagined the supervising teacher and the important visitors opening the door and, with a look of puzzlement on their faces, inspecting me standing there in the dark like a fool. She would probably ask, "Would you mind telling me what you are doing here, Mr. Bragg?" I would try to smile as normally as I could and, hoping to make the best of a bad situation, answer, "Oh, I'm waiting for a bus."

I began pounding on the door, knowing that my pupils, deaf though they were, could feel the vibrations.

After a while the door opened. Who else should open it but Larry. All the other children looked bewildered. Larry asked, "Why are you in there?"

"All right, I will tell you why I locked myself in. I just wanted to see if I could open the closet from inside, and found I couldn't. So don't you ever play hide-and-seek in there or you'll get stuck."

Larry raised his hand and said, "It's not true. You can open the door from inside."

"But I tried that and couldn't."

"It can be done. Let me show you how." He grabbed my hand and pulled me toward the closet. He opened the door and showed me a small lock in the back. He was obviously pleased with himself, and all I could do was nod my head in thanks.

The following Monday I wrote on the blackboard in large script, "Why did I lock myself in the closet?" Then I turned around, faced my pupils, and repeated the question in sign so they would all understand it. The purpose was to reinforce their knowledge of language and teach them how to reason. I could see I succeeded to some extent. I knew now that the strategy I had inadvertently adopted was working; it was a strategy of capitalizing on situations as they arose, including my experience in the closet, to interpret English words in dramatic and precise sign language—and vice versa.

I settled into life in California fairly easily. I joined the Oakland Club of the Deaf and made friends with a fun-loving group of deaf men and women. As I look back I perceive more clearly that the whole gang of us were rebelling about the misconceptions of the hearing society. In their eyes, deaf people were supposed to be miserable creatures who bore up under their so-called affliction with patience and composure. We felt like, and were, normal young people and the only thing that made us different from hearing people, and that also joined us in a common bond, was our native language, sign language. It was through this bond that we were able to lead lives of happy normalcy, in our own "deaf way." We were clannish, yes, but what else could we do when the barrier of communication between us and the hearing loomed so tall? We would go to great lengths and travel great distances just to be together, deaf among deaf.

One day I got a phone message from a former college friend, Ed Barber. He was coming to San Francisco and hoped I could meet him at the train station. I always liked Barber because he was a happy-go-lucky little guy with a great sense of humor. So I was glad to pick him up the next evening in the used 1948 green Packard convertible with a white top that I had bought recently to celebrate my independence.

The moment he got off the train he declared, "Where can we have some fun? Let's start right away, pal."

I liked his spirit and took him to meet Burley, my hearing girl friend, who was waiting for us. I had met her at an evening class at what was then San Francisco State College, and in the couple of months I had known her I had taught her the manual alphabet and how to sign. She kept notes of class lectures for me since the instructor spoke so rapidly and used such long words that, even if I were a good lipreader, which I am not, I could not understand him. Burley also interpreted for me when I discussed the progress of my master's thesis with my faculty advisers. She was a great help to me.

After we picked up Burley we went to a party. At the party Ed seemed to have no problems mixing with the others. He was only hard-of-hearing, not deaf, and his speech was good. But at one point when I found myself alone with him, he asked me if I could get him a date.

"What is the problem?" I countered. "There are plenty of women here. Why don't you hook one yourself?"

"I can if I want to. But they are not deaf."

"Oh, you want someone who's deaf? What happened? I thought you could speak well and hear some. Can't you?"

"Oh God, you don't know what it is like to be hard-of-hearing. It's always a struggle communicating with the hearies. Always there are mistakes, misunderstandings, embarrassments. With the deaf it is different. I don't feel handicapped with them."

"How ironic! I'm deaf myself, and Burley is hearing, yet we get along just fine."

Emergency Preparedness Game

Windy L. Hasson, "Emergency Preparedness Game," *Ensign*, Sept. 2002, 73

Often when I watch the news on television, I see reports of natural disasters. With each new report, I am reminded of the counsel given by Church leaders to be prepared. Since our family did not have an emergency supply kit and preparing one seemed overwhelming, I wanted to find a doable solution. As my husband and I counseled together, we realized that we didn't have to accomplish the task alone—we could enlist our children's help.

To involve everyone and make preparing for an emergency seem fun instead of daunting or upsetting, we decided to have a scavenger hunt as part of family home evening. Together we could gather items for an emergency preparedness kit. Considering family members' individual needs, I made a list of supplies for our search. For starters, the baby would need a bottle, formula, and diapers, while my husband would need sturdy clothes and work gloves. I also found ideas from information I had saved from Home, Family, and Personal Enrichment lessons.

At the start of our family night, we discussed possible natural disaster situations and the importance of being prepared so we don't have to be afraid (see D&C 38:30). After our discussion, we divided our family into teams and gave each group an empty laundry basket and part of our list. Then we had our scavenger hunt throughout the house, collecting the needed supplies. The children had a great time gathering the items and choosing which clothing to include. Within an hour, we had items for a complete emergency kit—tailored for our family's needs. What once had seemed an overwhelming task became a fun activity for our family, and we now feel better prepared should an emergency arise.—Windy L. Hasson, Celeste Ward, Las Vegas Nevada Sandstone Stake

The Church offers helpful suggestions for preparing emergency supplies in a booklet titled Essentials of Home Production and Storage *(item no. 32288; U.S. $.75), available in distribution centers. Regarding emergency storage, the booklet advises everyone to have portable containers with the following: water; food requiring no refrigeration or cooking; medications and critical medical histories as needed; change of clothing, including sturdy shoes and two pairs of socks; sanitary supplies; first aid booklet and equipment; candles; waterproof matches; ax; shovel; can opener; and blankets (see p. 7). The booklet also recommends preparing a portable packet with valuable family documents, such as family history records.*

"That's different. She can fingerspell and sign. She speaks your language. Get me a deaf girl with whom I can sign to my heart's content, and I can take off my damned hearing aid."

"I'm at your service. Tell me your preferences."

"All I want is someone who's nice and bright and with whom I can sign and neck."

"Let me think. I have it! Gabby!"

Ed was intrigued. "What is she like?" I told him that he would see for himself and to hurry as the evening was late. I explained the situation to Burley, who was very understanding, and she let us go.

In the car, as we drove back across Bay Bridge, Ed and I continued our conversation. Most deaf people are adept at driving with one hand while signing with the other and darting occasional glances at their companions to "read" their answers. We were no exceptions.

When we reached Telegraph Avenue in Berkeley, I parked near the restaurant where Gabby worked. We walked in and sat down. I looked for Gabby, who bused tables and poured coffee and tea for customers. The manager would not let her work as a regular waitress because she was deaf.

She put down her coffeepot on the nearest empty table and approached us with a broad smile on her face. We hugged and I introduced her to Ed.

I could see for myself that they clicked at once. They both were ebullient, spirited individuals. They chatted like old friends. She had to get up and do her chores, but in between she raced back to our table. She and Ed had so much to say to each other that I began to feel superfluous and excused myself. But Ed stopped me, asking how he would get back to the train station without me. That was the cue for Gabby to offer to drive him there in her car. Then once again she had to leave us to clear some tables. I bid good-bye to Ed, signing to him, "You forgot one more requirement: a deaf girl with a *car*." He laughed. "You're one hell of a pal. I'll be in debt to you forever." I left with the pleasant feeling of having introduced two very nice people to each other.

That was in September. From then on Ed came to San Francisco practically every weekend, but I rarely saw him—he and Gabby were too busy with each other. Toward Christmas, however, Gabby popped up in my apartment. I hardly recognized her, because her hair was back to its natural brown. When I asked her what had happened to her hair, she signed back, "I'm tired of being the blond bombshell. I want to be myself, my natural self."

"That's not you. That's not the Gabby I know," I objected.

"I know," she answered. "I want to be a typical American girl, sweet as apple pie."

"But it's not possible for you to change your personality overnight."

"Why not? Don't you like the way I look now?"

"I do. But I also liked the way you were and really are."

She laughed, "Don't worry. I'll never change. But I can act if I want to."

Ed did not know about the change of hair color, but Gabby told me she was going to write and tell him before his arrival for the big Christmas party at her house. At that instant I had a devilish idea and signed, "No, don't tell him just yet. I have an idea for livening up your party. Are you game?"

"Well, you have to tell me what's on your mind."

I told her my plan, and she agreed to go along with it.

On December 24 I drove across Bay Bridge to pick up Ed at the train station. He had arrived from Soledad laden with boxes of Christmas presents, which I placed in the trunk, and we raced off toward Gabby's house. On the way he signed to me that he could not wait to see Gabby. He had not seen her for two weeks, and it seemed to him like a year.

He asked me how many people were coming to Gabby's party, and I signed, "About thirty, including Joe Velez and Iggie Ingraham from the deaf club, Burley, and, oh, yes, Betty."

He grabbed my hand, "Betty who?"

"Don't you know? Gabby's sister."

He frowned. "Gabby has a sister? But she never told me."

"How strange. Gabby never told you?"

"Yes, strange. What does she look like?"

"She's pretty and three years younger than Gabby."

"Prettier?"

"See for yourself."

Ed became thoughtful as we drew near Gabby's house and parked. As we approached the door, I saw Joe peering from behind a curtain. I winked at him.

The party was in full blast. I waved a big hello on entering and hugged quite a few people. Ed greeted those he knew, and I introduced him to others. When I felt the time was ripe, I nodded conspiratorially at Joe and he vanished into the kitchen to give a signal to Gabby.

The door to the kitchen opened and Gabby appeared. Her hair was brown and she wore a red dress with a green belt. Her face had a demure expression, and her gait was different, more sedate, as I had coached her.

I got up. Ed jumped eagerly to his feet and I introduced him to her. "Meet Ed Barber, Gabby's boyfriend." And to Ed, "This is Betty, Gabby's sister I told you about."

"Enchanted," Ed signed enthusiastically and they shook hands. "Betty" signed that she was pleased to meet Ed—Gabby told me so much about you."

"Good or bad?" Ed asked. "Did she tell you the truth?"

"Oh, yes, not to worry. Everything she told me about you was good."

"I'm relieved. Where is she?"

"Oh, she's just back from shopping, upstairs, changing her dress. She'll be here soon. I better go up and see if she needs me. I'll tell her you are here."

Ed signed, "Tell her to take her time. The night is long from over."

"Betty" excused herself and walked decorously up the staircase, with Ed's admiring eyes following her. We all found this irresistibly hilarious, and some left the living room for the patio because they could not suppress their laughter. But Ed was so smitten with "Betty" that he did not notice anything.

When she vanished at the top of the stairs, he smacked his lips and said, "She's so cute, so different."

"How different?"

"A little shy, not outgoing like Gabby."

I almost burst out laughing, but Joe came to my rescue by waving to me, signing, "Come, get your drinks. Eggnog is served."

As we helped ourselves to the eggnog, Gabby tripped down the staircase. She was wearing a kimono and her head was swathed in a Turkish turban from which peeked a lock of blond hair. She spread her arms dramatically in delight at seeing us and embraced Ed, exclaiming, "Oh, I'm just back from shopping. Sorry I'm late. Hope you understand."

"Take your time," Ed signed.

She waved to everyone and turned to Ed, "I better go up. Betty is ironing my dress. She is such a darling."

Halfway up the stairs she stopped, turned around, and added, "Betty thinks you're cute."

He signed, "Tell Betty I think she's cute too."

Gabby's usual broad smile narrowed as she answered, "Be careful. I get jealous easily."

Ed stepped two paces forward as he answered, "Maybe that's why you never mentioned her to me before."

"But there's so much that you don't know about me. Be with you soon," and she climbed the stairs and disappeared from sight.

Ed turned toward me as I was coughing to conceal my laughter. Everyone was eavesdropping on the scene and likewise trying not to laugh, but Ed still did not notice anything. He walked back to the sofa in a daze and picked up his glass, sipping from it.

In a few minutes "Betty" came down shyly in her red dress and green belt. Ed again jumped up from his seat, asking, "Oh, you finished ironing?"

"Yes, but I have to go back to zip up her dress."

He commented, "You are such a good sister."

She smiled modestly, "Well, Gabby was always good to me," and walked toward the kitchen.

I followed her. Once in the kitchen her smile disappeared. She blurted out to me, "I can't go on. I want to stop now. I can't stand this masquerade any longer."

"You want to quit now?" I asked.

"Yes, I think it would be better, before. . . ." she hesitated.

"Before what?"

"Before he likes me too much."

"What are you talking about? He loves you."

"No. He seems to like me better than Gabby."

"But you are Gabby."

"I know, but I'm afraid Gabby will lose him to me, and I am not Betty."

"Oh, I see. Then let the curtain fall on the play."

So we walked back to the living room and "Betty" sat down near Ed, who asked her eagerly, "Where have you been hiding?"

She was confused. "Ed, I'm sorry." She could not go on.

"What is it?"

Her eyes widened. "You mean you know I have been hiding myself?"

"No, I mean you were hiding in the kitchen, weren't you?"

She was stuck for an answer. Everyone in the living room stopped breathing. Her lips trembling, she finally signed, "I mean I've been masquerading as Gabby's sister, which I am not."

Now Ed was confused. "Then who are you if you are not her sister?"

"Well, I'm—I'm Gabby."

Ed laughed. We thought he had finally got it through his head, but he answered, "Are you kidding? Gabby is still upstairs." He finally sensed something was wrong and looked at us. Everybody tried hard to keep from laughing, but I began to realize the situation was getting out of hand. Gabby looked at me tearfully and signed to me, "I can't. . . . Please make him understand."

I patted Ed on the shoulder. "Ed, look, don't blame it on her."

"Don't blame what on whom?"

I pointed at her. "Gabby. That is Gabby."

But Ed still objected. "No. I saw Gabby a while ago. She is upstairs."

I signed, "Ed. Blame it on me."

"What?"

"The joke that we played on you."

"Joke? What joke?"

I signed, "Betty isn't Betty. Betty is pure invention." I continued, "It was my idea."

But Ed persisted, "See, Betty is here," pointing at her.

I nodded, "This is Gabby with her natural hair color. She played at being a double for you tonight."

"But Gabby is up there."

"She had pinned on a lock of blond hair for you. You never saw them both at the same time, did you?"

Ed looked upstairs, then at Gabby. She just sat there, looking worried.

He exclaimed, "Oh, my God," and covered his eyes, then laughed so hard he almost split his sides. "How could I have been so damn gullible?" Gabby started to wring her hands and rushed outside to the patio. Ed ran after her.

I learned later what happened on the patio. Gabby signed to Ed that she felt terrible playing that trick, but he, laughing, signed back that he thought it was the best joke ever played on him. Then he grew serious when he saw that she was still pale and shaken. "I'm afraid you like Betty better than me," she said.

"Betty is you, so why can't I have both of you?"

Unlike fairy tales, which end happily, the romance between Ed and Gabby did not. However, they did live happily ever after, each having married someone else. And they remained good friends, which is not so unusual in the deaf world where people are more affectionate toward each other. At every opportunity we hug each other.

What also distinguishes us is preoccupation with our image because the hearing world is apt to judge all deaf people by the particular deaf person they happen to meet. If that person is intelligent and educated, so much the better for us. If the person is a moron, they think we all are morons. If it happens to be one of the few deaf people who lipread and speak well, they wonder why we others cannot do that too. And if the individual happens to have a car accident, they start thinking that the deaf should be deprived of their driving licenses, unaware that insurance statistics show the deaf to be better drivers.

When school closed for the summer after my first year of teaching, Iggie, Joe, and I left Berkeley in Iggie's Chevrolet convertible for a convention of teachers of the deaf in Washington State. Actually, Iggie and Joe were not teachers; they worked as printers for *The San Francisco Chronicle*, but they came along to meet their friends at that convention. Deaf people are very gregarious and will travel hundreds of miles for a chance to socialize with their fellow deaf friends.

On the way home, we drove toward Reno, where we were going to meet Gabby, Pat, and other members of our crowd. We tried to make the trip in one day. Iggie drove the first part of the day, Joe in the afternoon, and I at night.

At about three in the morning, seventy miles from Reno, I was driving on a narrow, winding road through the Sierra foothills. Joe was sleeping in the front passenger seat and Iggie was sleeping in the back seat. I kept blinking to stay awake, determined to get to Reno by dawn. As I was negotiating a long curve, the lights of an oncoming car blinded me. I lost control of the car and it careened.

One shoulder of the road descended steeply and the other was level. I steered to the level side, off the road. The car bounced for about one hundred feet on the uneven rocky surface, struck a boulder, turned over, then righted itself.

The car turned over so slowly that I had time to brace myself before the impact flattened the convertible top. Once again it turned over, and righted itself.

My first thought was to save Joe and Iggie before the car caught fire. I could not open the door. In the darkness only one headlight was shining, the other was smashed. I finally managed to push the door open and pulled Joe out onto the grass. Iggy's body was draped over the seat back so that I could not see its upper half and was not sure whether he had been decapitated. But when I pulled him out by his legs, he still had a head on his shoulders, thank God.

Both were alive but shivering from shock. I got a blanket from the trunk and covered them. Joe signed that his chest hurt. I did a quick inspection and found no bones broken, but he had a gash on his head. Iggie too was not seriously hurt, but his head also had a gash. Thank God that headlight worked, because otherwise we could not have communicated in the dark.

I took a shirt out of my bag, tore it in two, and bandaged their heads. Then, warning them not to move, I tottered back to the road to get help. Only then did I become aware of a wetness in my right hand. It was blood. Apparently, just as the car was about to hit the boulder, I had instinctively protected my head by propping my hand against the top of the convertible.

There was a deep cut in my palm, though no bone was broken. I wrapped it in a handkerchief and kneeled at the roadside, crying silently and feeling thankful that we all were alive. I searched my pockets for a pen and paper but, as usual, I had forgotten to carry any on me. More bad luck—how would I communicate with our rescuers?

The headlights of an oncoming car pierced the fog and I ran out onto the roadway waving my hands. The car stopped. Inside were an old woman and a young man. Pointing to my ears to show that I was deaf I mimed a car crash and simulated the motion of writing and patted my pockets to show that I had no pen.

I was lucky. They had probably met deaf people before and so knew what was needed. They produced pen and paper and I wrote down for them an explanation of what had happened. They did not invite me to get in, perhaps because they were a little scared of me, but they wrote me that when they arrived in Susanville, forty miles south, they would notify the police and the ambulance squad.

I walked back to Joe and Iggie, reassured them that help was coming, and after a while walked back to the road edge, where I lay down and awaited help.

Toward dawn, flashing lights signaled the arrival of the ambulance and a patrol car. I walked with them to show where Iggie and Joe were lying. One patrolman started to take pictures of the scene. I told him, "Please, no photographs. We want no publicity. Please, don't give deaf drivers a bad name." He eyed me up and down, looked at my friends lying there and said, "You asked for it." Then he wanted to see my driver's license. He scrutinized it and finally said, "Don't worry. The photographs are just my hobby," and let us go, to my great relief.

I rode in the ambulance with my friends to Susanville, where we were taken to the local hospital. I held their hands while the doctor sewed up their gashes and treated them for shock. When he was done with Joe and Iggie, he dealt with my badly cut hand. The doctor wanted Joe and Iggie to stay in the hospital for three days. Since they seemed to be okay and were resting comfortably, I left and hitchhiked to Reno, to the cabin where our friends were staying. From there I went to Berkeley, picked up my own car, and drove back to Susanville for Joe and Iggie.

In the fall of 1955, when I resumed my teaching duties, I continued going to night school at San Francisco State College, where I majored in education and minored in drama. But this did not fill the aching void I felt in my life. Something was missing. My acting career seemed to have come to a standstill. Joe Velez, a fellow amateur actor, and I became involved in variety shows to raise funds for the National Association of the Deaf, but still this was not the same thing as entering the real-life theater world. I attended plays in San Francisco with Burley, who interpreted the dialogue for me in the dark. I even took an extension course in playwriting and read all the plays I could lay my hands on. But all this still was not enough. I hit rock bottom. I did not feel alive and walked around in a fog. Then one day in February the sun rose and almost blinded me.

I happened to read in the *San Francisco Chronicle* an announcement about Marcel Marceau's debut in the United States. "World's greatest pantomimist!" This caught my attention. I read eagerly an article on Marceau in *Life* magazine as well. Was this destiny? After all, I was a mime myself. I had done mime from childhood on. During World War II, at age thirteen, I performed for hearing audiences to raise Red Cross funds. While working at the summer camp of the silver-haired man I performed my "Orchestra" act in front of five hundred hearing people. I had a burning desire to develop my talent with help from such a world class artist as Marceau. I knew what I had to do.

Wednesday was the big day—I had a ticket to a matinee performance of Marceau. All that morning teaching, it was an effort to remain patient, and my pupils were amused by my continual glances at the classroom clock. They called me a "clockwatcher," and I apologized. The morning seemed to last forever, but finally the hands of the clock stood at twelve-thirty. I left the classroom, practically ran toward my Packard and drove in a hard rain across the Bay Bridge to San Francisco. While on the bridge I saw a rainbow. Was it an omen? I parked my car near the Geary Theatre and entered. It looked as though every seat was filled. I elbowed my way to my seat up in the balcony, the best I could get. One good thing about it was that it offered me a bird's-eye view of the audience's reactions to a man who was not going to utter even one word for two hours and was thus for these two hours in a predicament similar to mine.

Finally the house lights went out. A spotlight illuminated the stage and then I saw him. His face was painted white and he was wearing a white costume. He was walking, yes, he was walking, but in place. I watched greedily every gesture, every expression he made; I was in the presence of a master. Now and then I looked at the audience; it too was in Marceau's thrall.

At intermission I left for the lobby. I could not hear the comments of the theatergoers, but I saw how animated their faces and movements were. Clearly, they too were captivated by the Frenchman. Afterward, when we went back to our seats, I watched Marceau act as Bip, his alter ego, with his foibles and pratfalls, the little man in a big world, with a touch of Charlie Chaplin. He never said a word, yet his mime spoke volumes.

The curtain descended. Applause and more applause. The audience left. I alone stayed in my seat, torn by conflicting feelings of hope and hopelessness. If Marceau could communicate with his hearing audience without uttering a word, why couldn't I, despite or because of my deafness? At the same time, I felt overpowered by his genius and despaired of ever equaling him.

I woke up from my musings and left the empty auditorium. With my umbrella unfurled, I walked through rainy streets as if in a trance, reviewing Marceau's performance. I didn't pay attention to where I was going, yet my feet led me again and again back to the Geary. I gathered up my courage and tried the doors to the theater. One was open. I went in. Inside it was dark except for the traditional lone bulb on a pole standing in the middle of the stage.

I walked down the center aisle, looking at the empty stage and trying to visualize myself alone on it. Suddenly Marceau appeared as if from nowhere and circled the stage, unaware of me. He stopped and raised his head, watching water leak from somewhere above. I approached, hoping he would notice me. He sensed my presence, took a few steps forward, looked at me, and began to speak.

I raised my hands, fingers to my ears and shook my head. He peered at me, understood, and looked up and eloquently mimed water leaking from above. I clapped. He made a slight bow. We were using our own special language.

He was short, with a perfectly formed body and wiry hair. His thick, dark-brown eyebrows nearly hid deeply sunk eyes. Even then, at the very beginning, I had a feeling that he saw me yet did not see me, that he was always absorbed in some thoughts of importance to himself alone. This was a feeling that always persisted in all my encounters with him afterward.

He gestured at me to join him on the stage. We shook hands. He said something, apparently in English with a French accent. It was difficult to lipread him. I gestured to him that I could not lipread him, so would it be okay to write? He nodded. I got out pen and paper and wrote that I was a schoolteacher but had done mime in my spare time all my life. Now I would like to learn the discipline. He wrote back asking me to perform for him. "Now? Here?" I asked. Sure, he gestured as if to say, "The stage is all yours." He turned a chair around and sat down, resting his elbows on its back.

I performed for him as if I were performing for the entire world. I took off my jacket and tie, unbuttoned my collar, and started out with my "Noah" act. I mimed Noah, his wife, his boat in pelting rain, and all the various animals in pairs, ending with the dove holding an olive leaf in its beak.

When I finished, Marceau nodded approvingly and asked for more. I could not believe it; he wanted more. I switched to my "A Game of Tennis" act in which I mimed alternately a big, husky player and his timid, little opponent.

In this act, my technique was directly opposite that of Marceau. In his "David and Goliath" act he used a panel behind which he would disappear to emerge on the other side as Goliath and vice versa. By contrast, I remained in one place but merely turned my body in the opposite direction when miming the other character. I later developed and elaborated this "cinematic" technique, which I termed Visual Vernacular. I think that this technique also captured Marceau's fancy.

Again he asked for more. I then did my "Orchestra" act, in which I mimed, in succession, the conductor, the violinist, the cellist, the cymbalist, the trombonist, and the pianist. The succession was so rapid that when I again mimed the conductor my arms grew visibly weaker and my movements became slower and slower until, as if completely fatigued, my arms dropped feebly, but I continued to conduct with rapid and rhythmic up, down, and sideways movements of my eyebrows alone.

When I finished, I was out of breath and perspiring. Marceau reflected for a while, then got up and wrote something while I dabbed my face and put on my tie and coat. He showed me the paper. It said, "I like what I saw. I invite you to study with me in Paris this summer, free of charge. When is your school out?"

On the evening of June 4, 1956, I boarded a plane for Paris. That trip remains crystal-clear in my mind. The following day I settled in a small hotel on the Left Bank. In the evening I put on casual clothes and walked to a café on the boulevard Saint-Germain. I ordered a glass of Saint Raphael wine. This was so far the most exciting day in my life. But as I sipped my wine and watched the drizzle, my thoughts turned gloomy. I remembered how my father, who had by then followed me to California and settled there, strenuously objected to my going to Paris. He had asked me what I expected to get out of it, and I answered that I did not know. He retorted that it was a waste of time and money. I countered that it was my own money and I wanted to invest it in my future with Marceau. In short, it was the usual bitter exchange.

It had been preceded by an equally bitter clash between my parents. I had happened to walk in on them during another of their one-sided verbal clashes, one-sided in that Father did all the violent arguing while Mother just bore up under it. I saw Father sign, "You don't understand me. You never did!" It was enough to root me to the spot. He noticed me and gestured rapidly. "Finish! Stop!" and they acted as if nothing had happened. A while later, however, when Mother left the living room to do some cooking, my father admitted to me something so personal that, while touched by this revelation so unusual on the part of a father toward a son, I felt at the same time a deep dismay. He complained to me, "You might not believe this, but she never once said to me, 'I love you.'"

As had become my practice lately, I tried to reconcile them. In the kitchen, I approached Mother and reported to her my father's words, asking why she would not tell him she loved him. She burst out, "I work to earn money for a more comfortable life for us. I keep the house. I do the bookkeeping. What more does he want from me?"

I asked, "Why don't you then say to him the simple thing, 'I love you'?"

But all she answered was, "Please, . . . it is between Father and me."

I got up and walked along the Seine. Suddenly I felt lonely for my father's support, which he had never given me. Then I thought of my mother, who had secretly encouraged me to go to Paris.

The following afternoon, I showed up at the Théâtre d'Ambigu where Marceau was then giving nightly performances. He embraced and kissed me on both cheeks, saying "Welcome to France" in English. I answered in my mangled French, "Merci beaucoup," a phrase that I had practiced uttering with a hearing friend. He introduced me to his seven supporting players and we sat down. He explained to me that he didn't hold regular classes but I was welcome to join his troupe in the afternoons and participate in the exercises, which were followed by individual improvisations.

His seven supporting players were at first defensive in their attitude toward me, but when, after doing warm-up and limbering exercises with them, I started improvising, their attitude changed.

Georges Segal, Marceau's star performer, took an interest in me. I taught him fingerspelling, and, as a result, he became my interpreter in the afternoons when Marceau lectured to us. Georges also became my friend. We ate out together, and on nights off he took me to parties. At the time, Marceau was the rage of France and many young people wanted to learn mime, which made Georges and me quite popular. At these parties there was music and lots of intellectual discussion.

After about a month Marceau told me that he wanted to start work on my breathing. "This is your big weakness. Even people in the back of the auditorium can hear you breathe."

I was startled and asked, "People can hear me breathe?"

"Yes, they can. In a big auditorium it makes a difference."

I felt like Molière's bourgeois gentleman when he was told that all his life he had been talking prose. Only the deaf can be ignorant of such simple truths. If not for Marceau I might never have known to this day about the relation of noise to breathing. I was reminded of Mr. Ryder's ludicrous and sad attempt to teach me and my fellow deaf pupils "the proper way" to laugh. But no, this situation was completely different, and I felt terribly grateful to Marceau. He demonstrated to me what he meant by miming a happy man frolicking and looking up at imaginary birds, which he mimed by fluttering his hands. Suddenly, a bird fell, dying. Marceau picked it up tenderly in his cupped hands, raised it to his face and breathed gently as if he himself were the dying bird. He gasped for air and expelled one last breath as it were.

Thus Marceau showed me how breathing is a very important element that must be in harmony with the moment and with the feeling expressed. Passion, for example, is associated with rapid and spasmodic breathing, while languor calls for gentle exhalations. This lesson has stayed with me ever since.

Every afternoon the seven players and I used to improvise under Marceau's watchful gaze. During that period I too came up with some new ideas. The technique I was developing differed from Marceau's. He was first and foremost an illusionist, a pure mime. He would, for example, simulate being pulled along by an imaginary dog on a leash or, characteristically, he would be resting his elbow on an imaginary shelf. I, however, added gestures to my mime, thus furthering the technique I now call Visual Vernacular. This technique, the basis of all my mime work then and now, derives from sign language, in which I have been steeped all my life. It follows the cinematic approach; in other words, I simulate what a camera can do—close-ups, long shots, zooming, panning, high angle and low angle shots, slow motion, and fast motion. The performer remains all the time within the film frame, so to speak, presenting a montage of crosscuts and cutaway views. For example, in my "The Hawk and the Squirrel" act, which I was to develop later, at one moment the performer is a hawk swooping down onto a squirrel (long shot); at the next he becomes the terrified squirrel (close-up), followed by the image of the hawk rising with the prey in its talons (high angle, panoramic view, fast motion).

Marceau would watch me keenly then discuss my act with his seven players, with Georges Segal interpreting his words to me. Otherwise, the Master never complimented or applauded me. Instead, he just smiled and nodded slightly. I could not, and to this day I cannot, figure out his response. Georges liked what I was doing and applauded me warmly when witnessing my improvisations.

However, I was surprised by Marceau's reaction to a request I made after spending about a month under his tutelage. One day I received a telegram from a friend of mine, Robert Freiman, then and now one of the two foremost deaf painters in the world. (The other is Morris Broderson, whose works also are part of the permanent collections of some of the world's major museums, such as the Museum of Modern Art and the Hirshhorn.) Robert was in London, giving a one-man show at the O'Hana Gallery, and asked me to join him for the weekend of July 4th. I asked Marceau to be excused early on Friday afternoon so that I could fly to London and return on Monday. He wrote in response, "Certainly, but be sure to come back." This was the only indication I got that he cared that I was there.

Robert met me at Heathrow and drove me to the O'Hana Gallery. I helped him put up his paintings, and in the evening, after a good dinner, he showed me around London.

At one point I saw a big poster with the headline "The Night of 100 Stars." It advertised a charity show at the Palladium at midnight the next day. Leading Hollywood and British actors—Laurence Olivier, Vivien Leigh, Tyrone Power, Bob Hope, and many others, were to be present at this charity benefit for an orphanage whose patron was Olivier. The ticket prices were steep, five pounds apiece, which was a lot of money for those times.

This was something I could not miss, seeing so many stars in one place in one evening. I persuaded Robert to go with me, and we bought our advance tickets at the nearest theatrical ticket office.

It was drizzling when we arrived at eleven the next night. The theater was still closed, and we had no umbrella. So we walked around the building to the back door in the hope of seeing some of those one hundred stars arrive. Lots of other people had the same idea, so we joined them in lining the streets and cheering the stars as they arrived in their limousines.

My clothes and Robert's were getting damp, so I told him to follow me and ask no questions. Giving him no time to object, I joined a procession of five people, apparently British actors, who got out of one of the limousines. With Bob trailing behind, I casually followed them, with the crowd on both sides of the streets cheering. When the guard at the back door saw us come, he opened the door. For a moment, Robert and I thought he was going to close it in our faces, but, saluting, he let us pass, too.

Once inside I furtively motioned to Bob not to sign, so that we would not attract attention. I moved my mouth as if I could hear. Bob, who is an expert lipreader, was stumped by my mouth movements and asked me what I was saying. It took him a while to realize that I was merely talking nonsense. "I'm only bluffing," I mouthed.

The backstage was crowded with actors and crew. We moved slowly from place to place watching the numerous celebrities while trying to act natural so that no one would spot us as outsiders. At one point we passed Laurence Olivier, Vivien Leigh, and John Mills rehearsing a tap dance. Then we walked on. I looked at my watch; the performance was to start in a couple of minutes. I motioned to Bob to follow me. He mouthed, "Outside?" "No," I mouthed, "see that door?" pointing to the door leading to the auditorium, which was guarded by a man in uniform. "Let's go there. You first."

He obediently wended his way there. As I followed him, I wrote on the back of my ticket in large script, "Guests of Sir Laurence Olivier." The guard opened the door for Bob, with me following and fanning myself nonchalantly with the tickets. I purposely let him steal a glance at the back of the ticket as we passed through so he would remember us when we returned backstage after the performances.

The auditorium was already filled except for a few seats in the front rows. Our tickets were for the balcony, but I proceeded to the orchestra seats. Nobody asked to see our tickets, so we just sat down.

A chorus of singers and dancers performed with the guest stars. Only two acts were memorable—the tap dance by Olivier, Leigh, and Mills, and the prancing of Tyrone Power with a top hat and a cane, surrounded by a bevy of chorus girls.

I noticed the people in the seats next to me looking through a thick program book and was seized with the desire to get one myself, not so much because I was deaf and could not hear the program announcements of the emcee as because I wanted to have a souvenir to bring home to my parents and friends. During the intermission I tried to buy a copy of the program in the lobby, but it was sold out. I tried the other side of the lobby, with the same results.

The performance was over at three o'clock in the morning. Afterwards a small crowd of autograph seekers and well-wishers gathered in front of the door leading backstage. A guard barred their way. I decided to forget the program for now and, with Bob in tow, approached the guard, who, when he saw me, bowed and opened the door to us. I walked in, nodding graciously. Once we were inside, Bob asked me how I had done it, and I showed him what I had written on the back of the tickets. He slapped his head in amazement.

Backstage a reception was in full blast. Flashbulbs were popping and waiters bearing trays with glasses of champagne wove their way through the throng. I picked up a glass and sipped from it. A photographer approached, and as I moved back to let him pass, I bumped into the person behind me, almost spilling my champagne.

We turned around and faced each other. That person was the man I had admired most, Laurence Olivier. He smiled politely and said something which I could not lipread. Thinking quickly, I got out paper and pen and wrote that my name was Bernard Bragg and I was a student of Marcel Marceau. This led to a comical misunderstanding because Olivier thought that, as a mime, I had sworn some kind of oath of silence. I spoke and gestured that I was deaf. He finally understood and asked if I could lipread, and I gestured, "A little." Then he commented that Marceau was a very fine mime. He asked where I was from; I wrote him that I was a schoolteacher from California, and that I taught deaf children. He thought it very interesting. He turned to his wife, Vivien Leigh, and called her over. She came and Olivier introduced us. I was enchanted to meet the woman who to me and the world was Scarlett O'Hara. Heaven knows how many times I had seen *Gone With the Wind*. Bob approached and, because he spoke well, he became my mouthpiece. I introduced him and spoke of his coming exhibition at the O'Hana Gallery. They kept asking us questions; apparently meeting two deaf artists was a novelty to them. Then a photographer barged in, so they excused themselves and followed him.

Bob and I circulated through the crowd, rubbing elbows with celebrities. I passed by Tyrone Power, who was again surrounded by chorus girls. Olivier came back and asked "Have you met Tyrone Power?" When I shook my head no, he called out to Power to come; Olivier introduced us and talked to him at some length, apparently about me because before he left he wished me good luck.

By this time it was four o'clock in the morning. I looked at Bob and gestured it was time to leave. We left by the same back door we had come in. The crowd of autograph seekers still packed the sidewalks outside. One woman, after looking hard at me, asked for my autograph. Good naturedly, I signed her program with a flourish. This reminded me that I still did not have my own copy of the program, and I told Bob we could not leave until I got it.

Bob groaned, "It's too late. Let's go back to the hotel." But I was insistent and walked around to the front entrance. The chief usher was still there, and he said all the programs were sold out but I could try in the morning at ten when the box office reopened. Back in my hotel room, I fell asleep, still unsure whether the events of the past night were dream or reality.

In the morning I told Bob I was going back to the Palladium for the program. "God, not again," he sighed, but he agreed to give me a ride. When we arrived, I saw the manager, but he said all the programs were sold out. When he saw how anxious I was about getting a copy, he suggested I go to the producers of the show and he gave me the address: 17 Greek Street, Soho.

I walked back to the car where Bob was waiting and showed him the address. "The program is there." He threw up his hands but signed, "Oh, okay." We meandered through the narrow streets of Soho until by some miracle we arrived at 17 Greek Street. Bob stayed in the car and made me promise I would be quick in getting back.

I entered the building, and my life changed. After I climbed the stairs to the top, I rang the doorbell. A woman opened the door, and I asked her about the program for the Night of 100 Stars. In the open space behind her I saw a stack of the programs and pointed at it to make sure she understood what I was saying.

She asked if I was a foreigner, because of my "deaf" voice, I guess. I answered no, pointed to my ears, and wrote down that I was deaf. I explained that I had seen the performance last night, but the programs were sold out and the box office manager told me to come here.

For some reason she looked amazed. She opened the door wide and gestured for me to come in. She also gestured for me to wait a moment while she sat down at her desk and dialed someone.

I wondered what was going on, especially because she kept looking at me while talking into the receiver. Suddenly a door that I had not noticed opened and an immaculately dressed, dark-complected man with slicked-back hair came in. He looked at me, and the secretary pointed at me. I spoke and gestured that I wanted a program. In reply he asked whether I could lipread. "Why? I only came for the program," I politely answered, and I wrote down for him that I was deaf, a schoolteacher from California, and a student of Marcel Marceau for the summer.

He smiled and wrote me back, to my astonishment, "You're heaven-sent." He asked me to sit down, and we had a long chat. It turned out that his name was Lance Hamilton and he was a theatrical producer. He had just received a call from David Miller, a Hollywood director, asking him to find a coach for teaching sign language to a blind-deaf actress in a film to be shot in England with Joan Crawford as the star. In that film, "The Story of Esther Costello," renamed in America "The Golden Virgin," a rich society woman, played by Joan Crawford, adopts the deaf-blind Esther and, while in London, hires a sign-language tutor for her.

He asked me to be that tutor. He told me that David Miller, the Hollywood director, was arriving in London three days later. Could I stay and wait for him? He added that this was a wonderful offer, the kind one gets once in a lifetime, as if I did not know that.

Suddenly the door opened and Bob strode in, white-faced with rage. "What's the big idea," he signed, "keeping me waiting?" I jumped up and introduced him to Hamilton, telling him that Bob was a much better lipreader and speaker than I. "Where's the program?" Bob asked, "Let's leave." But Hamilton suavely intervened, asking, "Can I invite you to tea in my apartment next door?"

I explained to Bob in terse signs the sudden turn in my fortunes, and he was mollified. Behind the hidden door was a large and luxuriously appointed living room. Inside, Hamilton introduced us to his partner, Charles Russell, a tall, blond man.

It turned out that the two men were personal representatives of Noel Coward. We discussed mime and Bob's coming exhibition. It helped that Bob could lipread and speak so well; he served as my go-between to facilitate the conversation.

After about an hour, Bob had to leave. Hamilton asked me if I would be interested in working in that Joan Crawford film. I answered that I would love to but I had promised Marceau to return to Paris. Hamilton argued that it would do no harm to ask Marceau for a postponement; after all, this was my chance of a lifetime.

I asked, "If I work for David Miller, where will I stay?"

To strengthen their argument, Ham and Charles, as I called them henceforth, added that I would be more than welcome to stay in their apartment, which had three bedrooms including one guest bedroom. They suggested that for now I go back to my hotel, think over their offer, and return the next day. "We can then wire Marceau asking for a postponement, not a cancellation."

I hesitated, but before I could answer, Charles asked if I could drive. "Sure," I said, "I have a driver's license."

Charles took out his car keys and tossed them to me, saying, "Drive my car to your hotel. Come back tomorrow." He walked down the stairs with me and Bob to show me where his car was parked. It was a brand-new black 1956 Thunderbird convertible with white leather seats.

I took a jaunt through the City and environs in the shining Thunderbird, and enjoyed the stares I drew. I felt very pleased with myself.

That evening, I dined out with Bob. After we discussed the pros and cons of Ham's offer, Bob signed that it was my decision alone. I, of course, decided in favor of accepting. I hoped that Marceau would understand.

In the morning I was back at 17 Greek Street. The secretary let me into Ham's apartment. I put down my carryall, which contained everything I had brought over from Paris, and mimed to Ham and Charles the actions of a movie director wearing a beret and dark glasses, operating a film camera, to show them that I was saying yes. Subsequently, Ham wired Marceau, but we never got a reply.

I spent the following two days wandering around London. Ham and Charles took me to see Noel Coward's play *South Sea Bubble,* which starred Vivien Leigh. After the play they asked me to wait by the stage door while they went to the star's dressing room door. Some time later, Vivien Leigh emerged in the company of her husband, Laurence Olivier. Ham and Charles were going to introduce us, but they did a doubletake on seeing Olivier and Leigh proceed toward me, shake my hand, and say, "Hello, Bernard." I told Vivien I loved her performance, and the couple bid me good-bye.

Ham and Charles looked at me incredulously and asked how I knew the famous couple. "We met at the Palladium, on the Night of a 100 Stars," I answered. "Who invited you?" "Oh, I invited myself," and then I proceeded to tell them how Bob and I had bamboozled our way inside and crashed the reception. They laughed, "And then the search for the program miraculously led you to us!"

The following day David Miller arrived. We had a long talk, in the course of which I explained to him the difference between the two-handed British and one-handed American fingerspelling systems. In my opinion, the one-handed system was more suited for communicating with the blind, since the blind person could place his hand over one hand of the person fingerspelling to him, in a kind of "underhand touch" system. Miller understood the problem and even said he wanted to write me into the script. Things looked good.

Soon afterward Ham and Charles took me along to the home of John Mills. While they were occupied in a business meeting, I browsed among the books in the living room. Someone tapped me on the shoulder. I turned around and saw a woman who fingerspelled to me in the two-handed English alphabet that she was Mills's wife, Mary. We got into a conversation and she confided to me that she was thinking of writing a play about a deaf person. "For me?" I asked, and we laughed. She asked if I felt left out among the hearing. "No, not really," I joked, "so long as I have a cigarette in one hand and a Scotch in another and, if I'm lucky, one person to chat with." "Why one person?" she asked. I explained that otherwise it would be too much for me to watch several different people talk at once.

I thought no more of this conversation, but a couple of days later Charles came back after answering a phone call and fingerspelled to me—for by then he had learned passably how to fingerspell—"What did you do to make Mary Mills fall in love with you?"

I did not know what he was talking about but my riposte was, "I fell in love with her first."

He then told me that Mary had called and specifically asked him to bring me along to the world premiere of the film *The Battleship and the Baby*, starring her husband, John Mills, and to the reception at her home afterward.

That was the first opening night I had ever attended. Since I had only planned to be in London for the weekend, I didn't have the proper clothes to wear. Charles and I were of the same height and build, and he had generously invited me to help myself to one of his several tuxedos with all the accessories.

I must admit that the best part of the film was arriving at the cinema in my black tie and being surrounded by celebrities in formal attire. The film itself I hardly remember, but the reception at John Mills's home afterward was memorable. As soon as I entered, Mary called out, "John, get a glass of Scotch for Bernard!" and she offered me a cigarette from a box.

Carrying the cigarette in one hand and sipping the Scotch from the other, I cursed myself for making that fatuous remark to Mary on my earlier visit, because I still felt left out. As if to rub salt into the wound, Mary got the character actor Lionel Jeffries to converse with me "person to person." He started talking to me, very slowly, and very clearly, so that I could lipread him fairly well. He had just finished playing the doctor to Kirk Douglas's Van Gogh in the film *Lust for Life*. When he mentioned this, I told him, more or less—I don't remember the exact phrase—that my father had oils. His eyes popped, "How many?" "Oh," I said, "four or five." "He must be bloody rich," Jeffries observed. I realized this must be a misunderstanding; I could not rely too much on my lipreading skills. So I whipped out pen and paper and wrote, "You said my father is rich. What did you think I said?"

"Didn't you say your father owned oil wells?"

Oh no! I explained that my father merely had painted copies of Van Gogh's works. When Jeffries realized what I had meant, he doubled up with laughter, so much so that everybody was looking at us.

At the same time, Olivier and Leigh entered the room, saw the scene, and asked what was so funny. Jeffries explained the situation to them, and they too laughed. I appreciated that, instead of feeling embarrassed for me because of my gaffe, they saw the funny side of it.

Olivier questioned me about sign language and I told and wrote him that it was a rich and sophisticated language in its own right; Shakespeare could be and was done in sign. He asked me to do Hamlet's "To be or not to be" soliloquy in sign. I never dreamed that I, a deaf man, would one day perform for the world's greatest Shakespearean actor. I performed in a corner of the room, and when I was through I could not lipread his response, but could only hope it was complimentary.

A few days later, Marilyn Monroe arrived in London; Olivier was to direct her in *The Prince and the Showgirl*. The press went into hysterics. This was a new world to me, this celebrity world, and I was still dazzled by the suddenness with which I had become part of it. I met and made friends with, among others, a youthful Roger Moore and Gordon Jackson. With Roger Moore and Ham, I toured southern England in the Thunderbird.

On one of our excursions, we met a group of fellow actors in a London restaurant. We were eating soup and talking at the same time. Gordon Jackson sat on my left. I was the only deaf person at that table and was having difficulty following the conversation. I was busy eating soup, but something to my side grabbed my attention. I saw Gordon pick up a cracker from the bread basket, place it on the palm of his hand and smash it against the elbow of his other arm. I almost choked on my soup and asked him to explain why he had done that. He chuckled, saying, "That's a Scottish superstition, a custom I grew up with. Scots are very superstitious, you know. They believe that if you happen to break a cracker into three pieces, that is a good omen. He added that one cannot cheat when using the elbow.

"This is incredible," I told him. "The sign for *cracker* looks exactly like what you just did. This sign must be 150 years old, and both of us are still carrying it on—you with your real crackers and me with my sign."

Finally Joan Crawford arrived in England. Ham, Charles, and I went to meet her at the Dorchester Hotel. All I remember of her appearance was her sparkling eyes and steely smile, and also that she moved like a queen, a haughty queen. She was accompanied by several men, including her husband. Charles introduced me to her and she talked to me. She talked so fast that I could not lipread a word. She seemed to be uneasy with me, as if she had never met a deaf person before.

The next day I received a note from her saying that she was looking forward to working with me. I still have that note.

Then the blow fell. A couple of days later Charles told me apologetically that I was being shut out of the production of *Esther Costello*. An English teacher of the deaf who had also applied for the tutoring job threatened to sue under British labor laws, which gave priority in employment to British subjects. These laws made exemptions for special skills, but the English teacher argued that, being a professional teacher of the deaf, he too had these skills. According to Charles, David Miller fought for me with British officials and tried to get me a labor permit, but failed.

I had a sinking feeling as I asked what that meant. Charles answered gently, "You are out of luck."

I had no choice but to accept it with the best grace I could muster. I called on the reserve of "veddy British" civility I had acquired during my stay in England, and bid them good-bye.

That was early in August. I still had a month to go before returning to Berkeley, so I decided to go back to Paris and Marceau—if he was still there; I did not know because he had not answered my telegram and phone calls. I had even written him a long letter explaining the whole situation. I did not expect it to be answered, and it was not.

Ham, Charles, Gordon Jackson, his wife, and several other friends saw me off when I departed for France. As the train moved, Charles ran to keep up with me, signing, "The movie is going to be a flop without you."

It was nice of him to say so, at any rate, and I waved gratefully to him and my other friends as the train picked up speed.

Once the train left the station, as I leaned on the open window, watching the buildings and towers of London pass from my view, I was suddenly jolted by the realization that something was missing. Oh, no! The program for the Night of 100 Stars! I had left it behind!

Thus ended my entrance into the world of glamour and glitter. Now when I think about it, I feel gratified that these stars accepted me as I was, with my deafness as part of me.

When I arrived in Paris, Marceau's theater was shut down for the month and he had taken off for parts unknown. I happened to visit an American Express office and saw a poster advertising a leisurely voyage aboard the S.S. Orcades from Le Havre to California via the Panama Canal. I decided to take it.

Once I was on the *Orcades*, somehow the word got around that I was a student of Marceau and had hobnobbed with celebrities in London. Everywhere I went I was greeted with smiles and waving hands. I was probably the only tourist-class passenger to be invited by the captain to eat at his table, and at his request I gave mime performances to the passengers.

When we disembarked at Long Beach, I and the actor Edmund Gwenn were interviewed by a television crew. My parents, who were waiting for me at the dockside, were astonished to see me with Gwenn and a television crew. Later, my picture with a headline announcing "American Mime, Marceau's Student, Comes Home," was published in a Long Beach newspaper.

Once at home in Berkeley I teamed up again with Joe Velez to do mime performances for deaf audiences. We had begun performing together in a production of *The Monkey's Paw*, which I also directed, at the 1955 NAD rally in the San Francisco Bay Area. Joe was a printer at the *San Francisco Chronicle* by profession, but he was also a gifted mime and actor by avocation. We did variety shows together for deaf audiences until one day he told me that his wife was going to have a baby and he could no longer be away from her in the evenings. Good sport that he was then, as always afterward, he added, "No need to hold your hand. You can succeed on your own as a solo mime."

Shortly afterward, in the summer of 1957, I got my first invitation to perform solo at a convention of teachers of the deaf in Knoxville, Tennessee. This turned out to be a big break for me; one job led to another. I performed in Miami, where the *Miami Herald* gave me a big write-up, and that led to my being invited to perform on television in Puerto Rico.

The write-up in the *Miami Herald* also led to a center spread in *Parade*, a national magazine. After the *Parade* article appeared, I received a wire from Richard Frey, the manager of The Backstage, a nightclub in San Francisco, offering me a job on weekend nights.

At The Backstage I was the second half of a double act, the first half being a singer named Joan Bereta. I made a new and good friend, Harry, who was a freelance photographer. I taught him to sign and fingerspell, never dreaming what dividends this would pay. It happened this way. I had finished my performance and bowed to the audience's applause. As I was exiting, Dick Frey stepped up onto the dais and said something that made them stop applauding. No sooner had I entered my dressing room than Harry rushed in and told me what Dick had said. It turned out that Dick told the audience, "Stop clapping. It's no use because he is deaf and cannot hear the applause."

I was stunned. I hurried back to the stage. Once there I mimed broadly to the audience that while my ears were stopped up my eyes were not, and that my eyes invited and appreciated applause. They understood all right and applauded me with even greater fervor than before.

Deaf people can easily be taken advantage of because of their deafness. Harry helped me avoid this pitfall more than once. One evening a *Life* magazine reporter and camera crew showed up at The Backstage as part of a feature they were doing on the ten top nightclub performers in the United States. It was late evening and I had one more show to go. I saw Frey talking with what looked like a camera crew, and this puzzled me because he didn't say anything to me. Anyway, after I returned to my dressing room, Dick showed up and told me to stay there and not go out until he called me, again without explaining what was happening.

This was very mysterious, but I thought no more of it until, moments later, Harry burst in and told me that the camera crew were from *Life* and wanted to interview me but Dick told them I was gone and suggested that they talk to Joan Bereta instead. I figured out instantly what was going on. Joan was Dick's protégée and he wanted her to have all the glory. At the same time I felt powerless to do anything about it.

Harry, however, did something about it on his own. He left the dressing room and approached one of the *Life* people, telling him, "Bernard Bragg is here, in the dressing room. He is deaf and does not know what is going on." The crewman approached the *Life* reporter, who was watching Joan as she sat on a stool and crooned to the accompaniment of a piano. He whispered something in the reporter's ear and, after Joan stopped singing, the reporter said to Dick, "We want to see Bragg. Could someone go get him?" So the same crewman and Harry, at whom Dick threw a dirty look, left and brought me out.

On February 18, 1958, my picture appeared in *Life* along with those of nine other top nightclub performers, including Mort Sahl, Elaine May, Mike Nichols, and Shelly Berman. Joan's picture was not included.

Dick gave me a bigger billing than Joan's, perhaps because my name had started to attract larger crowds. Then I met Marty, a young and quick-witted man who offered to become my agent. When Dick learned about Marty, he protested, saying, "You can't do that. Either work with me or sign with Marty." He left me no choice, so I quit.

As I was leaving, Dick's partner ran after me and whined, "Please don't leave us. I feel like my arm is being chopped off." I picked up an imaginary arm and sewed it onto her shoulder. She laughed and we embraced.

Marty proved to be as good as his word. He got me engagements at The hungry i nightclub, at the University of California, and, in the summer, in the Dahl Theatre and the Troubadour Club, both in Los Angeles. I was well received everywhere.

One result of my nightclub appearances was that I started to get offers to perform at private parties in Palo Alto and on Nob Hill in San Francisco. Most of the time I arrived just before my performance and left right afterward. Once in a while, though, I stayed and mingled with the guests.

At one lawn party I met a deaf man named Jeffers. He either did not know sign language or refused to use it because he was an oralist, but for that very reason I could lipread him pretty well. He mouthed his words very distinctly. During the course of our conversation he asked me point-blank, "Why can't you speak?"

I was flabbergasted to be asked such a question; I, who saw myself communicating with the world through my art. Finally, I mouthed my answer, "I never went to an oral school but had some oral training. Can you follow me?" He said yes, and we became friends after a fashion. I did not sign in his presence, out of consideration for the violence of his feelings against sign language, and through him I met a group of five or six rich deaf oralists. These people led the same lives as their wealthy hearing counterparts—golfing, traveling to Sun Valley in order to ski, attending charity balls. They had been taught not to view themselves as deaf, but they lived in a closed world of their own, mixing almost exclusively with each other—a contradiction that I was careful not to point out to them if I was to retain their goodwill.

At another party I met Janet Mason, who worked at the local educational station, KQED. She offered me a job, which I readily accepted. I had to show up at the studio only once a week, every Wednesday, so I did not have to give up teaching. When I arrived at the studio, I would put on my mime costume— a red and white striped shirt, navy-blue pantaloons, and ballet-like shoes— and paint my face mask. Unlike other mimes, who painted their necks and throats, I painted only my face. I acted out Aesop's fables and fairy tales in mime. This led to a flood of calls from children asking where "the quiet man" was and, as a result, I was offered my own weekly TV show, which was called "The Quiet Man."

This was one of the most creative periods in my life. I worked with a superb team that enjoyed experimentation and creative use of the camera. Two of my favorite shows I did for KQED were Dickens' "A Christmas Carol" and *Hamlet*. In "A Christmas Carol" I mimed all the characters: the cantankerous Scrooge, the humble Bob Cratchit, Tiny Tim, Young Scrooge, the Spirit of Christmas Past, and all the others. I did all this on the run, so to speak, dashing from one stage set to another in a big studio room with three cameras trained at me. As the camera panned I would hurriedly change characters by putting on or taking off various props and run to the next stage set where I would assume a new role.

In *Hamlet* I mimed the various characters, one after another, including Ophelia and the ghost of Hamlet's father. But this was a different kind of experiment: here I stayed in place, without running from one stage set to another. I kept myself within an imaginary film frame and switched from one character to another with lightning speed. It was here that I perfected my Visual Vernacular technique.

My appearances on KQED led to my being asked to teach and perform mime on a program produced by the National Educational network, the precursor of PBS. We created a fifteen-week series called "What's New," which lasted three or four years and was rebroadcast nationally.

Despite the success I was having, I felt walled in by the physical limitations of mime as an art. From the beginning I had departed from Marceau's classical pure mime by combining my mime with gestures similar to those of American Sign Language. I began to experiment with rendering songs into sign to the accompaniment of a voice interpreter and a piano. The audiences seemed to love it, and it has since become an accepted art form, but it was not my aim in life to become a song-and-dance man.

Adding to my discontent as an artist were the invitations I began to receive to psychology classes at Stanford University, where I was asked to act out on-the-spot suggestions thrown at me by students, who then analyzed my responses as part of their study of the creative process. They made me feel like a rare laboratory specimen.

My sensitivity got the better of me when a theater critic from the *Los Angeles Examiner* showed up in my dressing room to interview me. He asked if he could mention my deafness, which hit me the wrong way. I asked him, "If I were blind in one eye or had a mole on my left shoulder, would you mention it in the review?" He said nothing, but in his subsequent review, which was favorable, he made no mention of my deafness.

I was especially sensitive on this subject because in those days sign language was generally rejected as an inferior communication system. At the same time, it was my native language, one that I knew had beauty, richness, and dramatic power. Because of the ease of communication in sign language, I felt that my deafness was pulling me back toward the deaf world and away from the bigger, hearing world.

I happened to become friends with a psychiatrist Rod Gorney, who later became my manager for a time. He helped me to see that deafness is very much a part of who I am as well as part of my creativity, and that without it I would not be the artist I am. That was some consolation to me, but ultimately it threw into more glaring contrast my anomalous situation.

Even though I was now earning a respectable living from my mime perform-ances and making a name for myself, I was getting tired of spending hours alone between acts in my dressing room. I was not able to go out because removing and reapplying the white paint-mask I wore on my face was just too troublesome.

I could use mime with great effect on stage, but my everyday relations with the hearing world were more simplistic. At the California School for the Deaf I felt stimulated working with deaf children. We communicated in our own language, sign language, and that was why I kept my teaching job even when I was challenged to make a choice between teaching and performing.

The first time Allen Neubauer, the principal of the high school depart-ment, called me on the carpet, his usually pink face was purple with irritation, and he shook his finger in my face and accused me of "doing too much social work" with my pupils and "deviating from the school curriculum." He was angry because I had revised some of the required curriculum and incorporated basic psychology in my class work. I had weekly discussions with my students about basic human emotions, such as fear, envy, anger, and joy. They responded well to what I was doing, they even enjoyed writing their English papers. I kept the supervising teacher posted about what I was doing, and she had approved it. Not so Neubauer.

I tried to stay cool and argued, "I don't think so. I am trying to link my pupils' social problems to their verbal ability."

He glared at me ferociously. "No. What you are trying to do is teach your pupils psychology!"

"Yes, without using the term 'psychology.' We discuss and write about what's close to our hearts, real human emotions. My sixth graders are able to express freely on paper their fears, jealousies, frustrations, and suspicions. The purpose is to develop their English skills by motivating them."

His stare bored through me. "The curriculum does not specify that you are to bring emotions into the sixth grade."

I got up enough courage to object, "The curriculum specifies what I must teach, but it doesn't tell me how to motivate and inspire my pupils to write."

He stopped me with an imperious wave of his hand, "Go back to your classroom and stick to your curriculum."

That was only my first collision with him. Months later I was on the carpet again. This time Neubauer accused me of moonlighting because I was working in a nightclub on weekends and on television every Wednesday. I said I was only trying my hand at show business, but he would have none of it. He complained that this interfered with my teaching job. I asked him whether my pupils or my supervising teacher had complained. I told him I was at a loss to understand his objections.

He replied, "But people talk. Your name is in the press and on TV. People wonder if you're doing your job here properly."

I answered that I enjoyed both activities. "They never conflict. Acting is to me a diversion, like golf is to you."

"But I don't make money out of golf. You make money out of acting. Above all, you can't serve two masters."

Nothing was settled. I politely refused to give in to his demand to quit performing, but his threats hung over me like a sword and I left his office feeling angry and upset. It did not exactly make me feel any better when a few weeks later he humiliated me publicly.

This happened at the Teachers' Forum, the occasional gathering of teachers at my school for the purpose of discussing their teaching experiences and classroom conduct. I was describing a classroom experience with my pupil Ivan. I had caught him drawing a nude woman in revealing detail. Instead of punishing him or making a fuss over the whole thing, I complimented him on his drawing skill. After all, I justified myself to my fellow teachers, portraits of nude women are among the greatest masterpieces of art. So instead of reprimanding Ivan, I explained to him some anatomy and Da Vinci's principles of proportion. Then I asked my peers what they would have done in my place. Neubauer stood up, stepped onto the stage, and remarked, "Mr. Bragg may do well to write Dear Abby and ask her how to handle Ivan." Thereupon, he declared the meeting closed.

In the teachers' lounge the following day, Neubauer told me, "I understand you were upset over what I said at the forum yesterday. You aren't sure what I meant by my 'Dear Abby' comment."

I answered, "Truthfully, yes."

He said, "I know you discussed your frustrations with Miss Prince. She told me this morning. She spoke up for you."

Miss Prince was a sweet, older teacher, the most respected and best loved of the teachers at the school. She had approached me after the forum and told me how much she enjoyed my tale of Ivan. She said she would have blown her lid had she been in my place.

I said to Mr. Neubauer, "I had thought my story would lead to further discussion of the behavioral problems of deaf children in the classroom."

He was silent for a while, then said, "Well, there was not enough time left. Besides, it was my poor way of being funny. But I really do think you managed that situation with Ivan just fine."

We shook hands. I took it to mean that, while he still did not approve of my double life, he would no longer press me to make a choice between teaching and performing. But fate had already made the choice for me.

CHAPTER FOUR

The Premiere

I sometimes wonder if all the credit should go to fate? What is fate? Are not we masters of our own destiny? Perhaps half and half. How did fate lead me to the day in June 1966 when I received a letter from the man named David Hays, a Broadway set and lighting designer, asking me to join him in establishing the National Theatre of the Deaf? That theater was a dream I had long been trying to realize through my writing and lectures, the same dream that I had inherited from my father and Professor Hughes, the very dream that I shared with Bob Panara.

That dream had first begun to approach reality six years previously, in 1961, when I had received a letter from Raymond Levy, a Broadway "angel" who offered to help establish such a theater. I answered his letter and in the same year, after giving a performance in New York, I met Dr. Edna Levine, a psychologist with entrée to theatrical circles. She had picked up Levy's idea, also entertained by Anne Bancroft, of a professional theater of the deaf, and became sufficiently enthusiastic about it to apply for a $1,000,000 government grant. The grant was turned down, but she did not give up trying. We discussed the possibilities over a cup of tea at her home and agreed to keep in touch. Subsequently she again tried to get a government grant for the project. Once again, however, nothing came of it, until Hays came to her.

I n the summer of 1966, on the very day school closed, a letter from David Hays caught me unawares. As I reread the letter while walking across the school's central plaza, one phrase in its first paragraph stood out: "many fingers point at you."

Hays had recently become a vice-president of the Eugene O'Neill Theater Center in Connecticut and was casting about for a novel idea and program. When he learned of Edna Levine's failed efforts to obtain a grant to start a deaf theater group, he thought it worthwhile to give it a try and asked her to give it up to him. He was going to push it forward singlemindedly with all the energy at his disposal. She agreed, on one condition: "Get Bernard Bragg!"

There was one person above all I wanted to share this letter with. That was Kathee, my fiancee of three years, a black-haired girl with lovely brown eyes. I had first met her at a party given by Taras Denis when she had been teaching at Fanwood. We were immediately attracted to each other, as if we had known each other for a long time. She was such a fluent signer that at first I had thought she was deaf, too. The truth was she was hearing but had grown up in a deaf environment and been immersed in deaf culture because her father had been superintendent of the Illinois School for the Deaf and he and his family had lived in a house on the campus.

Before meeting Kathee I had been engaged to Linda, a cinematography student at the University of Southern California, but that did not last long; our worlds were too different. Now Kathee was something else; no other woman satisfied me so much in so many ways. I felt as if she was an extension of myself. Our personalities were very much alike and we shared many of the same interests, especially theater.

We had met in February 1963 at Fanwood, but by a fortunate coincidence the following fall she also got a teaching job at Berkeley. She taught in the classroom next to mine, and every weekend we would go to see a new play in San Francisco.

So of course, when I got Hays's letter I hurried to show it to her. I was practically jumping with joy. She read it, handed it back to me, and said, "Looks like you are getting what you were waiting for."

Hays's letter, heaven-sent as it was, arrived at a chaotic time for me. I was directing the play *Moments Preserved* by Eric Malzkuhn, a creative deaf playwright and actor who had written it especially for the National Association of the Deaf meeting in San Francisco. In 1943, Malzkuhn had been responsible for staging a Gallaudet production of *Arsenic and Old Lace* on Broadway. I was also rehearsing a solo mime show for Bimbo's, a nightclub in San Francisco, and taping a television program, "What's New." Yet somehow I managed to suspend everything and free myself for a week in order to fly to Waterford, Connecticut, and meet Hays.

When I arrived at Groton Airport I was welcomed with open arms by Edna Levine, who theatrically presented me to Hays, a short, sharp-faced man with intense dark-brown eyes. We shook hands and then, as Mrs. Hays said later, all hell broke loose. We spent extremely fruitful days together, swapping ideas and fleshing out the concept of the National Theatre of the Deaf, or NTD.

Yet all that time I kept thinking of Kathee. There had been something puzzling in the way she reacted to Hays's letter, but at the time I was too caught up in my good fortune to pursue it. I kept thinking about her on the plane back to San Francisco. I had a vague premonition of disaster, but shook it off, telling

Debuting in my first "costume" at age four months.

My parents Wolf and Jennie in their mid-twenties.

Wearing my school uniform at age seven.

"Tall Ship," long-lost painting by Wolf Bragg.

My father, *left*, at his best, acting in the play "Auf Wiedersehen" (which he also directed).

With fellow classmates and teacher Bob Panara (at my left, back row, *center*) at Fanwood in 1946.

My first grown-up toy—a 1948 green, white-top Packard convertible shown in front of the California School for the Deaf in Berkeley in 1953.

In my favorite role, Tartuffe, performed in 1951 while I was attending Gallaudet.

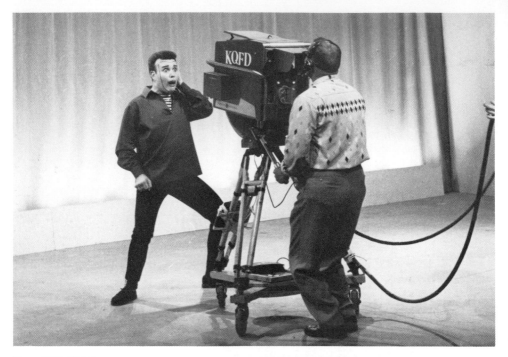

From 1958-1961 I
performed on the weekly
TV show, "The Quiet
Man," from station
KQED, San Francisco.

While teaching at the
California School for the
Deaf, I moonlighted with an
appearance at the "hungry i,"
a popular San Francisco
nightclub, circa 1959.

As part of my nightclub act I created a mask with make-up instead of full white face style used by other mimes. Here I improvised routines based on audience suggestions.

Marcel Marceau and I, teaching and learning from one another.

Joe Layton directing my song-and-dance number, "Gesticulate," for the 1967 NBC broadcast of "Experiment in TV."

In title role of *The Critic*, with Joe Velez
as Puff and June Russi as my wife.

Also, in the title role of Gianni
Schicchi on Broadway with the
NTD, 1968-1969.

Mixing with Israeli
dancers during a 1969
NTD tour of Israel.

Visiting Jaffa, Israel in 1969.
Standing left to right: Richard
Kendall, Audree Norton, me,
Ed Waterstreet, Linda Bove,
Mary Beth Miller. Kneeling:
Joe Velez.

Linda Bove and I appearing on Broadway in 1970 in *Songs from Milkwood* by Dylan Thomas.

Panel discussion at the World Federation of the Deaf in 1975. On my left is NTD cofounder, David Hays.

Appearing in NTD's 1971 production of *Woyzeck*, back row, left to right: Carol Fleming, Jane Norman, me, Pat Graybill, Phyllis Frelich. Front: Freda Norman, Ed Waterstreet, and Richard Kendall.

From *My Third Eye*, an extremely popular play developed by the NTD in 1972. Back row: me, Tim Scanlon, and Mary Beth Miller. Middle row (left to right): Ed Waterstreet, Joe Sarpy, and Pat Graybill. Front: Freda Norman.

Various expressions from the cast of *My Third Eye*. From left to right: me, Pat Graybill, Freda Norman, Tim Scanlon, Joe Sarpy, Ed Waterstreet, and Mary Beth Miller.

Cast of *My Third Eye*. Left to right: Peter Wolf, Bill Rhys, Jane Norman, Pat Graybill, Dorothy Miles, Ed Waterstreet, Phyllis Frelich, Richard Kendall, John Basinger, Carol Fleming, me, Freda Norman, Linda Bove, and Mary Beth Miller.

Rehearsing *Prometheus Bound* while artist-in-residence with the Moscow Theatre of Mimicry and Gesture in 1973.

Visiting a class of deaf students in Moscow (1973) and enjoying direct communication in Russian Sign Language.

During my world tour in 1977, I conducted a drama workshop with deaf Spanish actors in Madrid, translating poems into sign-mime.

Performing in New Delhi,
India in 1977.

Life after NTD: A scene from *Tales from a Clubroom*.

Coaching Jeff Bravin in "And Your Name Is Jonah."

Michael Bortman, Jeff Bravin, and I having a script conference during the filming of "And Your Name Is Jonah."

Wrap-up of "And Your Name Is Jonah" with Sally Struthers and Jeff Bravin in 1979.

My mother celebrating her eighty-third birthday.

Gallaudet's first deaf president, I. King Jordan, awards me an honorary doctoral degree, May 1988.

myself that she would be happy for me, and I was anxious to tell her about my exciting and creative discussions with Hays.

When I got home I found a note from her saying that she would not be able to see me for two weeks as she was tied up with her course work.

I kept busy in the meantime, teaching, acting, and corresponding with Hays. After two weeks, Kathee came to my apartment. I asked her why she looked so serious and wondered if she was okay. She signed, "I know you'll be shocked by what I am going to say. I came . . . I think . . . that we would be better off being apart."

"What do you mean?" I asked, stunned.

"I know how much you love theater."

"But so do you."

But she said, "It's not the same thing. You belong to theater. I cannot fit in your life."

We kept talking in this vein for some time until finally she declared, "Let me be honest with you. There is someone else, a man I've been seeing for a long time, and I am going to marry him."

When I asked who he was, she explained that he served in the Coast Guard. He lived on the floor below her apartment, and they had become friends. She ended her explanation, signing, "I want you to know that I will always love you."

I was too stunned to respond. Finally, I brought myself to say, "But I always thought . . ." She interrupted me, "So did I, but from now on the NTD will be your life."

I argued, "There is room in my life for you."

She shook her head, "No. You'll understand years from now. I hope we can remain friends. I want always to be your friend."

Thus she stepped out of my life, though not out of my mind. To this day she remains my dear friend.

I plunged back into other things in my life. Hays and I continued our correspondence. We discussed the new grant proposal for the NTD and our ideas about what such a theater should be like and what kind of sign language should be adapted to it.

One week before Christmas I flew to New York. Hays took me to a huge dance studio and introduced me to Joe Layton, the Broadway director and choreographer who had staged *Gone With the Wind* in Tokyo and London and had directed, among other things, the film *Annie*. His forte was musicals, as he graphically demonstrated to me. Layton immediately asked me to demonstrate to him what I could do. I reached into my repertoire of songs and poems and did Poe's "Annabel Lee," Shakespeare's "The Seven Ages of Man," "I

Left My Heart in San Francisco," and other pieces, accompanied by the pianist who was conveniently there.

Layton kept asking for more. He straddled the chair with his elbows resting on its back, which reminded me of a similar favorite pose of Marceau in 1956. Finally, I did a passage from *Oklahoma* and stopped.

Layton's reaction was disappointing. He turned both thumbs down. Through a sign language interpreter he commented, "That was not very exciting visually. You just stand in place and wave your hands."

"But," I protested, "what about the music? The piano accompaniment? My hands move to keep step with the music, 'eye music,' so to speak. Didn't you notice?"

He answered, "Don't take it to heart. I'm not criticizing that. What I meant was lack of movement on your part. You have legs. Use them."

"Oh, you want me to sign with my legs?" I asked, half-jokingly."

"No, I want you to move your legs around."

So he started to teach me how to move around while signing. He imparted to me the valuable lesson that I should move my legs in the same direction as my arms, even when pirouetting, and that I could make leaps like a ballet dancer when signing.

When the holidays were over I flew back to Berkeley. Shortly afterward Hays informed me that NBC Television was going to tape an hour-long show in sign language, "Experiment in TV." He asked me to help pick deaf performers for it.

Hays chose Gene Lasko, who had previously worked with Arthur Penn on, among other hits, the film *Bonnie and Clyde*, to direct various segments of the NBC show, and Joe Layton to choreograph three numbers. Lasko flew to Berkeley to see me and for three days we worked together on the program, which was mainly to include selections from *Hamlet, The Prince of Denmark* and scenes from the play *All the Way Home*.

The deaf actors and actresses I had helped pick at the time subsequently became the core of the NTD ensemble, and some of them went their own way to become famous elsewhere: Audree Norton appeared on the TV show "Mannix," Phyllis Frelich won a Tony award for her performance in *Children of a Lesser God*. Julianna Fjeld won an Emmy award as the producer of *Love Is Never Silent*, Ed Waterstreet starred in *Love Is Never Silent* and now is a freelance director, Linda Bove has been a regular on *Sesame Street* for many years, and Gil Eastman won an Emmy award for hosting the TV show *Deaf Mosaic*. In addition, there was Lou Fant, a hearing man and a superb signer, who has made a name for himself on stage and screen as a character actor.

My performance was to be taped in the barn of the O'Neill Theater Center. Two cameras were set up, one downstairs and one on the stair landing from which I was to sign the first half of my song—"Gesticulate" from *Kismet*. I practiced for almost two weeks with Joe Layton who choreographed my sign-dance movements, and then the taping started.

I was the last to be taped and everybody was anxious to finish on schedule. That was when trouble started. I was standing on the stair landing with everybody watching me, including Joe Layton, who stood behind the camera. He shouted, "Lights! Music! Camera!" and counted to four on his fingers. That was the signal for me to begin, and I pranced, leaped, and climbed onto the railing, signing with my free hand, "Sweet hand, swift hand, spinner of fable and fantasy, faithful friend of my art, would they rend us apart."

It so happened that a rope was tied to a railing post. The other end of the rope touched the ground. This gave Layton a last-minute idea. He shouted to me through an interpreter, "Slide down that rope!" and motioned to Gleason, a heavyset lighting man, to hold the other end of the rope downstairs and stretch it slantwise so it would be easier for me to slide down to the ground.

When I signed, "Up! Into the sky, and we did fly," I grabbed the rope and was about to slide downward on it, when I suddenly froze, looking at the rope and at Gleason, who held its other end almost vertically instead of diagonally.

Layton, Hays, and some television crewmen rushed upstairs toward me, asking, "What happened?" "Why didn't you slide?" "Why don't you move?"

I was so embarrassed that I felt my face blush, but I stood my ground and protested that the cloth wrapped around the rope was not thick enough to protect my hands—the invaluable hands of a deaf person. Layton's face betrayed impatience. He started talking rapidly to Hays and others, so rapidly that I could not lipread him. He probably was not intentionally rude but just forgot about my deafness. Then he turned to me, "All right. We'll wrap thicker cloth around the rope. Remember, we don't have much time."

Somebody brought a length of cloth, which was wrapped around the rope, and Layton hurried back to his post behind the camera. Once more he shouted, "Lights! Music! Camera!" and counted to four on his fingers. I leaped onto the railing, grabbed the rope—and froze again. I just could not bring myself to slide down it.

There was a big blow-up. Hays rushed toward me, shouting, "What happened? Why did you stop?" I told him lamely that I still did not think the rope covering was thick enough.

I had never seen him so furious before. He muttered something that I did not catch. I stepped down, feeling frustrated, but also feeling that I just could not trust my hands, my most precious possession, to that rope.

Hays shouted some expletive. "I'll show you how! I will do it myself!"

He leaped onto the railing, grabbed the rope, and slid down it. Everything seemed to be fine, but when he landed on the barn floor, his body suddenly jackknifed. A stunned crowd surrounded him. He groaned and held out his hands, palms up. There were large red welts on them and we could almost see smoke rising from them. I watched this scene from the second floor, casually looking the other way and flicking off an imaginary piece of lint from the sleeve of my black sweater.

Joe called for a five-minute break and instructed a crew member to get more canvas, which was rolled around the rope until it was twice as thick. Then he asked me, "Ready?"

I nodded. He called out once more, "Lights! Music! Camera!" and counted on four fingers. When he straightened out his fourth finger, I "belted out" my song with redoubled energy, leaped onto the railing, grabbed the rope, whose other end this time was held by four more crew members in a much more gently sloping position, and slid down it. The moment my feet reached the ground I pirouetted and, ending my song, spread my arms wide as if embracing the world and fingerspelled each letter of "Gesticulate" to the beat of the music, with my hands intact.

The NBC special triggered a brouhaha which was not made public but which to this day is still remembered by the deaf community. There is an organization in Washington, D.C., devoted to the promotion of oralism, the A. G. Bell Association. It is richly endowed with funds, for it had been bequeathed fabulous riches by its founder, Alexander Graham Bell himself, a strong advocate of oralism who happened to invent the telephone while pursuing one of his ideas for improving the speech ability of the deaf.

The head of the A. G. Bell Association in 1967, Dr. Fellendorf, was so outraged when he heard that NBC was going to produce a program in sign language that he wrote a letter of protest to the producers, expressing his fears that sign language would pollute innocent deaf children and affect adversely their attitude toward learning speech. This threatened to be a battle royal, but fortunately we won it by not turning it into a battle. Instead we got the support of educators of the deaf all over the nation. As a result, NBC decided to ignore Fellendorf and put the show on the air for all the world to see.

Those were heady days. Not long afterward I received a wire from Hays, "We got it!" meaning that our grant proposal for the NTD was approved by the United States Department of Health, Education, and Welfare, owing largely to its sympathetic consideration by a key official, Mary Switzer. Thus, the NTD came into being. Its first play, Puccini's opera Gianni Schicchi, *had been adapted to the NTD style of acting-cum-signing in the absence of music, under the direction of Joe Layton. This one-act adaptation, along with several other pieces that together made up an evening's performance, made the NTD so successful that in the second year of its existence the company performed on Broadway to enthusiastic reviews, and the following year it went on a national tour with the same repertoire.*

Near the end of that tour, on a humid, spring day, we appeared in a special one-nighter for Washington VIPs, other supporters of the fledgling NTD, deaf leaders, and, mostly, hearing audiences. That also was when the NTD almost lost its face.

I stood on stage with the blinding klieg light on my face. In that light I did not even have to cross my eyes in order to see how long my nose was, I could see it straight ahead, since its tip protruded a full three and a half inches. I raised my head so that my nose would point higher in the air and look even more proud and defiant, ready to accept any and all challenges.

No, I was not playing Cyrano de Bergerac. Cyrano was not even remotely related to the character I was playing at the time. The foxy gentleman farmer Gianni Schicchi was a more boisterous version of Mosca, the parasite in *Volpone*, on which Puccini's work was based.

I was wearing not only this white proboscis but also a black velvet hat with a long red feather, and a heavy black robe cut in seventeenth-century fashion. Even under normal circumstances the wearer of these garments was enfolded in a hothouse environment, but tonight the circumstances were not normal— the air-conditioning was not working properly.

I had begun to perspire under my heavy costume. Suddenly, as I was hopping on and off the sumptuous fourposter bed on stage with the other actors chasing me, I felt something crack in the ridge between my eyes. I felt a stab of fear in my stomach. I began silently to pray that the nose would stay in place at least until the end of the play. Otherwise, it would be curtains for the NTD; the audience would forget the whole purpose of the NTD and what it stood for. Only the nose would be remembered. I could not let that happen.

My anxiety increased as I felt the crack spreading. At the same time, droplets of sweat trickled into the crack and began to weigh down my nose, which grew heavier and heavier and started to droop. It was going to fall off any moment. I had to stop it from falling somehow, so while prancing and swaggering around the stage, with the whole gang of gaudily dressed characters stumbling after me, now and then I would stop to place my index finger on the tip of my nose as if plunged in deep thought. Alternately, I would shove the flat of my hand against the bottom of the nose to push it up more firmly while at the same time dramatically sweeping the air with my other hand and declaiming about the money to be left by the dying old "Volpone," lying on his fourposter bed, the nightcap half-covering his face.

The audience was mystified by my gestures. The hearing spectators thought I was using signs, while the dear ones tried to figure out what I was trying to convey.

The moment I had been dreading arrived. June Russi, one of the actresses, threw a bird cage at me, as she did every night. Always before, I knew when to expect this missile and reacted with split-second timing, catching it before it struck me. Tonight, however, was different. The drooping nose distracted me so much that I was off by a fraction of a second in responding to June's throw. That was enough for the bird cage to hit me squarely on the nose and knock it off.

As the long white nose shot into the air, I thought idly of Longfellow's lines, "I shot an arrow into the air, It fell to earth, I knew not where." But as it spiraled downward, everyone could see where it fell; and in fact it fell right in the center of the stage. All the actors froze in their tracks, wondering what that nose was doing on the floor.

After the nose landed with its tip in the air, still looking defiant, my fellow actors transferred their gaze to me. Right in the center of my whited face there was a big hole where once the long white nose had jutted. I retained my pose near the bed, my arms akimbo, but inwardly I wished I could sink through the floor and escape to some faraway place and stay there forever. The game was up; I had just dealt a mortal blow to the NTD in its infancy—it had lost its nose.

Oh well, I thought, I might as well do something to break up this tableau before its horrible outcome. I looked at Charles, a fellow actor, arched my eyebrows superciliously, and beckoned to him with a lordly gesture. Fortunately, was he, professional enough to stay in character, he approached me with a shambling gait and a humbly bowed back.

I commanded him, "Go, get it and give it to me." He obediently retrieved the ill-fated nose and brought it back to me, placing it in the palm of my hand.

I raised my hand triumphantly for everyone to see the nose.

That instant I knew what I had to do next. I strutted toward Charles and clamped the nose on his own nose. He grasped the plan at once and carried it off brilliantly by backing away from me while at the same time bowing and scraping.

The stage emptied. I was alone. The play was ending. I delivered my final speech with the required braggadocio and, in the best cavalier manner, I bowed from the waist and swept the floor with my velvet hat and red feather.

The curtain fell. My fellow actors trooped back onto the stage and we formed a line, holding each other's hands. When the curtain rose, we were greeted by a wild ovation. We took three curtain calls. After the curtain fell for the last time, Gene Lasko, by then a director for the NTD, appeared and walked wordlessly toward me. I did not know what to expect, but when he came near me, he embraced me.

So the NTD survived the loss of its nose and finished its national tour to triumphant acclaim.

Our ensemble traveled across America achieving success after success, and we grew as talented deaf actors joined us. Some also left us, notably Audree Norton, a shining star of the NTD and dear friend of mine ever since Gallaudet days. She was the first deaf actress to break through to hearing audiences by appearing on "Mannix," a popular television series broadcast by CBS.

Another one who fell by the wayside was my close friend Joe Velez, a gifted actor who did much to make the NTD famous. He left the NTD after two years to be with his wife and two very young children in California, but for the next three years we kept in close touch. When our troupe toured the Northeast, he took a vacation and flew in just to keep us company for old times' sake.

One night, in Birmingham, New York, the whole NTD troupe went to the movies. Joe and I sat next to one another. We did not know what the film, *Bang the Drum Slowly*, was about. Our aim was to watch two fine actors, Robert DeNiro and Jon Voight, in action. As actors ourselves, we took a professional interest in their movements and facial expressions. Slowly, however, as we began to pick up the various visual cues relating to DeNiro's hospital stay, the treatment he was receiving, and his changing, emaciated, and languid appearance, the realization began to seep in that it could be nothing else than cancer. I do not know which one of us realized it first, but when the shock of recognition hit me I could sense a certain stiffening of Joe's posture that it also hit him.

We sat in the cinema in darkness, our eyes riveted on the screen. We were very quiet, hardly moving. I avoided looking at him, and he, too, I realized, avoided looking at me. We both knew only too well our reactions to what we were seeing on the screen, an almost exact repetition of the story of our lives.

Now that we knew, we stuck it out by silent agreement and stayed till the bitter end, although we kept hoping it would be a happy end. The film was about two close friends, both baseball players. DeNiro was the catcher, and was slowly dying of cancer. Voight was the pitcher.

The relationship between these two characters was identical to Joe's and mine. We could readily change places with them. We too were close friends and teammates and Joe was dying of cancer.

I experienced a desolating sense of helplessness as I watched the drama unfolding on the screen. I fought back my tears, hoping that Joe did not notice, and kept praying that DeNiro would get better. I suspected Joe was hoping for the same thing. What we needed at that moment was hope. But the film ended with the pitcher saying good-bye to the catcher as he was going home because his life in baseball was over. Joe's life in the theater was over too.

When the film ended and the credit list scrolled up on the screen, I rose rapidly before the house lights went on and left my seat. I ran toward the exit and leaned against the wall, my eyes filled with tears. Suddenly, I felt someone touch my shoulder. It was Joe, who said, "Come on. I'm hungry. Let's have a hamburger." That was his subtle way of comforting me. Strange, I thought, I should be comforting him.

Joe is now long dead. But his memory is alive in me. That's one of those things that keep me going. His greatest legacy to me is his saying, "Glad I made it."

I had first met him in California in 1952 after my graduation from Gallaudet College. I was teaching at the California School for the Deaf at Berkeley and got to know Joe one evening while visiting a club of the deaf in Oakland. We instantly liked each other and quickly discovered we both loved theater with a strong and enduring passion. Joe was then a linotype operator for the *San Francisco Chronicle*.

We became pals and went together to see movies and plays. We were great movie buffs and enjoyed imitating movie actors. We loved going to plays, too, although we could not hear a word of dialogue. It was enough, actually more than enough, for us to watch the actors move and express emotions. We usually were familiar with the plays, but we even went to see new plays whose published versions were not yet available.

One day Joe said to me, "You know so much about drama, literature, and other things. You're lucky to have gone to college." It turned out that he himself had taken the admission exams to Gallaudet twice and failed them both times. I urged him to try a third time, but he said he did not think he could make it, he was too weak in algebra and English. So I said, "Take the exam a third, a fourth, a fifth time until you finally pass." He was still skeptical, so I suggested that he ask Leo Jacobs, a popular deaf teacher, to give him private tutoring lessons for a year and added that three of my fellow teachers at the California School for the Deaf would also be happy to help (and I was right).

For the next ten months Joe worked days and studied nights, until he was near complete exhaustion. But it was worth it. I will never forget the afternoon when Joe barged into my classroom shouting with large triumphant signs, "I made it!"

He left for the East, stayed at Gallaudet until graduation and, while there, met Bonnie, a lovely young woman from Idaho, whom he married. On returning to California they settled down in the San Francisco Bay area where they had two children, a boy and a girl. They were beautiful people, and I enjoyed being in their company.

Soon after Joe moved back to California we decided to team up as actors, and we began to appear in amateur theatricals to raise funds for the National Association of the Deaf. We did this for several years, until Joe decided he needed to spend more time with his family.

When I was asked to go to Waterford, Connecticut, to help set up the NTD, Joe wanted to come, too. I tried to get him in but had no success. When the NTD opened its first summer school, Joe signed up for an acting class. I tried to persuade David Hays and Gene Lasko to hire Joe as part of the regular troupe, but they were reluctant. Finally, Lasko agreed to watch Joe more closely in his acting class. At the end of summer school Joe was offered a job in the troupe.

Within two years Joe became one of the NTD's star performers. His rendition of Lewis Carroll's poem "Jabberwocky" made him famous, but he also attracted attention in his regular roles. We toured Europe and the United States and got wonderful reviews. Clive Barnes, for example, wrote in the *New York Times*: "Much of the individual acting was admirable. I liked particularly the dark intensity of Joe Velez as the tragic hero in the Japanese piece ["The Tale of Kasane"], and Bernard Bragg was a joy to behold as the impudent scoundrel [Gianni] Schicchi."

We even got onto Broadway for the second time, after *Gianni Schicchi*, in a performance of Sheridan's *The Critic*. Clive Barnes again singled us out. We could not believe we had done it again, yet it was true. "Glad we made it," Joe said.

The one drawback was the low actors' pay at the NTD. Joe had a family to support in California, so he left the NTD, much to my regret, and his, too. His parting words to me were, "Don't worry. Someday when the kids are old enough, I'll come back."

Two years later he fell ill. The doctors thought he needed stomach surgery, but when they opened his stomach and saw what was inside, they hastily sewed him up. Every kind of treatment was tried to stem the spread of cancer: chemotherapy, injections, drugs. Joe was a fighter and did not give up. Now and then he experienced remissions, altogether three of them. It was during his third remission in 1974 that he had joined our NTD troupe in upstate New York for two weeks, just to be with us.

At the end of these two weeks we gave a party for him. The entire troupe got up early in the morning to have breakfast with Joe and bid him farewell. His taxi arrived at the motel and we all hugged him. When he came to me, he embraced me wordlessly.

As Joe's taxi left, I thought of the film we had seen the week before and wondered why our lives had to be just like that movie.

The following year I flew to California to visit Joe. Bonnie greeted me at the door and we hugged. She told me that Joe had been looking forward to my visit. He came out of his bedroom, taking slow, tiny steps like an old man. His face was ravaged and he looked some twenty-five pounds lighter. We hugged, although there was not much for me to hug. We sat down and, as I fought to hold back my tears, he bombarded me with questions about the National Theatre of the Deaf and myself.

That was in early August. The NTD was scheduled to give guest performances at the University of California in Berkeley in late November. Joe closed his eyes and counted on his fingers the number of months before the NTD would be in California. Four months. His eyes opened. He said he would be there to see the performance. His exhaustion visibly increased. Bonnie, who was observing him keenly, said it was time for another shot of morphine and began to escort him back to his bedroom. At the door he turned and said, "See you in November." I signed yes, but I thought to myself that this would probably be the last time I saw him.

I was wrong. In November, when the NTD arrived in Berkeley to perform *The Dybbuk*, Joe was still alive. I and three other NTD actors, Linda Bove, Ed Waterstreet, and Freda Norman, longtime friends of Joe, rented a car and drove to his house.

Joe had lost even more weight in the last four months. His body was wasted away and his face was skull-like. Even so, he was very happy to see us. We sat down and I told him of a plan I had been considering for some time about getting a scholarship fund established in his name. He inclined his head as if to say thank you. We had to leave soon for the run-through. On the way out he told us, "I'll be there to see you tomorrow night." He would be making his first public appearance in many months. I told him to come backstage first, to the greenroom, and then I would lead him and his family to their front-row seats.

In the early afternoon I called David Hays long distance, through an interpreter, asking if I could go on stage just before the performance and dedicate the play to Joe. He agreed, adding, "Be sure and make it short and in good taste." I replied, "You can count on it."

The next evening I waited at the back door for Joe and his family to arrive. The children helped Joe out of the car. He was wearing a thick yellow pullover under his sport jacket, apparently to make him look less thin. His face was nearly like a death's heard mask, yet his eyes glowed with excitement.

Once they were in the greenroom, Joe said to Bonnie, "Time for another shot," and they went to a restroom. After she administered the injection, we led him and his family to the auditorium, to the first row. Then I climbed to the stage and waited in front of the curtain with an interpreter who spoke for me, until the house lights went out and some stage lights came on. All I signed was: "Good evening, ladies and gentlemen. The performance tonight is dedicated to Joe M. Velez, probably better known as Mr. Jabberwocky." I extended my hand in his direction. He raised himself with difficulty, assisted by Bonnie, and the whole audience, two thousand strong, rose and applauded him. He turned around to face them and gave them the sign for "I love you," with the little finger, index finger, and thumb extended.

The lights went out, the curtain went up, and the performance started. Afterward, we met again in the greenroom, where everyone hugged Joe good-bye. Everyone cried, but Joe kept smiling. Then Bonnie and the kids went to get the car. The others drifted out too, leaving Joe and me alone. I began to escort Joe outside, but he stopped and faced the darkened stage and the empty auditorium. We remained silent for a moment. He turned to look at me and he signed very slowly, "Glad I made it."

He left the theater leaning on my arm. The car was waiting. We embraced and his children helped him in. I stood there alone watching the car leave. When Joe arrived home, he went straight to bed and he never got up again. He died two weeks later. A part of the NTD died with him.

The NTD continued to grow in stature over the years and became more internationally known as well. In 1972 we participated in a theater festival in Belgrade, Yugoslavia, during the International Games of the Deaf. The NTD and the then Moscow Theatre of Mimicry and Gesture were the only professional theaters of the deaf then operating. My fellow American actors and I seized the opportunity to watch the Russians perform, but their sign language turned out to be so different from ours that we could not understand the dialogue at all. The Russians had the same experience while watching our performance.

Offstage, however, we found it much easier to understand each other's sign language and we got along very well. This paid a dividend at the banquet on the final night of the festival. Hays knew no Russian and his counterpart hearing director of the Russian theater spoke no English. In order to communicate with each other, the Russian director talked to a lipreading Russian deaf actor, who signed the message in Russian Sign Language to me, and I in turn relayed that message to Hays in English. When Hays wanted to say something, he had to take the converse route. We enjoyed turning the tables on our hearing directors who, isolated from each other by mutual incomprehension, looked on with puzzlement at the forest of our flying hands.

One unexpected result of this banquet was that it gave rise to the idea of an exchange of actors between the NTD and the Moscow theater. When the idea became formalized, I asked Hays to let me go to Russia, and he agreed. As it happened, the NTD was scheduled to tape a CBS show in England in late November 1973 and after that I was free to fly to Russia.

"I turned down the lamp and then I slept." As I signed these last lines of Dylan Thomas's "A Child's Christmas in Wales," I stepped off the camera's field of view. It was over. My fellow actors shook hands with me. I left Pinewood Studios to the accompaniment of a chorus of signed good-byes, "Don't let the KGB catch you," "No monkey business," and "Don't defect to the Russkies."

In the cool November morning at Heathrow Airport I boarded an Aeroflot plane for the land of Stanislavsky. Only one American before me had ever performed with a Russian cast—the famous black actor Ira Frederick Aldridge, who performed in Russia more than one hundred years ago.

The plane landed at Sheremetyevo Airport in a blinding snowstorm. I stepped down the ramp, bundled in the extra-warm clothes I had purchased in London. I was whisked through customs with the help of Vladimir Fufayev, president of the All-Union Association of the Deaf. A look at the magic card, or whatever it was that he was carrying in his wallet, was enough for the customs officer to wave me on.

Once past customs I was met by Fufayev's assistants. Like Fufayev himself, they recognized me immediately from the pictures they had received. They drove me to Hotel Peking, where a table set with food and drink awaited us in my room. We ate and took turns proposing toasts. In between the toasts Comrade Fufayev monopolized the conversation. I could not understand his Russian signs very well, but I could tell he was full of friendliness and good cheer. That evening they took me to Red Square. It was an unforgettable spectacle—the falling snowflakes, the red neon star, and the guards in front of Lenin's Tomb.

The following day my new friends escorted me to the airport and placed me on a plane to Riga. At the airport in Riga, I was met by Michael Slipchenko, an actor who was to show me the ropes and teach me Russian Sign Language. Slipchenko was the other exchange actor; he was scheduled to spend six weeks with the NTD.

At the hotel restaurant, I studied him attentively. He had the same build as I and appeared to be about the same age, in his early forties. I could not understand his Russian signs, save for a few elementary ones I had remembered from Yugoslavia, so we carried on the conversation in mimicry and gestures. Luckily, we had no problems communicating. I made clear to him my desire to learn Russian Sign Language from him by a kind of total immersion, rather than from dictionaries, and he agreed. I would point at the table, at the chair, at myself, and at other objects, and in this way within a few hours I learned as many as fifty signs from him.

After dinner he took me to a performance of Griboyedov's *Woe from Wit*, given by the Moscow Theatre of Mimicry and Gesture then touring in Riga. What I saw took me by surprise. The actors, all deaf, faced the audience instead of each other and clearly enunciated every word, using very few signs, apparently so the deaf audience could lipread them better. As Michael explained to me, they were not actually uttering the words aloud, they were merely "lip-synching" the words while four or five interpreters seated in the orchestra pit were pronouncing the words to match the mouthing.

This was completely different from the practice of the National Theatre of the Deaf in the United States, where the interpreters are part of the cast, perform on stage together with deaf actors, sign with abandon themselves, and at the same time recite the lines for both themselves and the deaf actors. In our troupe the deaf actors do not even mouth the English words.

After the performance, Michael took me backstage and introduced me to the troupe and its artistic director, a hearing man named Viktor Znamerovsky. I shook hands formally with them all, and when they asked me to comment on their performance, I signed diplomatically that I was very impressed with the energy they had displayed in their acting. They were likable people. Their variety of temperaments matched that in my National Theatre of the Deaf troupe, and I thought I could work with them very well.

They were surprised and pleased at the rapidity with which I was picking up their sign language, and I gestured to them that the credit belonged to Michael, who looked gratified. I agreed with Viktor that for the first few days I would just be watching the rehearsals of the play in which I was to act, Aeschylus's *Prometheus Bound*, until I felt ready to take an active part.

The following morning I had breakfast with Michael at the hotel restaurant. He helped me order from the menu while at the same time teaching me the Russian signs for "tea," "egg," "bread," and the like. We then walked to the theater, where Viktor gave me copies of the Russian- and English-language scripts of *Prometheus*. I was to be Hermes, the messenger of Zeus.

I practiced my Russian Sign Language lines with Michael's help. I agreed with Viktor that I would memorize my lines in English and sign them in Russian. I told him, with Michael interpreting, that I felt challenged by this whole business.

In the evenings I watched the various plays in the troupe's repertoire, and on weekends I attended the matinees for children. The house was always full, the tickets were very cheap, and the audiences were enthusiastic. Yet from my observations of the troupe's acting style I concluded that if the audiences loved this kind of theater so much, they must be really starving for culture. Here the actors faced the audiences; they rarely showed their profiles, not even while talking, or rather mouthing words, to each other. Never had I seen anything more curious. They used skimpy signs, more like gestures, and they never raised their hands in front of their faces, apparently so that their mouthing would remain visible. Their postures were stiff and their gestures rigidly declamatory in a manner that was half-Racine and half-Kabuki.

While I was in Riga, I also attended some plays performed in "hearing" theaters, where the actors behaved much more naturally and I could witness Russian theater in all of its glory. I realized then that the Russian deaf troupe was an exception rather than the rule; its stiff posturing simply mirrored the indigenous oralist trend and was intended to make it easier for deaf audiences to lipread the dialogue. Still, as an exchange artist, I felt I had come to learn, not to criticize.

The rehearsals of *Prometheus Bound* began. I sat in the auditorium watching Ostap, the tall, thin, heavy-lidded actor who had the role of Hermes, the role I was to take over. After three days Viktor asked me to take over Ostap's part. I climbed onto the platform meant to be a rock crag, above the stage and above the actor playing Prometheus, Dmitri. He was leaning against a large boulder, with his chained arms outstretched. When the actor playing Zeus gave me my cue by turning his thumb down, I descended the staircase to the stage level. My eyes were then in line with Dmitri's feet. While descending, I caught myself imitating Ostap's swagger, and this realization distressed me. As I signed my lines to Dmitri, I committed my first breach of propriety; I looked up at him instead of facing the auditorium.

Viktor stopped the rehearsal and climbed on stage with Michael in his wake. He looked upset and I thought he was going to complain about my deviationist act, but instead, he declared that the interpreter in the orchestra pit could not follow my lines because I was not mouthing my words in Russian. He then asked if I could mouth them in Russian.

The question really floored me. Could Viktor be so naive as to suppose that I could "mouth my lines in Russian," just like that? I patiently explained to Viktor, via Michael, that it would take me years and years to accomplish this feat of verbalization, which for deaf people is far from being as simple and easy as learning a foreign sign language. Then I asked why the interpreter could not simply follow my Russian signs. He could not, Viktor explained, because he was trained to follow mouth movements rather than signs.

This looked like the beginning of a long argument, and Viktor declared a break in the rehearsal. The actors walked off stage and plopped down onto seats in the auditorium, watching us on stage.

I had an idea. I suggested to Viktor that Ostap sit with the voice interpreter in the orchestra pit and speak my lines in Russian while I signed my lines on stage in American Sign Language. This way I could express my emotions as Hermes truthfully and with sincerity.

Viktor said he liked my idea but there was a problem: what about Dmitri, the actor playing Prometheus? He did not know American Sign Language, so how could he maintain a meaningful dialogue with me? Simple, I answered; he and I could practice until he became familiar with my lines in American Sign Language and I became familiar with his lines in Russian Sign Language.

So Dmitri and I began to practice on our own every afternoon. He soon got to understand my lines perfectly and I his; I foresaw no more problems. We worked well together and I felt extremely gratified.

But my expectations were overturned during the dress rehearsal, two days before opening night. That was the first time Dmitri and I had rehearsed on stage together rather than in a dressing room and the first time in costume.

Wearing a shining breastplate and a gilded laurel wreath, I waited for Zeus to give me my thumb-down cue. While waiting I was thinking, Should I imitate the troupe's acting style or should I do it my way? After all, was it not the purpose of cultural exchange for artists to exchange their experience?

Descending the staircase, I approached Dmitri, signing, "Wise of thy wit and bitter of thy tongue."

From his height he continued to stare tragically straight ahead into space above the empty seats of the auditorium, his arms extended and chained to the rock. He ignored me, though I knew he could see me. I moved closer to him. He still did not look at me. So I waved my hand to attract his attention.

He inclined his face downward to look at me and, frowning and puzzled, asked me what I was doing. "Hello, I am here," I gestured. He gestured back,

"Yes, I know. So?" I gestured, "I thought you didn't know, because I tried to catch your eye." But he answered, "You don't have to. Just go ahead and sign your lines."

"Without your looking at me?"

"Sure. That's the way we do it."

In the meantime Viktor climbed on stage with Michael in tow and asked what the problem was. I told him that I considered eye contact extremely important, but he disagreed, saying that Prometheus should listen (yes, that was the verb Viktor used as if he did not realize that this was a theater of the deaf) while staring into space. He added, "We actors don't look at each other; we don't have to, most of the time."

But I countered, "Yes, that's fine for hearing actors like yourself, and this may be a good custom on the Russian deaf stage, but we deaf people have to depend on eye contact."

Viktor, even though he signed and began to look as if he wished I were back in America, did not object and asked Dmitri to please give it a try and look at me while I was signing my lines."

I climbed back onto the fake rock crag. Zeus turned his thumb down and, on that signal, I descended majestically down the staircase and approached Prometheus, signing my lines.

A disaster! He again stared straight ahead without looking down at me. I lost my patience and tapped his buskin-clad foot with a finger. He looked down. I waved, "I'm here." He was angry. "Why can't you do your part and I mine? That's the way I have been acting for years and nobody ever found anything wrong with it."

This had to happen, the ugly American bit, and I was embarrassed. He was right. After all, I was only a guest in his country and could not dictate to others what was to be done.

But Viktor came to my rescue; to this day I do not know why. He said to Dmitri, "Try just once more to see what it is like."

Dmitri nodded uncertainly. We all went back to our places. Zeus gave the signal and once again I descended the staircase until I reached Dmitri.

He turned his face toward me as I began to sign in American Sign Language, "Wise of thy wit and bitter of thy tongue, thou pilferer of fire, speak out, and nothing hide."

He signed back in Russian Sign Language, this time facing me eye to eye, "Great swelling words thou speakest, and thy pride soars, for a servant, to no vulgar pitch."

His face was transformed. It was colored with emotion and his eyes shone. I responded with the same fever pitch, "Yet even by such stubbornness before to this ill haven were thy fortune steered."

And so, with eloquent signs and sweeping gestures, we hurled lines at each other until the end of the scene, with Dmitri no longer a wax figure but a real, rancorous, and defiant Prometheus, and myself a minatory and admonishing Hermes.

When it was over, we both were exhausted. We looked at each other, grateful and happy. It was only then that I turned to look at the auditorium and saw that Viktor, all the members of the cast, and even the technicians and carpenters, had gotten up from their seats and were applauding us vigorously.

Viktor climbed onto the stage and asked Dmitri how he was feeling. "Very emotional," Dmitri answered. "Did you experience that emotion before?" Dmitri shook his head and, after a pause, looking at me, signed, "I must admit there is something to it." I gestured to him that I was glad we finally felt each other's emotions. And Michael, with whom I had shared my feelings all that time, signed to Dmitri, "That is where our compatriot Stanislavsky comes in. Instead of pretending that you are a hearing person who listens to words, you establish close contact with other actors by looking at them in the eye."

On opening night we received a standing ovation. Still, I was not sure about the audience because I had seen it applaud those stylized Racine-Kabuki performances. But of one thing I could be sure; my fellow actors did appreciate and like the difference in acting style.

My Russian experience was capped by yet another surprise meeting with Marcel Marceau. I had heard he was in Moscow, so I asked the desk clerk at my hotel to call the other hotels to try to find him. He was at the Hotel Peking; I ran over there and found Marceau sitting in the lobby. He did not recognize me at first because I was wearing a mustache and a fur hat, looking very Russian, so I said, "Tell me you don't know me," and at the unmistakable sound of my voice he smiled and we hugged each other. He asked me to go along with him to a banquet to which he had been invited by the troupe of the Moscow Mime Theatre.

The Russian mimes welcomed us into the banquet hall. We sat at a long table laden with delicacies and bottles of vodka and liqueurs. The Russians started to take turns toasting the great French artist and the great American artist and drinking to international amity and peace. Our glasses were refilled each time a new toast was proposed, and since there were altogether twenty-five of us, we gradually became drunk. An interpreter, a thin-faced woman who was remarkably skilled, translated the utterances of her compatriots into French for Marceau's benefit and wrote them down in English for me.

When Marceau's turn came, he stood up and delivered a speech in the same vein, while the interpreter busily scribbled it for my benefit. He toasted eloquently the great Russian artists and the art of pantomime; his speech lasted longer than any of the others. He downed his glass of vodka with his head tilted back in the Russian manner and then pointed at me.

It was my turn. The interpreter looked nonplussed; her knowledge of languages did not include sign language. She offered me pen and paper, but I waved them away as I stood up. Among these mimes, I was the only one to propose a toast entirely in mime. I pointed at each of them in turn, then made a gesture of gathering them all together into a ball in the palm of my hand, picked up that ball, pressed it against my heart, and bowed. When I sat down, Marceau stood up and declared that mine was the most eloquent speech made at that gathering. I do not remember what happened next. In fact, I woke up with a frightful headache the next morning in my hotel room. I will never again believe that vodka causes no hangover.

Two years later in 1975, Michael Slipchenko came to us at the NTD and took over my role as the father of the unlucky bride in Ansky's The Dybbuk. *He delivered his lines in Russian Sign Language and played his role to perfection.*

He had rapidly adapted himself not only to the American style of acting but also to the American lifestyle. He told me he would not be the same person when he went back home to Russia, now that he had gotten a taste of freedom and the American way of life; yet he had to go back—he had been picked to go to the United States in the first place because he was a party member, and he had left his wife and little daughter at home in Russia.

He brought me a gift from Russia—a pair of authentic bast (tree-bark) shoes that had belonged to his grandfather. He had found them in the loft of the family farmhouse. He cleaned and wiped them so that they looked like new.

When he was leaving for his homeland I gave him a clock with a picture of the ocean and the inscription, "Time Flies but Memories Last." To be with him was a pleasure, and I was sad to see him go.

Soon afterward I witnessed a tragedy that struck a fellow actor. Sometimes an illness is not as slow and drawn out as it had been with Joe Velez. Instead it flares briefly, disappears, and ominously reappears, thundering toward a climactic explosion that leaves spectators shaken. We at the NTD were not spectators but participants in a spectacle whose main protagonist, Dorothy Miles, enacted what was almost her self-immolation. The spectacle was performed in sign, but its meaning, the outcry of a human being who could not cope with reality, was universal. To this day I do not know what she was protesting against and what kind of deep trouble she was experiencing, but whatever it was, I know that her being among people deaf like herself did prove of therapeutic value.

I happened to look back and saw David Hays waving at me frantically and signing, "Very important." Oh, no, here goes my afternoon swim! I took one last longing look at the beach and walked back across the dunes to where he stood.

"What happened?"

He looked serious and worried. "It's Dorothy. More trouble. I need your help."

As we walked back to the Mansion, as everyone called the O'Neill Theatre Center which housed the National Theatre of the Deaf, he explained that he had received a phone call from the Reverend Mr. Curtis about Dorothy. The minister was worried about her because she had behaved strangely that afternoon at the church picnic in Hartford. Everyone at the picnic wore a name card, but Dorothy wore three cards, each with a different name, one of them her own. Having just staged a play about the deaf with the help of the local deaf community theater, a play which she also had written herself, she was besieged by autograph seekers at the picnic. She asked each in turn which of those three names they wanted on the autograph. They did not understand her question, naturally, and reacted in different ways, some embarrassed, others upset. A crowd had collected about her while she kept defiantly asking which one of those three names they wanted her to be.

The Rev. Mr. Curtis saw what was happening and called a psychologist friend of his, who came at once to observe her from a distance. The Rev. Mr. Curtis interpreted Dorothy's signing to him, and he concluded that this was "an explosive case. Get her to a hospital, and quick!" That was why The Rev. Mr. Curtis had called David, who now came for my help, since I was a close friend of Dorothy's.

By now we were entering the Mansion. Once inside David's office I told him that I remembered how haggard and high-strung Dorothy had looked at the end of the recent NTD tour to California. She had just received her master's degree in theater education and was excited about teaching drama in the fall. "We must get her all the help we can, for her sake," I said.

I no longer minded losing my last swim before the NTD summer school began. Dorothy's condition was more important. We were in Waterford, about an hour's drive to Hartford. It was 4:00 P.M. and, according to David, The Reverend Mr. Curtis had called him at 3:30. I asked David where Dorothy was now, still in Hartford or on the way back, and he answered, "That's what I'm trying to find out. I want you to alert Dorothy's close friends to keep an eye on her. Please let me know immediately when she arrives. I feel the best course would be for us all to get together and bring her to a hospital."

I agreed and left him while he made some telephone calls. I drove off to warn Dorothy's friends to watch out for her. Tim, Freda, Ho, Art, and Nikki arrived at the Mansion one by one after I contacted them, and we gathered in David's office. By now it was seven o'clock and still no news. Where could Dorothy be? Someone asked, "Should we call the police?" But someone else counseled patience. Suddenly the phone rang. David picked it up. He listened intently, then responded, "Hold her there. Don't let her go." He hung up the phone and said, "Dorothy is back. She's at Gloria's home. Let's go there."

Gloria was David's secretary, a matronly woman whom everyone liked and trusted. We all piled into David's van. While he drove, I advised the others to take off their watches, rings, and necklaces so that no one would get hurt if force were needed, although we all hoped we could get Dorothy to the hospital peacefully. I added that she should sit in the center of the van so we could prevent her escaping, and we must try to humor her.

We reached Gloria's apartment building, all feeling uncomfortable but under the compulsion to do something to help Dorothy. The door opened. Gloria, looking ashen, beckoned us inside. Behind her stood her husband, John. We rapidly filed into the living room. Dorothy was there reading a script of *The Tempest*, signing it to herself as if in a dream. She did not look up. She was wearing a long-sleeved red Chinese robe. She was on the last page of the script, and when she signed the last line, she finally looked at us and signed with a commanding air, "Thank you for coming," as if she had planned it all in advance and expected us. "I'll now cast you all," she continued. She pointed at me, "You're Prospero, dear Bernard." To Freda, who had in the meantime sat down on the floor, "You're his daughter, Miranda." She then looked at the husky black Ho: "You're Caliban." Her gaze shifted to Tim, who stood leaning on the back of a chair. "You're Ariel, who else?" And indeed, with his curly hair and boyish face, Tim looked the perfect Ariel. She then looked at David and signed, "You know, I'm taking over as their director."

Her eyes glittered and there was a kind of grandeur about her. She was Dorothy, yet not Dorothy. She was possessed. It was all so unreal. Such a lovely woman. She had the typically English straight nose and delicately sculptured face. When she had joined our troupe several years previously it had not taken her long to throw off the shackles of her oral upbringing and absorb sign language with astonishing speed and fluency. She had joined the NTD as a wardrobe mistress and worked her way up to costume designer and then playwright and actress. She was also a gifted poet and a brilliant watercolor painter. Such a brilliant and creative person, and now possessed by the devil of mental illness.

We all stared at her with fear and concern, feeling powerless. She pointed at Art and signed, "You'll be stage manager." He stood like a statue and did not answer. Suddenly, Nikki, the interpreter, burst into tears. Dorothy, smiling, approached her, kneeled at her side, and began to stroke her hair, "I forgive you. You're crying with happiness." She got up and looked at us. Her gaze fastened on Tim, who, trembling, was the first of us to say something. He blurted out, "You're ill."

We were stunned. I furtively shushed Tim, "No! Humor her," but Dorothy replied, "No, I'm fine. I'm not ill. Can't you see how happy I am? I've never been happier in my whole life."

Tim ignored me and signed to her, "No, not true." Then David broke in, signing with a false bonhomie, "Let's throw a party." Dorothy turned around. "Yes!" She solemnly spread her arms high. "Yes, let's celebrate."

We all jumped to our feet and David suggested, "Let's go. Straight to the Mansion." We filed out in a line, which I led, thumping an imaginary drum and playing an imaginary pipe. Art picked up Dorothy and carried her tenderly in his arms in the middle of the procession as it emerged from the building and advanced toward the van. All of us got into the van except Nikki, who had her own car. David started the van, but Dorothy cried out, "Wait! Where's Nikki?" I chimed in, "Nikki is in her car. She's driving to the hospital. Her husband cut his finger. Let's go join them." "Right," Dorothy replied. "Let's go there first and pick up Joe. He must be with us at the party."

David drove while Dorothy gaily signed ditties from *South Pacific*, her favorite musical. The instant we entered the waiting room at the St. Lawrence Hospital, Dorothy flopped onto a chair and became very quiet, looking exhausted. But she did not stay there long; the doctor was already waiting for her. David had called Dr. Neilsen, a tall Swede and a good friend of our troupe, and had forewarned him. He approached Dorothy slowly, inclined his head, and bowed. "Hello, Doctor," she greeted him. In reply, he said only, "Please follow me," firmly but not curtly. She got up and followed him down the hallway. I grabbed Nikki's hand and we two followed them, while the others stayed in the lobby.

At a doorway, Dr. Neilsen gestured, "Please wait in this room." She went in but almost immediately came out, puzzled, "Where's Joe?"

"He's not here," said Dr. Neilsen, stone-faced. "Please go in and stay there!"

She looked at the tearful Nikki, who signed to her, "Please understand. We all love you very much and want you to get well."

Dorothy's expression showed that she realized she had been tricked. Suddenly she looked like a trapped and frightened animal, glancing around as if trying to escape, but she was now surrounded by us.

She lunged at Nikki and slapped her very hard, so quickly that I didn't have time to intervene. Cradling her slapped cheek in her hand, Nikki signed shudderingly, "That's okay. That's okay."

Dr. Neilsen pointed sternly at the door and said, "Go in now."

Dorothy backed away, all the while looking at the group standing in the hallway. No longer a trapped animal but a lady desperately mustering all the dignity possible, she signed, "I'm not sick. You all are sick." She extended her arms as if to have them manacled. "Take me. Take me." Dr. Neilsen again pointed his finger at the door, wordlessly this time. She entered the room, holding her head high. Dr. Neilsen closed the door.

Nikki, still sobbing, walked back to the waiting room with me, leaning on my arm. Suddenly, the lobby door opened and two police officers rushed in and started to talk excitedly to the receptionist. David heard them and walked over to the desk. Nikki began to interpret their conversation for us. The police officers said that they were looking for Dorothy in order to arrest her. On her way back to Waterford, Dorothy had stopped at a grocery store to buy cigarettes. On leaving she bumped into a woman, whom she pushed and slapped. The woman had called the police, who were now looking for Dorothy.

"You're five minutes too late, gentlemen," said David. "She was just admitted to this hospital and is under medical supervision."

We all sighed with relief as the two police officers beat a retreat after checking with the receptionist and declaring that they would wait until Dorothy's discharge. They left the hospital, and so did we.

The next morning summer school opened. The Mansion swarmed with newcomers and we all had our hands full. But just before noon David came to tell me that Dorothy's psychiatrist had called and asked for her friends to come and visit her right away. That would be the best medicine for Dorothy, the doctor said.

I was the first person to go to see her. I took her a vase with a single red rose in it. When I walked into her room she was lying in bed with her eyes closed, but almost at once she sensed my presence and opened them.

She sat up and signed, "Hello, Bernard. You came to test my mind?"

"I came here to see how you are," I answered, offering her the rose.

I could see she was touched; the needlelike sharpness in her eyes had softened. I added, "That's from us."

She hugged me, then she told me that all the while she had known what was happening but felt powerless to stop it. However, she had had a long talk with her psychiatrist and believed she would be fine again.

I asked her whom else she would like to see, and she said Tim, Nikki, Freda, Art, and Ho. They were coming, I assured her, and on this note I left her.

Even now I think of her with admiration and love. She is back home in England reestablishing her roots and putting the past behind her.

CHAPTER FIVE

Reviews

Life on the road, while traveling with the NTD, brought me many intriguing encounters, some of which in one way or another had roots stretching far back into my past. It was almost as if my past kept trying to catch up with me, wherever I was—the Midwest, California, or even Scotland. In Scotland, in 1975, the ghost of my grandfather caught up with me.

From Glasgow we proceeded to Aberdeen in a rented car. I was driving. Richard, a fellow actor, and I had a few days free before the rehearsals in London. To while away the time, and because the occasion was right, I began to tell Richard about my Jewish-Scots grandfather. "My grandfather was a cabinetmaker by trade, but he always loved farming and worked on a dairy farm thirty miles west of Aberdeen. He and his family moved to the States when my father was four."

I kept reminiscing. It was my grandfather, Louis Bragg, who named me Bernard, but I had not known it until one day when I was thirteen. My parents were at work, so I was home alone. Out of idle curiosity I opened the green metal box in which they kept their most important papers. I saw a hospital wristband with the name "Bragg" on it. It was an old-fashioned band, made of beads. Then I saw a birth certificate bearing the name "Nathan Bragg" and my own birthdate. I felt unnerved. Could it be that I was not the real son of my parents but a foundling or an adoptive child? All day long I was perplexed and worried. When my parents returned home, my mother went into the kitchen to prepare dinner and so did not notice how strange and quiet I was, but my father did. He asked me, "What is wrong with you? You are not yourself." I hesitated. "Come on," he urged me.

So I said, "Okay, but first please forgive me for opening the green box."

He commanded, "Tell me what you saw in that box."

I answered, "I found a birth certificate there, but I'm not sure whether it is mine or someone else's."

"What do you mean, someone else's?" my father asked.

"Yes, someone else whose name is Nathan."

My father and my mother, who had in the meantime joined us, looked at each other. He bowed his head. I was on the verge of bursting into tears. So I was a foundling! But Father started to smile, "Yes, I remember now." And Mother joined in, "Yes, we should have told you long ago."

I interrupted, "I don't want to know. Don't tell me."

My father gestured at me to stay put. "Relax. It's nothing." Then he told me what happened. When I was born he had been working in Philadelphia as a house painter. He took an overnight train and arrived at the hospital in Brooklyn the day after my birth. A nurse greeted him and asked him to give her a name for my birth certificate. He was stumped and asked, "Is it a boy or a girl?" When she said it was a boy, he thought of Nathan Hale. Since Mother had no objections, that was the name he gave to the nurse. But two weeks later, when Mother brought me home, my grandfather came to visit us in Brooklyn from his farm in Sharon, Connecticut. He asked my father, "Wolf, what is his name?" and when Father answered, "Nathan," he pounded the table with his fist and roared, "No, it's Bernard!"

I was relieved. So I was their real son after all. But this also made me feel closer to my grandfather. As I kept driving I remarked to Richard, "You want to know how it came about that I was named Bernard? Hereby hangs another tale. When my grandparents were a young couple, they had a baby boy named Bernard. He was younger than my father. One day my grandmother had to go shopping in town; she took the older children and left little Bernard in her husband's care. He left the baby in the barn, in what he had thought to be a safe place, and went to attend to some urgent farm chore. Not long after, he noticed smoke billowing from the barn. He dropped the rake and, terrified, rushed inside the barn and groped in the smoke for Bernard, picked him up and, holding him in the crook of his left arm, ran outside and collapsed on the ground.

"But when he came to, wracked by the pain in his burned left arm, his heart almost burst when he saw that the thing he was gripping convulsively was no longer a living being but a blackened, charred piece of flesh.

"By that time neighboring farmers flocked to where he lay and picked him up. Given the state of medical science in those days, he spent the next four years, on and off, in a hospital, where he kept getting skin grafts for his arm and hand. His left arm became permanently disabled. It remained crooked and had a clawlike projection where his hand should have been."

By now we had reached Edinburgh. We passed it and kept going north, up the coast. I kept reminiscing.

"When I was growing up, every summer I used to go to my grandfather's farm in Sharon. I helped him feed cows, bring in wood, and do countless other farm chores. I followed him everywhere. I felt real contentment in his presence.

"I remember particularly one Passover Seder when the whole family, including my aunts and uncles, sat down around a big table and my grandfather read from the prayer book, turning its pages over, one after another as he finished each. At one moment, when my grandmother left for the kitchen, he skipped three pages of the prayer book without ceasing to pray. Soon afterward my grandmother returned to the living room, sat down, listened for a minute, and expressionlessly turned those three pages back. He continued praying as if nothing had happened, except that he glanced expressively at me and sighed.

"You can see how close I was to my grandfather. Closer even than to my own father, though strangely enough I could communicate more easily with my father because he was deaf like me. Although my grandfather knew no sign language, a wink from him, a pat on the head from him, meant so much more to me and I felt such great intimacy with him.

"I didn't have the same feeling about my grandmother. She was a straight-backed woman, proud of her Viennese descent; her own father had been ennobled by Emperor Franz Joseph. I always have wondered how she and my grandfather met. She was bitter too because the family sank into a kind of poverty after Grandfather burned his hand in the fire. I suppose what also made her bitter was the strain of deafness in the family. She must have taken it as a kind of personal curse. At any rate she was always as distant with me as with my father.

"I can remember sharing only one moment of tenderness with my grandmother, and that was the day of my grandfather's funeral. He died when I was thirteen years old. My parents and I had gone to see my grandparents that day. My grandmother came out of my grandfather's room and spread her hands in a gesture of resignation and despair. I knew then he had died. The next scene I remember is standing and crying beside my grandfather's coffin, which was draped with a flag bearing the Star of David. My grandmother mechanically smoothed the flag over the coffin, then she came over to me and hugged me. She began to sway and cry with me.

"I stood there thinking that my grandfather had lived with his guilt a long time; maybe that was why he gave me so much love and attention. The motorcade of four or five cars was ready to follow the hearse. But my father ordered me to stay, against my protestations. Perhaps he was frightened by the intensity of my grief. Everyone left, and I lay down on the ground and buried my face in the grass, feeling lost and alone.''

We were approaching Aberdeen and I concentrated on driving through the city's outskirts. I signed to Richard, "This is the city where my grandfather used to live and my father was born. Wonder if I can find my father's birthplace. I have his address here. We could ask a cop. You could interpret for me." Richard, who was only hard of hearing, not deaf, nodded, "Of course. But why is this so important to you?"

"Well, I don't know. But I feel this is a way of my getting closer to my grandfather. Do you mind tagging along?"

"Not at all. I am curious too."

We entered Aberdeen. We were going to look for a place to stay overnight, but the city was so lovely and clean that I proposed to Richard that we first sightsee a little in the car. He agreed. We wandered through neighborhoods, soaking in the scenery. We eventually found ourselves on a lovely, winding street. The houses were surrounded by beautiful gardens. The entire street bespoke tradition and an idyllic way of life, and we found it enchanting. At one point I happened to look at the street sign—it said Wallfield Crescent. This gave me a shock. Slowly I drove on toward the next corner and stopped in front of a house. It was number 5—the house my grandfather had lived in before moving to his farm. With shaking hands I showed the slip with the address to Richard. "Look, this is the place." He looked at the slip. Then he looked up at the street sign and the house number and exclaimed, "How in the world did you find it, without a map, and without asking a cop?"

I confessed to him that I did not know and felt a little scared about it myself. Incidentally, later I happened to see a big wall map of Aberdeen, the third largest city in Scotland, and found 5 Wallfield Crescent only after a long search conducted with the aid of a local inhabitant, who scratched his head when he could not find it easily.

I got out of the car and photographed the three-story gray stone house with its brick ornamentation. Richard raised his head and began talking. I followed his gaze and saw a woman in a second-story window. As Richard interpreted it to me, she was wondering why I was photographing the house and where we were from. She invited us to her apartment and offered us tea. We learned that she had a daughter living in California, only ten miles from where my parents had lived. I could not learn anything from her about my grandfather, but as we left, I stole a peek at the open door to a bedroom. Inside stood a massive old-fashioned bed, and I thought, rather wishfully, that this perhaps was where my father had been born.

We decided to find an inn near my grandfather's old farm, thirty miles west of Aberdeen. On the way I told Richard about my visit three years previously with my biographer, Helen Powers, in Connecticut. She had asked me if I wanted to see my grandfather's grave, and I was astonished that she knew where it was. "I didn't write your biography for nothing," she answered, smiling. She drove me to Beth Israel Cemetery outside Danbury, Connecticut. After we entered the cemetery and walked a certain distance, she stopped and told me to go on by myself. "Walk to the fence. It is the fourth grave from the corner." I found it easily and read the inscription, "Louis Bragg, 1863–1942." The grave was overgrown with grass. I picked up a small rock and, as is the Jewish custom, placed it on the grave—a gesture that had taken me some thirty years to accomplish.

Richard and I found an inn just before dark. We had a good dinner and spent the remainder of the evening in the bar, where we chatted with the locals. I asked the innkeeper if there was a farm nearby. He told me there had been one just across the nearby stream.

For some reason, I woke up at five o'clock the next morning and could not get back to sleep again. I got up and dressed quietly so as not to wake Richard. In the hallway just beside the outer door, I picked up a walking stick.

Outside it was still dark. I crossed the road and white bridge and walked through a grove of trees. Shivering in the chill air, I followed a cowpath through the early-morning mist. In the distance the sky began to brighten. I breathed in the sweet fragrance of grass and trees, mingled with the smell of manure, as I followed the winding path. Suddenly, I felt my grandfather's presence.

"Grandpa," I said to myself, "I know you are here."

No response. But a moment later I felt bathed in a blast of warm air which dissipated the chill. It came and went like an exhalation of a very dear presence.

The yellow-white disk of the rising sun was now completely above the horizon. I turned around and sensed that the presence was gone.

"Thank you, Grandpa. Good-bye."

There was one thrilling moment when I had felt terribly close to my father— and that is the moment I want to remember, however much my other memories of him are those of conflicts. He was a gifted, talented, and charming man. He was also a tragic figure, in some respects, and I suppose that somewhere along the way I decided that where he had failed I would succeed. What else could be the source of my strong and lasting motivation—against so many odds?

I drove in pouring rain all the way from New London, Connecticut, to New York, feeling annoyed with my Aunt Lena because she had asked me to come see her in this awful weather. However, she needed my help, and that was that. She had misplaced some important papers and, because of her poor vision, had asked me to help locate them.

She had recently given up her apartment expecting to get a better one, but the deal fell through and she was temporarily staying at the home of Belle, her sister-in-law, also deaf, whom she did not trust enough to ask for help in finding those papers. I had never visited Belle before, and what I found there left me shaken.

I reached New York, parked, rode up the elevator to Belle's apartment, and pushed that white flashing-light button. The door opened and my aunt and Belle hugged me affectionately.

I went with Aunt Lena to her room and soon enough retrieved the stock certificate receipt she was looking for. She thanked me and asked me to stay for a while. We went into the living room, where my aunt and Belle urged me to eat something. Until then I had not taken a good look at the living room. But as we were chatting, something began to gnaw at me. Finally my gaze fastened on a painting hanging on the opposite wall. I kept looking at it at intervals during our conversation. At some point I excused myself and approached it for a closer look—and a thrill of recognition.

The painting depicted a tall, full-masted ship riding a wave in a stormy, green sea. I kept staring at it. Suddenly I noticed Belle standing behind me and smiling. I told her I did not know why but this painting looked familiar to me.

She laughed, "It should. Your father painted it. Don't you remember?"

"My father?" I looked again at the painting and saw his signature, Wolf Bragg, in the dark green water in a corner.

It brought back bittersweet memories, not just of the tall ship but of the years before. My father had been a house painter during the Depression. When I was three, I watched him paint, in exchange for our rent, the walls of the apartment building in which we were then living. I picked up a paintbrush and tried to daub a wall with it. When he saw what I was doing, he grabbed the paintbrush from my hand, accidentally smearing my cheek with white paint, and gestured violently that I should never touch that brush again. I was frightened and held back my tears until my mother came and led me away. When I grew up I asked my mother why he had reacted so violently. She answered that he was afraid I would follow in his footsteps and become a house painter myself, and he wanted me to have a better life than that.

When I was ten, he started to paint on canvases instead of walls. It became his favorite hobby. I loved to watch him paint and once I gathered enough courage to ask him if I could learn to paint too. He laughed and said he had never gone to an art school himself but learned on his own. I told him that he had a natural talent for painting which I did not have. He answered, "You don't know until you start painting yourself." He looked at me half-critically and gave me a small square of canvas with a little brush and a paint pot as if he were doling out to me something precious. "Go ahead. Paint anything." I painted from imagination a flower that looked like a daisy and showed it to him, wanting his approval. But he was not pleased with my work and criticized it for lacking shading. I admired his expertise and knew in my heart that I could never equal him but felt happy that I had an artist for a father. He liked sports too, so, in order to please him, I took up basketball, baseball, and football, but my heart was never in them.

When I was eleven, my father began to paint the tall ship. I sat and watched him brush in every detail, from knots in the ship's rigging to the white spumes on the green waves. The painting seized my imagination, and I never tired of looking at it. Every Friday when I came home from school, I looked for it. That was how I noticed immediately its disappearance one day. I looked all over the house, but it was nowhere to be found.

I asked my mother about it, and she said, "Oh, your father donated it to the Hebrew Association of the Deaf to be raffled off. They need to collect money to support social services for the deaf."

I was heartbroken and complained, "Why the tall ship? It was my favorite painting. Why not some other painting?"

"Don't feel bad," Mother said. "He'll paint many more."

"But they won't be the same. I loved that painting. I even dreamed of leaping from spar to spar on that tall ship like a swashbuckling pirate." But I had to resign myself to the fact, and I consoled myself with the thought that Father would indeed produce more paintings.

But I was wrong. For the next thirty-five years my father never once put brush to canvas, for a reason that I failed to understand and he would not explain.

Years passed. Now and then I begged my father to paint again. He, however, kept answering, "Please, don't talk about it."

One year when we were all still living in California, I bought a box of oil paints and an easel. When Hanukkah came, my parents and I opened our gifts. The paints and easel were my gift to him. When he unwrapped them, he asked me, "Why?"

"You know why." I answered. And I added that I thought this might inspire him to paint again.

Father responded that he could not understand why I was so anxious for him to take up painting again.

I said, "Perhaps because I feel in myself a passion for painting but lack your talent." He remained silent and his face was drawn as I added, "You've got the talent but lack the passion."

He answered, "I wish I had your passion. You wish you had my talent."

"I'm here with you. Isn't that enough to inspire you to paint?"

"I can't paint for you. I have to paint for myself."

"Do it then. I hope some day soon you'll open this box and set up the easel."

His final comment was, "Who knows?" He put them away in a garage.

More years passed. Whenever I visited my parents, I looked into the garage. The unopened box and the easel always lay there.

Later, after I had moved back East, my parents came to visit me. Father began to complain about the blank walls in my new house. I told him it would be nice if I had some paintings from him to hang on the walls. "There you go again, harping on me," he answered. "You started it," I said, "but okay, I promise never to mention it again." And on that note our conversation ended.

And now I was in Belle's apartment looking at the very same painting of the tall ship that I had last seen when I was eleven.

I turned to Belle and asked, "How did you get it? Did you win it at a raffle?"

"No," she answered. "Somebody else won it and loaned it to me. Later, he died, so I've been keeping it for many years."

"This is the painting I dreamed of, the favorite painting of my childhood."

She smiled and said, "You can have it. Take it home with you tonight."

"No. It's yours."

"No, it's more yours than mine and I want you to have it. I love it, but I can see you love it even more, so please take it with you."

I took the painting and kissed both women good-bye. I could not wait to reach New London—to find the "right" spot for this painting. On arriving I quickly hung the painting in the living room, stepped back, and gazed at it admiringly, feeling grateful to fate.

A few months later my parents flew in from Florida to visit me. They had followed me back East and temporarily moved into my house in Connecticut. After my father was retired, they decided to move to Florida because many of their friends from New York had moved there.

When my father saw the painting in my living room, he froze in his tracks and exclaimed, "But that's mine!"

I said, "No, it's not yours. It's mine now." And I added that I had always wanted to have one of his paintings. He asked me how I had gotten it. I replied, "It fell into my lap," and then I told him the whole story.

He kept looking at the painting. Finally, he commented, "I never realized I was that good." Then he looked at me and said, "That's the greatest story I ever heard."

Six months later, in December, I flew to Florida to see my parents.

My mother opened the door. She embraced and shushed me simultaneously.

"Why? What? Where's Father?"

"Go see for yourself. He's in the sunroom."

I crossed the living room and saw my father in an old paint-stained shirt busily applying a paintbrush to a canvas. The box with the paints I had given him years ago was open.

During a trip to California in 1982, I experienced a living, breathing reminder of how interwoven are the lives of deaf people and the hearing people who join their community. I also realized how a chance meeting in the past can plant the seed of the future.

While in California in December 1982, I attended a Christmas party at the home of an old friend. Some fifty guests were present and everyone was signing. With fingers fluttering and hands flying, people engaged in animated conversations that absorbed them completely.

I knew some of the people and could tell that some of the guests were hearing, but they signed with the same relish as the deaf. I wondered what fate had joined the lives of the hearing guests with those of the deaf. Were their parents deaf perhaps, or was their interest in the deaf aroused in some other unforeseen way?

A tall man with a shock of brown hair, dressed like a stockbroker, materialized in front of me. He saw with amusement that I did not recognize him. Without introducing himself, he signed, "I have a story to tell you."

I took his direct approach in stride and told him to go ahead with his story as other guests began to congregate around us.

"There was a young hearing man," he began, and I could see that his signing was fluid and competent. He could almost be taken for a deaf man, but he was probably the son of deaf parents. "The young man lived in a small town some one hundred miles from Tempe, Arizona. His name was Charles and he was an ordinary high school kid. He was the kind of American teenager who one might meet anywhere in America, in Arizona, Ohio, or Oregon, the kind who loved sports and had no particular career goal at that time in his life. One day he went to the town library to do research on a science assignment. When he finished, he closed his books, got up, and on the way out stopped at his favorite shelf, the biographies. A book caught his eye. Its title was *Signs of Silence,* by Helen Powers.

"Now Charles had until then never met a deaf person in his life and he knew nothing about the deaf and their world. He was curious and leafed through this book, which was a biography of Bernard Bragg and of the National Theatre of the Deaf. The book fascinated him, so he sat down and did not stop reading until he reached the end. Then he got up and placed the book back on the shelf. That seemed to be the end of it.

"But three days later he read in a Tempe newspaper an announcement that the National Theatre of the Deaf was giving a performance of *My Third Eye*. Your name was featured in the announcement. What an incredible coincidence, he thought, and he was deeply stirred.

"He rushed back to the library and successfully pleaded with the librarian to let him borrow Powers's book so he could have it autographed. Then, when he got home he asked to borrow his father's car so he could drive to Tempe.

"His father normally did not allow Charles to borrow the car for a long drive, but after the young man showed him both the book and the announcement, he found this to be an unusual circumstance and agreed to his son's request.

"Charles drove to Tempe. Inside the theater he saw a sight he would not soon forget. He had never before seen deaf people, and now all at once he saw a large group of them conversing in lively gestures. And when the lights dimmed and the play began, the signing on stage opened a new enchanting and magic world to him."

The man in the brown suit continued, "After the play, the actors came out front to meet the audience and sign autographs. You stood surrounded by a group of deaf and hearing people, both strangers and old friends. The stage manager appeared and reminded the actors individually to hurry to the bus, which was scheduled to leave in ten minutes; he had a very strict rule about the bus departing on time.

"As you were about to bid good-bye to those around you, you noticed a young man in the back who kept watching you and trying to catch your attention. He held up a copy of *Signs of Silence*.

"The stage manager once again beckoned to you, but you could not ignore that young man who wanted an autograph, so you asked the people around you if they did not mind making way for the young man.

"The stage manager was growing frantic, 'Hurry! Everyone is on the bus except you!'

"You were about to leave, but when the young man came up to you, you said, 'Just a minute, I promise.'

"You signed a greeting to the young man, but he obviously knew no sign language. You looked around, 'An interpreter, please.' One young hearing daughter of deaf parents raised her hand, and interpreted what the boy said about his discovery in the library and how he had gotten the librarian's permission. You asked him how far it was to his hometown from Tempe, and he said, 'About one hundred miles.' You autographed his book and signed, 'It took me three thousand miles to meet you, and it took you one hundred miles, but you made a special effort, so we could say that we met almost halfway.'

"You then excused yourself and ran to the bus. The young man drove back home that night with the autographed book on the seat."

He stopped as if ending the story, but I could tell there was more. I asked, "So what happened afterward? Finish it and tell us the end and what became of him? Where is he now?"

The man answered, "You met him again."

"Did I? Where? When?"

"Just now. Right before you. The same young man, older now, stands before you."

"So it is you! I thought so."

He smiled and nodded. We embraced, and I commented, "How could I have recognized you at first? Your signs are so fluent. That young man I met could barely make a gesture."

"Thanks. I'm director of interpreting services in the Bay Area. I also train sign language interpreters."

Just then I happened to glance at a pretty young woman standing next to him. He introduced her as his wife and also an interpreter. He said, "I love it. Working with deaf people is my whole life. Thank you."

"Thank yourself," I answered, "Halfway."

Not all encounters are as gratifying. There was one occasion, also in California, when catching up with the past degenerated into a farce. Even now, when I think of it, I don't know whether to laugh or to feel depressed.

From my table I surveyed the vast banquet room below. Many of the faces were familiar to me. They belonged to my former fellow teachers at the California School for the Deaf at Berkeley, the school I had abandoned because I went on to something I loved more—theater. I had mixed feelings about this evening.

I was seated at the head table, which stood on a three-foot-tall dais. It was the table for the guests of honor at this teachers' convention, and all of them, except me and the actress Nanette Fabray, were luminaries in the world of deafness-related professionals; in plain English, they were prominent hearing people who worked with the deaf. I was seated between the acknowledged leaders of the two opposing schools of thought on education of the deaf. On my left was the eminent educator Dr. William Stout, a fanatical champion of pure oralism, and on my right was Dr. Edward C. Merrill, the president of Gallaudet College, who espoused the philosophy of total communication (the use of sign language, speech, lipreading, residual hearing, and any other appropriate method to achieve communication).

They differed just as drastically in their looks and manner. Dr. Stout's whole appearance was that of a man who could brook no contradiction. Dr. Merrill, by contrast, was a courtly southerner to whom diplomatic language was second nature. Whatever private feelings he may have had, he always concealed them with his smooth manner.

There were quite a few unfavorable anecdotes in circulation about Dr. Stout. It was said that at the school where he ruled with an iron hand he would not let deaf children use a single gesture. There was one story of a time he happened to meet a deaf pupil who was covering his groin with his hands to indicate that he was in a hurry to go to the lavatory. Dr. Stout slapped the boy's hands away and made him pronounce the words, "May I go to the toilet?" He was dissatisfied with the way the boy enunciated the word "toilet" and forced him to say it again and again, placing the boy's hand under his chin to indicate the expulsion of breath associated with uttering the consonant *t*. By the time Stout was half-way satisfied, the boy had wet his pants.

I had had a run-in with him myself a few years previously when we were on the same television program. I did my bit to remove the stigma of unsightliness from sign language by demonstrating its beauty and flexibility. I signed, among other things, several Japanese haiku. Dr. Stout was there, too, but in the waiting room (or greenroom), where he watched my performance on a monitor. As I left the studio, Stout and his assistant from an oral school brushed past me, frozen-faced, without giving me a sign of recognition. I stayed in the greenroom and watched Stout on the monitor while my interpreter signed to me his words. It was the same old rigmarole about the importance of speech to living a normal life in society, as if he did not know, or rather refused to accept the fact that some profoundly deaf people never develop a normal speaking voice. After a while I had had enough, so I turned to my interpreter and said, "We're wasting our time. Let's go!"

Glancing around the head table I noticed I was the only deaf person. Was that in some way symbolic? Was I the token deaf there? Throughout the banquet Dr. Stout did not acknowledge my presence, except at the beginning when by accident we had almost knocked our heads together as we sat down. He had made a remark to me, but what happened was very strange. I could see that his diction and enunciation were extremely clear and our faces were at most only six inches apart when he spoke, yet I could not understand a word. Suddenly I realized why—only his lower jaw moved when he spoke. His face above the upper lip remained stiff and his eyes regarded me with a discomfiting, fixed stare.

Clearly, though, the gentleman was making a polite remark. So I smiled politely at him and gestured deprecatingly as if to say, "Don't mention it." On seeing my gesture he stiffened, as if his posture were not already stiff enough, and from then on he consistently avoided any contact with me. It was the typical reaction of an oralist, to whom any sign is anathema.

One person noticed the incident and smiled compassionately at me. That was the man who had given me my first teaching job, Dr. Elwood A. Stevenson, the superintendent of the California School for the Deaf at Berkeley. He had deaf parents, so had known sign language from early childhood. He was among the most progressive superintendents of schools for the deaf; he favored the use of sign at his school and the hiring of deaf teachers. In addition, his wife, Edith, was the daughter of deaf parents. Her father, Dr. Schuyler Long, was the author of one of the first dictionaries of sign language.

Then my thoughts took another tack because of what I noticed while scrutinizing the banquet participants seated at the round tables below the dais. Down among them was Neubauer, the principal of the high school department at the California School for the Deaf at Berkeley. There was no mistaking his jowls and bushy eyebrows, and even now in the late 1970s, he still wore his bushy hair—grayer now—in the crew-cut style, looking more than ever like a southern police chief rather than a school administrator.

As soon as we made eye contact, he waved to me and got up from his table. Oh no, I thought, as I saw him waddle in my direction, smiling and waving. Seeing him brought back old memories. Neubauer was the man who tried to prevent me from developing creative ways of teaching deaf children. He also had wanted me to choose between teaching and acting. I remembered his admonition, "You can't serve two masters," and smiled.

Neubauer stopped in front of the dais, barely a foot away from me, only his head and torso visible above the table. He energetically pumped my hand, repeating words to the effect that he was "Very happy, very happy, very proud of your wonderful success." As he was shaking my hand, his elbow accidentally knocked over a wine glass. The wine spread in a wide red stain on the tablecloth. I shrugged as if to say "don't worry" and took a napkin to mop the stain up, but Neubauer snatched the napkin from me and began to pat the tablecloth with it.

Embarrassed by this display of servility, I tried to grab the napkin away from him, but he doggedly held on to it. He won this tug-of-war and, beaming, he asserted, "No problem. Let me do it, let me do it."

He finished the mopping-up operation and declared, "Let me refill your glass." He grabbed a bottle from a passing waiter and deftly poured the wine right to the rim of the glass. When he finished, he said jovially, "Good to see you again after so many years. We all are so proud of you."

He turned away and walked back to his table. Once seated, he waved at me, and I waved back.

Then it was time for Nanette Fabray and me to go on stage. I pushed my chair back and got up. I nodded to Dr. Stout on my right and to Dr. Merrill on my left, and walked on stage with Miss Fabray.

Standing in the spotlight, I slowly raised my arms. There was no room now in me for mixed feelings or even for awareness of the audience, of the people in my past—both those who believed in me and understood the deaf and those who did not. It was they, all together, who composed the world from which I sprang.

Inspiration took over, and I started to sign the lines from "The Impossible Dream," while Nanette sang, "To reach the unreachable star. . . ."

CHAPTER SIX

The World Tour

The ten years from 1967 to 1977 that I spent with the National Theatre of the Deaf were a time of excitement and delight, but they also were a time of frustration and struggle as I grew increasingly wary of the NTD's growing orientation toward hearing rather than deaf audiences. True, the NTD contributed greatly to removing the stigma of ugliness from sign language, but that to me is not the purpose of theater; good theater enlightens the audience to basic human truths. One man, of course, stood behind that policy of selling the NTD to the general public: David Hays.

These ten years now seem like a blur to me—with some exceptions, such as my participation in memorable workshops directed by Peter Brook in nonverbal communication, Joe Chaikin in the expression of anger and other true feelings and thoughts, and Jean-Louis Barrault in the ancient art of pantomime. The cycle of rehearsals, tours, and summer school, repeated itself in rapid succession. I acted out on stage the dramas of others but lived through no profound personal dramas of my own.

Moreover, while I delighted in acting and working with professional deaf actors, I missed the individuality I had given up to become part of the ensemble. I missed, too, being able to communicate directly with audiences who appreciate sign language alone. I started to feel uncomfortable performing before audiences that were 90 percent hearing. To them, sign language was just a waving of hands. They seemed to be more interested in seeing how well deaf actors could move on stage and how good their facial expressions and body language were, than they were in discovering what the plays had to say, or in our talents as artists.

I suppose the breaking-point came in 1976 when we staged Four Saints in Three Acts.

Gertrude Stein's *Four Saints in Three Acts*, a notoriously difficult and verbose play, had been staged only once before, in Hartford, Connecticut, in the 1930s, with black actors; even then it had a very short run. Hays decided to revive it and direct it himself. Since producing and directing are each demanding jobs, it is difficult for one person to do both. The result, in this instance, was predictable. Neither the actors nor the audiences were happy with the production.

On opening night in Hartford we got something less than enthusiastic applause. When the curtain fell, Hays bounded onto the stage and blasted the hell out of us. He was given to outbursts, but we had never seen him so furious. He criticized everyone except me for making wrong stage movements and acting listlessly. Then he told everyone to leave except me. "Hurry, go to the bus!" (We were about to leave on a national tour.) When we were left alone he turned to me and screamed, so loudly that even I could hear the noise, "You really know how to upstage everyone with every little trick for yours! You are an actor with 1,001 tricks!"

I was in shock and I boiled with anger, wondering why he had waited until everyone else left before blowing up at me.

He continued, "Damn it! You smile too much."

I just couldn't believe what he was saying. I answered, "You wanted us to act naive and be all smiles. We simply followed your directions. Don't you remember?" I added, "How do we measure smiles? How much less or more of a smile should I show?"

"You know damn well!" he shouted, and continued ranting.

I realized the futility of arguing with him. He was notorious for his confrontations, on which he thrived. So I just turned and walked away. On the bus I wondered what was eating him. I hadn't seen him so furious in ten years.

Two months later, when our troupe was in Phoenix, Hays flew in and visited me in my dressing room. I had just finished applying makeup and was ready to go on stage when he stopped me. "I have arranged for your sabbatical," he announced.

I was thunderstruck and asked, "Why?"

"Ten years is long enough. I think you need a break."

I finally said, "I don't think I need it."

But he answered, "Go away. Do anything you please. And then when you come back next year you will be refreshed."

I protested, "You want me to be refreshed? But I thought I always was fresh. I'm not burned out at all. What gave you that idea?" And I added, trying to lighten the moment, "I still have my 1,001 tricks. What will I do all year?"

But he was adamant. "Go, travel."

I took his advice and planned a trip around the world. Before I left, Hays gave me a contract that stipulated I would receive half-pay during my sabbatical year. I gave it a cursory look, signed it, and shook his hand, but when I got home I read it more closely and found, to my astonishment, that it contained no clause binding me to come back to the NTD. This thought nagged at me throughout my trip. It was up to me alone to decide whether I wanted to spend another ten years of my life with Hays and his company.

Airborne! I was flying to the Old World, courtesy of the United States Department of State, the Ford Foundation, the National Association of the Deaf, and the International Theatre Institute. In the fall of 1977 I left on a six-month tour as the American goodwill ambassador to deaf and hearing people in twenty-five countries. I was representing NTD and was scheduled to give lectures and performances everywhere I landed. My first stopover was in Ireland.

When I landed in Dublin a limousine provided by the American consulate picked me up and took me to my hotel. All the arrangements had already been made for me. The United States Information Agency Speaker Program had cabled Irish leaders of the deaf to meet me in my hotel at four that afternoon.

I was a little uncertain of my ability to communicate with the Irish deaf, since their sign language is different from American, and six letters of their alphabet are fingerspelled differently as well. But my apprehensions were put to rest for a while. Mother Shawn, who greeted me in Irish Sign Language, signed so fluently that it was easy for me to understand her. She introduced me to the three other people in the delegation.

The only man in the group was Father O'Connors, a young priest with an ever-lingering smile on his face, who worked with deaf parishioners. Next to him stood Mrs. Ivors, a middle-aged woman wearing a tailored business suit who had an authoritative air about her. It turned out that she was the president of the National Association for the Deaf in Ireland. Aha, I thought to myself, struck by the paternalistic *for*. How different from the United States with its National Association *of* the Deaf. The fourth person was Molly, a self-effacing, meek young woman in her early twenties, the daughter of Mrs. Ivors, and the only deaf member of the welcoming delegation.

Mother Shawn herself, or more exactly Mother Superior Shawn, was a rotund figure in a nun's habit, with a cherubic expression on her round, grandmotherly face. She headed the local school for the deaf at Cabra as well as the education department at Dublin's University College, in addition to holding other posts; she was also *the* authority on deafness in Ireland.

During the course of our conversation Mother Shawn praised Molly, saying that they were very proud of her success—she had very good speech and a good "nonmenial" job. "Look at our Molly. She speaks well. We started her very early."

Molly smiled and listened to their praise but made no response. I looked at sweet, lovely Molly and wondered how much of our conversation she was understanding. I knew the type well: an oralist who smiles understandingly and whose eyes convincingly glint with comprehension as if he or she knows what people are saying, but who actually understands little or nothing. I wasn't surprised, then, that she remained silent and smiling throughout my conversation with the other three. She was being spoken for.

I felt sad and a kind of kinship with Molly. I had often been in her position, being talked of approvingly as if I were a laboratory animal that had negotiated an intricate maze, while I sat by passively, glad for the praise, totally unaware of the insult to self-respect and dignity this praise implied. I now know that when someone says, "Look at Henry. He's happy," and Henry is sitting in the room trying cooperatively to look the picture of human contentment, the whole scene has to be taken with a massive grain of salt.

Mother Shawn talked nonstop. She was the obvious leader of the group, and I could see the others were deferential. Father O'Connors had trouble getting a word in edgewise, while Molly's mother, that hearing president of the Irish Association for the Deaf, kept nodding.

I was disappointed but not shocked to find these leaders of the deaf were not deaf themselves. All the same, I was struck by the irony of the situation; while every one of the seven Presidents of the National Association of the Deaf in the States was deaf, Mrs. Ivors, the president of the Irish deaf, was hearing and didn't know any sign.

Mother Shawn started to question me about my credentials, although she already knew them from the news release that the American consulate had passed on to her. Then she asked me about my views on education of the deaf and oralism.

This was when I made one of the worst mistakes of my life. The way they talked of Molly and her response, or rather her lack of response, should have forewarned me, but I stupidly plunged ahead. I had deduced, wrongly, from Mother Shawn's skill in signing, that she was on our side. I therefore answered Mother Shawn's questions with complete candor, arguing that the deaf should be permitted to use their own native sign language, develop their own culture, and stand on their own feet. I added that I was in favor of total communication, which includes sign language, rather than of oralism alone.

As I went on, her expression became more and more frosty, and she told me bluntly where she stood—she was a confirmed oralist! My eyes darted toward Molly; the placid smile remained glued to her face—she was completely out of it.

I was bowled over by Mother Shawn's declaration, since she was signing so skillfully. The situation seemed to be different from that in the United States, where oralists either do not know sign language or, if they know it, refuse to use it. I asked her why she was using signs if she was against them.

She answered, "We use sign language with deaf people who never had the opportunity of learning speech in their infancy. What a shame. Too late for them now. But with babies and little children there is still time, and I am against using sign language in their presence."

In other words, she was against letting deaf children develop their natural language abilities and advocated letting them grow up in a repressive environment that would stifle their vocabulary and their ability to express themselves. How many lives of deaf children were and are being ruined by this attitude! For a moment, I was tempted to point this out to her, but one does not argue with people like her. Besides, I was supposed to be a diplomat. So I repressed the urge.

Mother Shawn continued, "I would hate to teach signs to young deaf children because signs are so attractive that deaf children would find speech and lipreading all the more distasteful and difficult to learn."

I thought to myself, How many times have I heard the same old line from oralists back home. Funny how they and Mother Shawn unwittingly admit the attractiveness, the glamour, of sign language. Again, I chose not to respond.

Then she begin to review with me the schedule for my stay in Ireland. I was to appear on television, give press interviews, tour a school for the deaf, conduct a seminar at Dublin University, present a lecture to the general public and another to the Dublin deaf community, and have lunch with professionals working with the deaf and another lunch with parents of deaf children. She said she would check the entire program out, have it confirmed, and get back to me in three or four days. I thought to myself, "Three days all to myself, great!"

Then she briskly bade me good-bye, averting her face just a bit too prematurely—a clinching portent whose full significance I realized only days later. I shook hands with them all. Before leaving, Father O'Connors finally got in his shilling's worth and asked me if I would be interested in attending his mass on Sunday, the next day. I said I would be happy to.

The next morning a taxi brought me to the local deaf club. I found my way to the room converted for celebrating mass and entered quietly while Father O'Connors was officiating in front of a portable altar.

I sat in the left-hand section, but after a while I realized something was wrong. Glancing about, I noticed only women around me; they were snickering and stealing glances at me, and I realized that I was the only man in that section. I happened to catch the gaze of a smiling young man in the right-hand section and gestured to him politely, "Oops. My mistake. Wrong section. I'll move over."

But he cheerfully signed, in American Sign Language, "No, that's okay. You're American."

After mass the portable altar was removed and the seats were rearranged more informally to make the place look like a club room. The smiling young man introduced himself. His name was Hugh, and he knew American Sign Language because he had worked in Cleveland as a tailor. He came back to Ireland in order to marry his sweetheart and classmate, a pretty brown-haired woman named Mary. He introduced me to her as well as to several other people in the room.

They readily accepted me in their group, and over the next three days they showed me the sights of Dublin and their homes. I knew perfectly well how lucky I was to get to know such wonderful and well-read people. I could and did discuss with them James Joyce, Sean O'Casey, and W. B. Yeats.

There was one thing I failed to understand: Why was it that not one of these articulate and intelligent deaf people was a leader of the deaf? Why did they display such impotence? In the United States people like these would hold positions of leadership in the deaf community and be well-paid professionals. But, with the exception of Mary, who was a teacher of the deaf, my newfound literate friends were carpenters, tailors, and factory workers. For a time I desisted from bringing up the subject, however my curiosity got the better of me and I broached the subject to them, as tactfully as I could.

They were not offended at all, but became visibly saddened. Finally, Mary answered, "We can't talk with them. We can't communicate with them." By "them" they meant the hearing people who administered programs for the deaf. I told them how in my country deaf people had their own deaf leaders, held leading positions in the vocational rehabilitation and school systems, and developed a thriving and rich artistic culture of their own. I could see that I was depressing them by telling them what they already knew, so I added that I was sure their turn would come sooner or later. They expressed their doubts.

The next day was the fourth day since I had seen Mother Shawn, and I still had not heard from her. Later that afternoon I received a message from her to the effect that my entire program was canceled and she had to fly to England. It ended with, "Sorry, maybe you can go to the deaf club and give a demonstration in mime."

That was the inauspicious beginning of my world tour. I was so upset that it took me a while to compose myself. That evening, my newfound friends came to visit me in my hotel room. We all went downstairs to have drinks in the hotel pub. They were excited about my coming television, press, and other appearances and wanted to know the exact schedule so they could be present.

Until then I had remained silent, not knowing whether to discuss my news with them. Perhaps it would be wise to take my disappointment and anger with me, I thought. If I spoke now, I might cause them and myself untold trouble.

But my hand was forced when Tony, a printer, asked me when I expected to appear on television. He was looking forward to the show and had even written to the station inquiring about it but had not yet received a reply. Mine would be the first appearance by a deaf person on Irish television, he said.

Against my better judgment, I showed them the message from Mother Shawn. The paper passed from hand to hand. There was a storm around me— hands flew with shock, anger, and a sense of betrayal. Tony said he remembered that I was to give a lecture at University College; Hugh said that if my visit to the deaf school was impossible today, I could surely have gone there tomorrow. But Mary, who taught at the school, added that there had been no word of my scheduled visit.

The bar was closing and we went to my room to continue our discussion. I felt terribly guilty for showing them the letter and upsetting them so deeply. Finally, Mary said, "How disappointing, but not very surprising."

"What do you mean?"

"Mother Shawn controls all of Ireland as far as the deaf are concerned."

Then Mary described how Mother Shawn had raised her. Mary happened to one of the very few exceptional deaf children with a natural talent for speech and lipreading, and so Mother Shawn was very proud of her and took her along as a prize exhibit to lecture demonstrations all over the country. During every demonstration Mother Shawn would ask Mary a set of standard questions, such as what her name was, where she was born, what school she was attending, and so on. The last and most important question was, "What language do you dream in?" Mary would always answer, "I dream in spoken language."

I interrupted and asked Mary what she meant by "spoken language." It sounded nonsensical, considering that Mary was deaf and could not hear speech. Oh, she was just quoting Mother Shawn, Mary answered, blushing, and she admitted that to her "spoken language" actually meant words that she had lipread rather than heard, which made more sense. Anyway, she continued, to Mother Shawn this question was important as proof that the deaf mind is "capable of learning speech," whatever that meant.

I interjected that Mary was what we deaf in America call a "decoy." My friends were intrigued and asked me to explain. I told them that this term was first introduced by the American deaf writer Albert Ballin, a renowned acting coach in Hollywood during the 1920s. It meant a deaf pupil with special gifts of speech and lipreading who is exhibited to hearing audiences as proof that oralism can help all deaf people. My friends looked at each other with amazement, laughed, and said they simply loved this term.

Mary had lived in Cleveland for a time in order to study at a Catholic teacher training college and to be with Hugh. When she returned to Ireland, she became the only deaf teacher of the deaf in that country, though at the price of agreeing not to use sign language in her classes. Mother Shawn asked her again to be present at a demonstration lecture. When the time came to ask her what language she dreamed in, Mary answered candidly, "I used to dream in spoken language, but ever since I married a deaf man who signs, I've been dreaming in sign language."

Mother Shawn never forgave Mary for this comment, and she stopped asking her to go along for her demonstrations and lectures.

When Mary finished her story, Hugh exploded "Mother Shawn advised a deaf couple not to sign to their own deaf child, for if they did the child supposedly would never learn to speak. The gullible fools! They listened to her, and now they can't communicate with their own son. It's not so much stupid as monstrous!"

"I wish I could be of some help," I signed to my friends, "But I guess there's nothing I can do. I'm only a visitor here and cannot butt in."

But Hugh, who had gotten a taste of deaf life in America and knew what it is like for the deaf to stand up and fight for their own rights, suggested that I go to the American consulate and show them the message from Mother Shawn.

Oh boy! I thought to myself. Now I'm in trouble. I'm supposed to be a diplomat, a goodwill ambassador of the American government, and instead I've unwittingly become a foreign agitator, a troublemaker to the powers that be. So much for the luxury of venting one's anger. But, it was too late for me to withdraw, so I answered that I would be happy to do it if Hugh came along. It would be good for the Irish deaf to speak up for themselves, I said. And besides, it was Hugh's idea and he was inspired.

Then Mary, caught up in the excitement, said that she would call a friend who worked for a widely read Irish newspaper, the *Irish Independent*, and get him to interview me. She asked if I would agree to it. I was already too much involved, but I nodded yes. Thus, the "conspiracy" was formed.

The next day, Hugh and I went to the American consulate, where we were received by the public relations officer. We communicated with him in writing. Hugh asked why the program was changed and why I was being prevented from sharing my dramatic skills and my experience as a deaf educator simply because of an arbitrary decision by Mother Shawn.

The public relations officer responded that he was in the foreign service and, since the cancellation of the program was requested by Mother Shawn, the consulate could do nothing about it. Hugh argued that this was suppression of free speech, but the man politely apologized to us for his inability to do anything about the matter and suggested that it would be best if I were simply to go ahead with my lecture to the club of the deaf. That was it. We got up, thanked him for his time, and left.

That evening I went to the clubhouse. There were about two hundred deaf people in the auditorium. The Pantomime Theatre of the Deaf presented three short sketches, and then it was my turn. First, I praised the mime troupe for their concentration and made some introductory remarks. Then I took a deep breath and plunged into my performance. After that I gave them a brief talk about the purpose of my world tour and my experiences and observations in the United States.

Afterward everyone came up to me to shake my hand. Father O'Connors joined us, and Hugh asked him pointblank why my television appearance had been canceled. He replied that it was agreed between Mother Shawn and me that I would not perform for television. I looked at him directly and said simply, "Don't you remember my last words to Mother Shawn and you in the hotel lobby, 'Okay, I'll do mime on TV'?" Looking pained and dropping his habitual smile he said yes, he remembered. He offered no explanation and I did not press him for any.

Stan, one of the club members, asked Father O'Connors why I was not to visit the school for the deaf and perform for deaf children, as they would certainly enjoy my presentation. Father O'Connors suggested I visit the school on Saturday. It was very clear to me that most of the children would be home for the weekend, so I politely declined, declaring that I was interested in meeting children, not touring the school.

Then Father O'Connors disappeared. A discussion began among the twenty people who had remained. I was asked about the jobs available to the deaf in the United States. When I answered truthfully that the deaf in America included lawyers, school administrators, editors, and even government officials, a deaf man commented that in Ireland only vocational training was provided to the deaf. Others in the group complained about the inability of the Irish deaf to have a voice in their own affairs and in the decisions concerning them. I got the feeling I had started something that was quickly getting out of control. Some in the crowd commented that they were appalled by Mother Shawn's ban of my work in their country. This placed me in a still more delicate position, and, therefore, I decided not to comment. By that time I was totally exhausted and soon returned to my hotel to sleep.

The next morning I awoke still feeling numb with outrage. No publicity! Appearances canceled! It was incredible to me that anyone could have that kind of power. In the lobby, I was handed a message from the columnist whom Mary had contacted. He wanted to interview me in the afternoon. What luck!

He arrived with Mary, who served as the interpreter. We had a long talk. I tried to be very factual about the information I gave him and told him nothing of the disappointment I felt at not being able to perform or lecture at the university or visit a school for the deaf. Then Mary explained the background to him, but I asked him not to mention it in the published version of the interview, in the interest of international friendship. Afterward I did several mime skits for him, and he wished me well and left.

Later that night, Hugh, Mary, Tony, and I went to a pub and shared a few rounds of Guinness. We looked forward to the publication of my interview. As Hugh said, we thought it would be a catalyst for the Irish deaf to help them move toward representation in the Irish Association for the Deaf and more control of their lives.

Two days later I was at the airport, waiting for my flight to Madrid. My friends were seeing me off. Their combined seven children inspired me to do a special performance that attracted attention from the crowd in the terminal. We had a good time. Suddenly, Hugh, who had disappeared for a while, ran up waving a copy of the *Irish Independent* containing my interview.

I read the text, which discussed my life as a successful deaf actor and mime who had come to Ireland in order to share his skills and experience. It expressed regret because I had arrived too late to participate in the annual theater festival, and the writer said he hoped that I would be invited to that festival next year. Nothing about Mother Shawn. Good man, I thought, and sighed with relief. Altogether, it was a neat interview, and it was symbolic in that it was the first time a deaf artist had been discussed in the Irish press.

I said to my friends, "Well, that's not much really, but you people got what you wanted. We made it." They congratulated me, but I replied, quite truthfully, "Wait a minute. Congratulate yourselves. It was you who accomplished it."

It was time to board the plane. We embraced, and I told them, "I've heard a lot about the Irish fighting spirit . . . and now I have seen it." There were mixed smiles and tears.

After these unexpected experiences in Ireland I hoped I could settle down to carrying out my mission of spreading the idea of deaf theater abroad and informing others about the achievements of the American deaf. Most of all, I wanted to show hearing people that the deaf people could stand on their own feet.

I also thought I could now look forward to relaxing while traveling from one
country to another and possibly leaving my deafness behind, at least during
those moments. But no, wherever I went, deafness followed me like a shadow.
And where it did not follow me, it waited ahead of me, as in Portugal.

The plane had stopped over in Madrid en route to my destination, Marseilles. I watched new passengers boarding. Most of them were Spanish but even so, I thought, most of them were multilingual Europeans. Unlike me, they probably had no problems communicating.

I was in a self-critical mood because of the experience I had had in Lisbon earlier in the day. Before boarding the plane I had to pass through a customs inspection. The inspector, a wizened little man in an ill-fitting uniform, asked me if I had anything to declare—at least that was what I thought he had asked. I handed him the signed customs form, but it apparently was not enough for him because he asked me another question. When I got out my pen and paper and wrote him in English that I was deaf and asked if he could write down his question, he inspected my writing for a long time, like a man who was just learning to read, and kept glancing at me suspiciously.

I had to overcome his impasse somehow, so I pointed at my ears to show that I was deaf. His eyes rolled up, showing impatience and frustration. He twisted his mouth in a tight-lipped grimace of annoyance, as if cursing himself for his bad luck in coming upon a deaf person. I took a deep breath, telling myself, "Ah, here comes trouble." He looked around as if he wanted to get away from me and find someone else to take his place. Then he looked at me and . . . It still pains me to describe what he did. He interrogatively placed an index finger on each ear. When I nodded, he stretched out his pink tongue, placed one index finger on its tip and, again interrogatively, stared at me goggle-eyed. At the same time, he shook his head at me in a gesture of negation. I took this to mean, "Don't you read lips?"

The vulgarity of his pantomime was disarming. I made my gestures as restrained as possible, trying to retain a shred of dignity. My neck burned and I became aware of the stares of a small crowd. A change also took place in the inspector's attitude. From being a stern police officer questioning a suspect, he turned into a buffoon. At the same time his eyes became positively human in expression, gleaming with that kindness one extends to circus freaks and the incapacitated, and he let me pass after glancing at the contents of my flight bag.

It was over, and I saluted him cordially, trying to make the best of it. He gave me a benign smile in return. But the faces of the people watching me remained blank.

As I proceeded to the waiting plane, I was stopped by a woman in the crowd. "I see that you're deaf," she spoke in English. I could readily read her lips and felt elated. The small crowd still stood there and this gave me a chance to restore my image, to show them that deaf and hearing people could communicate. "Yes, I am," I answered, deliberately choosing simple words that were easier for me to pronounce. I could tell she understood me.

The woman was fashionably dressed and of undetermined nationality; she could have been English or American or Portuguese. A boy of about eight stood next to her. She pointed to him and said, "He's deaf too."

I waved hello at the boy and gestured, asking him how old he was, when suddenly my hand was pushed down gently by his mother, who said, "Please don't sign to him. I don't want my boy to learn sign language."

"Why not?" I asked in my best speaking voice.

"He'd never be able to learn speech then." She added, "You know speech is very important."

"So is communication," I replied, thinking that this was a much greater barrier. She did not understand my speech. I had to write it down on paper for her. At the same time I glanced at the departure board. The line with my flight was flashing. I pointed at it and hurried toward my plane, waving good-bye to the woman and the boy.

I was brought back to reality by the other passengers boarding the plane. I looked out of the window at the deep blue Sunday skies. The airport was familiar because I had been to Madrid just ten days earlier, giving lectures, workshops, and press and television interviews. It was a wonderful experience, and it had been duplicated in Portugal, until that embarrassing scene at the Lisbon airport.

A Spanish woman in her thirties asked me whether the seat next to me was free. I motioned welcomingly at the seat and she sat down. She was slender, fashionably dressed, and had a mane of black hair.

After a while she started talking to me. I nodded and composed my face into that sincere and understanding kind of smile that deaf people wear when they do not understand what is said to them. I was too tired to write her that I knew no Spanish or Portuguese or even that I was deaf. I thought ironically that travel has no advantages for the deaf.

Just before take-off, a flight attendant came by bearing a stack of Madrid Sunday newspapers. He offered me one, but I waved him off. My fellow passenger took one and started reading it as the plane began to climb.

When she opened the Sunday newsmagazine I stole a glance at it and was startled to see that the whole center section was full of photographs and articles about me. I held my breath and watched the woman from the corner of my eye.

She studied my photographs and then turned toward me to study my profile. She again looked at the pictures. Then I felt her tap me on the shoulder. I looked at her inquiringly. She pointed her index finger at me and then at the largest of my photographs, glancing at me as if to ask, "Is that you?" I nodded. She burst into a smile. I was amused and waited to see what would happen next. She called the flight attendant as he was going down the aisle, showed him the pictures, and pointed at me. Her voice must have been loud, because people near us turned their heads to look at me.

Word spread throughout the cabin. People far in the back got up and craned their necks to get a better look at me. The passengers started to pass around copies of the newspaper. Some waved to me, and a few young people came up and asked me to autograph their copies of the section.

I felt gratified, but only momentarily, for the mental image of the little boy with his wondering gaze crept into my mind and stayed there.

I witnessed misconceptions and misunderstandings about the deaf every-where I traveled. I also found that in most countries, hearing people still dominated the programs and services for deaf people. This is a deadly mix that condemns most deaf people to menial jobs and estranges deaf intellec-tuals from the deaf world. Even in Western Europe, supposedly the most liberal part of the world next to the United States as far as treatment of the deaf is concerned, governments act as self-appointed mentors and guard-ians, suppress deaf leaders, and deny deaf people their emancipation by controlling their education—and those who control the education of the deaf control their destiny.

This governmental domination is even more pronounced in the Communist bloc, as I found out during my sojourn in Minsk.

Once again I was back in Soviet Russia. As before, I was met by an official welcoming delegation, headed by the same Comrade Fufayev, who gave me the royal treatment. My destination this time was Minsk, the capital of Belorussia. I was going to the hinterlands and perhaps there I would meet the real Mother Russia, or her Belorussian variety. Most importantly, I wanted to work with Russian deaf actors again.

When I arrived in Minsk no one met me at the airport except a uniformed official who checked my passport and wanted to know why I was there. I showed him my itinerary from the American embassy and my hotel reservation and explained to him, through gesture, that I expected someone to meet me, but he just shrugged his shoulders—a "know-nothing" gesture which Rus-sians seem to perform even more eloquently than the French. Outside the airport terminal I waited for a while, hoping that Feliks Shlinkonik, the founder of the Minsk Rukh Mime Theatre, whom I had met in Moscow in 1973, was only delayed.

Half an hour passed without a sign of Feliks. It was freezing October weather, so I gave up waiting and took a cab to my hotel, where there was no message for me either. Once I settled in my room, I went back to the desk clerk and asked for an English speaker. They found a woman who could write and read English and I asked her to call the Rukh Mime Theatre. She called, but no one there had heard of me. I was puzzled. The woman wrote down the address for me in Russian and English, and I took a cab to the theater at the Palace of Culture.

By then it was five o'clock. I left the taxi and walked up the main staircase to a huge lobby. People passed me, but no one gave me a look. I might as well have been a ghost. A uniformed woman to whom I showed the slip of paper from the hotel gave me the cold shoulder and walked on. I climbed to the second floor and found myself in a huge hallway. I knocked at the first door I saw and opened it, but the room was empty. I knocked at another door, which opened right away. When I pointed to my ear to identify myself as deaf to the woman standing in the doorway, she started signing to me.

I explained to her in Russian Sign Language, which I recollected very quickly, that I was from the United States and was looking for the local theater group, and asked if she could please lead me to them. She gestured for me to wait while she asked her boss to see me. I sat down and waited and waited. Finally, after an hour, she returned to the anteroom and said there was no letter about me from Moscow and the director was in a meeting and could not see me. I asked her if I could at least see the head of the mime theater, Feliks Shlinkonik. But she replied, "Sorry, I can't help you," and closed the door on me.

In the hallway I saw a deaf couple signing. What luck! I went up to them and asked them where the mime theater was. They took me there. As I walked in, a rehearsal was just beginning. I introduced myself to the actors and one of them suddenly recognized me from the pictures he had seen of my appearance in *Prometheus Bound* with the Moscow Theatre of Mimicry and Gesture. Once he told the others about me, they became more friendly. We chatted for a while, and I finally asked them about Feliks. He was not in that day and would not be coming in until after the weekend, they answered.

For some time now I had been aware of being watched by a short, stocky man. When he smiled, his eyes narrowed to tiny slits. He had been lounging in his chair as if he were sitting by a pool, but when he saw me ask for Feliks, he got up and came toward me with a springy step.

"I'm Ivan, Feliks's friend," he introduced himself and, as we shook hands, he added, "Any friend of Feliks is my friend." I took an immediate liking to him and was more than happy when he offered to drive me to Feliks's home.

We climbed into his little Zaporozhets and sputtered off. He maneuvered his car at breakneck speed like a jockey, and my heart immediately rose to my mouth and stayed there throughout the ride. By the time we arrived at Feliks's home it was dark; no one was in, so Ivan left a message under the door.

Ivan invited me to dinner at a restaurant, where we got to talk. He signed what might be called the sign language of the street—graphic, earthy, and affable, so very Russian. The food was very Russian too; it seemed they put sour cream or mushrooms or both into every dish.

After dinner he took me to his closet-sized efficiency apartment where he showed me an album of pictures of his travels. He was a photographer and had become something of a celebrity when he traveled on a motorcycle across the vast territory of the fifteen Soviet republics. This was a "first" for a deaf person, and it gained him a lot of publicity from various local newspapers. Apparently that was how he got his Zaporozhets, a rare feat for the average Soviet, let alone a deaf Soviet. Ivan commented, "Russia is big. You took planes, I took motorcycles, but we both were in the newspapers." We laughed.

We drove back to Feliks's home, but he still was not in, so we drove to the train station, the only place open at that hour, and had coffee and cake in the buffet. There were about one hundred people sleeping in the waiting room. It was an unforgettable scene. Even when my energy had long since dwindled, Ivan refused to quit looking for Feliks. He left me at my hotel and drove off in search of Feliks.

At ten the next morning I felt a pounding noise on the door. I opened it and both Feliks and Ivan stood there. Tall, with curly black hair, unmistakably Jewish, Feliks signed that he was very surprised to see me in Minsk because no one had informed him I was coming. I answered that it must be some bureaucratic mixup, a comment that they did not know whether to laugh at or be embarrassed by.

We three had breakfast together in the hotel dining room. Then they said that since there was no official welcome for me in Minsk, they would take it on themselves to give me an unofficial welcome, be my unofficial hosts, and show me around the city. There was not much to see. The whole city, which had been razed in the Second World War, was now built up with row after row of monotonous two- and three-story blocklike apartment buildings, some a plain gray concrete and others a mustard-yellow color. They also drove me to

Khayta, the site of a memorial to two million slaughtered Russians. The sight of row after row of tombstones was quite powerful.

In the evening they took me to the Palace of Culture to watch a rehearsal. The Rukh, founded by Feliks in 1965, is an amateur theater; the nineteen performers make their living as factory workers, technicians, shoemakers, and the like. The name "Rukh" means "the permanent search." That evening the group was rehearsing for its appearance in the upcoming Warsaw Festival.

I watched the run-through with great interest. Their style was imitative of other pantomime theaters I had seen in Eastern Europe. The themes ranged from work, love, and marriage, to war, revolution, and communism. The presentations were symmetrical, melodramatic, and stylized.

After the rehearsal they asked me what I thought of the program and what had impressed me the most. I complimented the group on its professionalism and said that I had been very impressed with "Khayta," the story of the Nazi massacre. The lighting, set, movement, and dances for that piece were hauntingly moving. I added that it would be very exciting to see the ensemble create something out of their own experience as deaf people, something from their own deaf culture. I demonstrated my Visual Vernacular technique, not to convert the Rukh company to my style, but rather to inspire them to develop indigenous theatrical forms of their own, and I could see from their faces that they had been given something to think about.

The following two days I also spent with Feliks and Ivan. I was worried that they might lose their jobs, but they reassured me that they were not playing hooky but had special permission to take time off. In the evenings we attended the rehearsal, after which the actors again asked me to give them demonstrations.

On the third day, Feliks and Ivan took me to another hall in the Palace of Culture, where we watched a rehearsal by another deaf amateur troupe. The director was a hearing woman in her sixties who had worked with deaf performers for seven years but still was unable to sign. She used an interpreter to communicate with the actors. Although she told me she was a disciple of Stanislavsky, she did not seem to apply his teachings in her work with this company. She told the actors exactly how to express themselves, often giving them examples to imitate. The result was a style of acting that leaned more to the melodramatic.

Out of the corner of my eye I noticed a woman walking toward me. I looked more closely and discovered she was the same woman who had shut the door in my face at the Palace of Culture. She was accompanied by a pigeon-chested man with a lame foot, and a dangling, limp arm; he was obviously a very important person judging from his tailored, form-fitting suit and gleaming black shoes. He had a cherubic, potato-nosed face. She pointed me out to him and introduced us. He turned out to be the department director who was too busy to see me three days ago. He could not sign, but this did not surprise me; it seemed as if every hearing official "in charge" of the deaf knew no sign language. He shook my hand jovially with his left hand and spoke to me while the woman interpreted for him. The letter from Moscow announcing my visit had arrived and they were giving a reception in my honor the next day at the Palace of Culture. The reception would be in the evening, which suited me perfectly since I was leaving the morning after. I told them I would be honored to accept.

The following evening Feliks, Ivan, and I went back to the Palace of Culture. The reception was held in the same office whose door had been shut in my face only a few days before. Long trestle tables covered with white tablecloths filled the room. They were laden with schmaltz herring, herring in cream sauce, herring in dill sauce, herring in mustard, and several other varieties of herring, as well as caviar, Moscow sausage, ham, cheese, apples, rolls, bottles of vodka, wine, Crimean champagne, and mineral water. The director embraced me like a long-lost cousin and led me to the place of honor at the central table after introducing me to various dignitaries whose unpronounceable names I forgot immediately. Before the party, Feliks and Ivan told me that the director was a former two-star general and that his infirmities were the result of war injuries. That he was a World War II hero appeared to be his only qualification for being appointed to supervise the affairs of the Belorussian deaf.

The director welcomed me to Minsk and proposed a toast in my honor. His stern face was wreathed in smiles. The toast actually turned out to be a long-winded and flowery but oddly sincere speech in which he apologized to "the dear guest" for the misunderstanding with the letter. He hoped "from the bottom of my heart" that I was enjoying my sojourn in Minsk, a city "resurrected from the ashes of its destruction by the Hitlerite invaders and rebuilt so as to provide ultramodern housing with all comforts" to its inhabitants.

We all downed our glasses of vodka, following it up with a piece of herring on a toothpick. By then I knew enough about Russian customs to propose a toast in honor of the Department for the Affairs of Defectives at the Ministry of Culture and Art, Belorussian Soviet Socialist Republic, for its outstanding contributions to the cause of the deaf. (Yes, "Defectives," because that is the Russian term for the physically handicapped—*defektivnyye.*)

There were other toasts— virtual round robin of toasts. I lost count after a while. How I managed to remain on my feet and exchange handshakes, embraces, and kisses with so many newfound friends when the reception was over, I'll never know. I don't remember much of what happened next. I do remember clambering out of the little Zaporozhets as it chugged to a stop in front of the airport terminal. As I shook hands with Ivan and Feliks, I told them, "You two make wonderful goodwill ambassadors for your country, without paperwork and without documents." We hugged each other wondering if we would ever meet again.

There was one other and even more memorable journey I made to the socialist bloc, this time to Czechoslovakia, for the International Mime Festival in Brno. I met wonderful human beings and experienced for myself the lunatic quality of a system that directs the destinies of deaf people.

My arrival in Vienna was much different than my arrival in Minsk. Since I was a "visiting dignitary" the American embassy assigned Felizitas Freitag, an Austrian employee of the embassy, to be my interpreter and guide. She planned and monitored my schedule and generally smoothed things for me. She was a delightful person, a pleasure to be with.

The day of my departure for Czechoslovakia, Felizitas took me to the train station. We looked silently at each other. "Good-bye, my Girl Friday," I signed. She held my hand and fingerspelled, "I'll be here when you come back."

"Same platform?" She nodded. We embraced and kissed. I boarded the train and waved to her as it lurched forward and began to gain speed. Her warm presence faded away as the train rushed through the darkness. I found myself shivering from the increasing cold; there was no heat on the train. The cold became so unbearable that I had to take a turtleneck sweater out of my suitcase and put it on. Then I put on my leather jacket and, over it, my raincoat. Still, I shivered; I was so cold I could not concentrate on reading or writing.

The train slowed down and came to a full halt. An Austrian guard came in to check my passport because we were about to cross the border. After a long wait, the train started to move again. I paced up and down in the compartment, trying to keep warm. The train again slowed down as it entered a zone of bright lights. A station sign said, "Břeclav." I looked out of the window and saw something that reminded me of wartime films about Nazi Germany. Reels of barbed wire ran alongside the station, and soldiers with machine guns at the ready stood on both sides of the train. This was definitely not like Russia.

Three uniformed men appeared at the door of my compartment. One of them entered while the other two stood outside in the corridor. The soldier said something to me, and in reply I gestured to him that I was deaf and showed him my passport, which stated so. I wanted him to know about my deafness at the very outset so that he would not think my silence odd. I had a letter of invitation to prove that I was going to Brno for an international deaf mime festival. I showed him that too. He scrutinized it as he did the passport, his face showing no reaction. Then he sternly motioned for me to open my suitcase. I did, and he rummaged through it, turning everything upside down and not bothering to put my belongings back in place. His inspection over, he turned around and strode toward the door of the compartment without a word or a gesture. At the door, he turned back, checked the entire compartment with his eyes, and noticed that he had overlooked my carry-on bag. He again approached me and pointed at it imperiously. I picked it up and put it down on the seat with a gesture of impatience. I was more upset than scared and decided that he should open it himself.

He unzipped the bag, took out my camera, and gestured to ask if it was loaded with film. I shook my head no, but he opened the camera case to make sure I was not lying. He rummaged some more and found the copies of *Newsweek* and *Time* that I had bought in Vienna. One of the covers showed a picture of tanks in Red Square on the recent anniversary of the October Revolution. As he leafed through it, his companions entered the compartment and looked on over his shoulders. Then he put both magazines under his arm with a movement that was as economical, self-assured, and resolute as all his other movements, and began to walk out.

He stopped when I shouted. I was outraged. He was taking my property and the principle of the thing blinded me to the danger of the situation. I pointed at the magazines and gestured that they were mine, thumping my chest with the flat of my hand.

In reply he shook his finger in my face menacingly, as if I was a little boy doing something forbidden. He left the compartment and shortly afterward I saw him outside on the platform. The train began to move again. I sat there stunned that my property had been confiscated. This was something I had previously seen only in movies or on television. I was not sure whether or not I was dreaming.

After what happened, I could not sleep. I just sat there feeling upset and restless until I felt the train stop. From the window I could see the station sign—it was Brno. I had arrived in the middle of the night and the station was deserted. I had expected someone to meet me because I had informed festival officials of the time of my arrival. I emerged onto the vast square in front of the station and saw a solitary taxi, but when I waved at it, it sped off. No one else was in sight on this cold and damp November night. Suddenly, I noticed a man with a nondescript face stepping into a shabby little car just outside the station. I hurried toward him and showed him my hotel reservation. I pointed to the illuminated sign nearby, "Taxi," and held out my hands and shook my head negatively. Then I rubbed my fingers to indicate that I would pay him for driving me to the hotel. He opened the door of his car and beckoned me inside. He even helped me put my bags in the trunk.

When we reached Hotel Slovan he carried my bags inside the lobby. I offered him a dollar bill but he would not accept it and, tipping his hat, he left. I ran after him and offered my hand to show my gratitude. He looked both ways before shaking it. I watched that mysterious stranger leave.

I checked in with the night clerk, and then rode the slow-moving elevator to the fourth floor. I walked down a dimly lit hallway until I located a door with my number on it. Inside was a bare, unheated room with a single unshaded dim light bulb hanging from the ceiling. There was a bed that looked like a cot, a rickety table, and an old chair. The floor was linoleum. The bathroom looked just as desolate, with a single thin cotton towel hanging on a bar, coarse toilet paper, and no soap.

I became apprehensive and, for the first time, missed the security of my life in the free world. I was even afraid to turn off the light and plunge into darkness, so I left it on. After putting on my pajamas, and over them my turtleneck sweater, I lay down on the bed, covered myself with the thin dark-gray blanket, and rested my head on a pillow that felt like it was stuffed with straw. But I could not sleep with that bare bulb on. Finally I turned the light off and, exhausted, drifted into a fitful sleep.

When I woke up, it was freezing cold. Through the window I saw only a brick wall and had to look up to see the sky, which was cloudy and gray. I took a shower, hoping for hot water, but no such luck. I dressed quickly and went down to the lobby.

It was crowded. I felt relieved to see so many people for a change, especially because they were signing like mad. Some officials approached me and I introduced myself to them. They apologized for not meeting me at the train station, without explaining why, then they began to introduce me all around.

Apparently I was the only Westerner there. All the deaf people I met were Czechs, Poles, East Germans, Russians, and Yugoslavs, here for the biennial mime festival. I began to mingle with them and soon I noticed that they stayed together in their national groups. Each group had a hearing leader who kept an eye on them. I circulated from group to group feeling a sense of freedom I had always taken for granted.

When we went to the dining room upstairs, I saw the same pattern as in the lobby; each national group sat at a separate table. I noticed an acquaintance, a Yugoslav named Zdenek, whom I had first met in 1965 in Zagreb when I performed on Yugoslav television. We embraced and he invited me to sit down with him. The Yugoslav group seemed different, more liberal and relaxed than the other groups.

Someone tapped me on the shoulder. A tall man with lank blond hair introduced himself as Paur and said he was to be my interpreter. We began to chat and I found out that he was the hearing son of deaf parents. He told me that the festival would begin once "the authorities," the high government officials who had organized the festival, arrived from Prague in the evening.

After lunch I took a long walk in the city. I looked at medieval churches, palaces, burghers' homes. The air was full of dust and smoke from factory smokestacks. Drably dressed people strolled aimlessly on streets that were almost devoid of cars.

Later in the afternoon, Paur picked me up and took me to a meeting where the overall program for the one-week festival was discussed. The festival committee had invited me to be one of the jurors for the contest program, and I had no idea of what I was in for. Paur also told me that I was the only professional mime at the festival.

I met several more people at this meeting, including Matilda, a beautiful woman in her early forties with reddish brown hair and warm features, and we took an immediate liking to each other. She was married, but her husband had stayed in Prague. She introduced me to a friend of hers, a Czech mime, who wanted to give me a demonstration of his art.

After the meeting, when everybody had left except Matilda and the Czech mime, he leapt onto the raised stage while we two sat down and watched him. He gave a faithful rendition of Marcel Marceau's famous skit, "Seven Ages of Man." He crawled like a baby, frisked and gamboled like a boy, strode vigorously like a young man. So far so good, I thought. But when he reached "maturity," he knotted one end of an imaginary rope into a noose, tied the other end to an imaginary beam, stood on an imaginary chair, slipped the knot over his neck, and simulated kicking the chair from under his feet; his neck seemed to snap and his tongue dangled as if he had strangled to death. His performance was so lifelike, I was stunned. Then he stepped down from the stage and sat down next to me as if nothing had happened. He was obviously making a political statement, but not one of us mentioned it. I simply shook hands with him.

That evening I went to the deaf club with Paur. It consisted of several separate rooms on the second floor of a downtown building. It was so cold inside that all of us kept our coats on. The rooms were dim, and in the largest room there was a counter that served as the bar.

I began to mingle in the crowd. Several people asked me about my life in America and I, in turn, asked them about life in their countries. I also talked about the bonds linking the deaf, my love of art and especially mime, and the problems of deafness that we all shared, such as the frustration of having oralism forced down our throats and having the hearing put us down and make us second-class citizens.

Then I described the achievements of the deaf in America; how we have our own deaf leaders and our own deaf teachers who are permitted to teach in sign language, who serve as role models to deaf children, and who earn the respect of the hearing; how we fought and won a long time ago the right to drive; how our employment opportunities are so plentiful. Deaf people in the socialist bloc were in these respects where the American deaf had stood some forty years ago, as I found out from my new friends. The schools in Czechoslovakia employed no deaf teachers, sign language was prohibited as a medium of instruction, and there were no deaf Czechoslovak leaders.

As the evening wore on and the conversations flowed, we noticed that we were having no problem communicating, even though we came from different countries. While discrete signs varied from country to country, our facial expressions and body language were so similar that we could understand each other. This confirmed my observation that whatever the country and whatever its sign language, deaf people all over the world share the same love for sign language and the same experience of apartness from the hearing majority.

The constant conversation with an ever-changing little crowd, lively and exciting as it was, gradually wore me out, so I waved good night to everyone and left with Paur, who showed me the way back to Hotel Slovan.

The next morning, I noticed a group of new arrivals sitting at a separate table in the dining room. They caught my attention at once because of the striking tableau they posed. I saw a lovely looking blond woman surrounded by eight elderly men who were treating her with obvious deference. She was in her late thirties and looked like a fashion model, a society lady, or a movie actress, or all three in one—an amazing sight in Czechoslovakia. Her cascading blond hair was perfectly coiffured and she wore a black tailored suit with a silk scarf wound around her neck. What was a Hollywood vision doing in the land of "socialist reality"? I asked Paur about this strange group and he told me they were the officials from Prague. The woman was a top administrator in charge of the deaf at the Department of Care for the Disabled in Prague, and the others were her colleagues. They had approved the funding for the festival and were responsible for the invitations to foreign mime groups.

At different times I noticed the group looking at me. They seemed to regard me as a curiosity. The regal-looking woman glanced at me. Our eyes met. She nodded slightly at me, and I reciprocated her nod.

In the afternoon the mime festival began. The contest was divided into three categories: individual mimes, two-person sketches, and group presentations. Most of these Eastern European mimes used an illusionist style imitative of Marceau and his predecessor Etienne de Croix. Their skits included such routines as emulating a robot's stiff gait, leaning on an invisible railing, being propelled along by an imaginary leashed dog, climbing an imaginary rope, and touching invisible walls with the palms. The performances were, on the whole, something less than extraordinary. There were two exceptions—the Russian mime group, whose technique, energy, and vitality, in my opinion, put them at the top of every category; and the Czech group's presentation of Gogol's "The Overcoat."

During the intermission I gave a demonstration of my own work, and I concluded by conveying to the audience all the good wishes of the American National Association of the Deaf. All that time I was aware of the fixed gaze of the blond who, together with the old men, occupied the front row center seats.

When the intermission was over, the jurors, a representative from each country and me, spent nearly two hours debating. We finally decided to give awards to everyone rather than have anyone go home without at least a "face-saver." The jurors' meeting adjourned with the members congratulating each other on a job well done. I was all smiles and kept my opinion to myself.

Since the awards ceremony was a main event of the festival, the auditorium was packed that evening. Afterward, we went to the club of the deaf. The Czech mime group made nearly everyone drink from the trophy cup they had won, which I found out was a tradition there. I managed to drink from it without spilling a drop, and everyone applauded. I was really enjoying myself when Paur came over and asked me to go over to the room reserved for hearing officials and VIPs. I did not like the idea, but could not think of a reason to refuse.

We walked in and once again I saw the lovely blond seated at the head of the table surrounded by her elderly retinue. The table was laden with pastries, coffee, and bottles of vodka. Paur told me that the woman had asked to meet me.

She got up and came toward me. In the semidarkness I could see only her beautiful face. Paur introduced us formally. Her name was Bozena Hradnickova. I offered her my hand; she smiled and stretched out hers. I felt a shiver down in my back as I saw the stump at the end of her arm. She let it drop and offered me her left hand, on which only the thumb and the index finger remained. I placed both of my hands over that poor mutilated hand and shook it sincerely. I hoped she could tell that this gesture meant that what matters is who we are and not our physical handicaps.

She was the first to start the conversation. With Paur interpreting, she said she had heard a lot about me and was greatly impressed by my performance in the afternoon. In my mind, I wondered how her hands came to be so cruelly maimed. I studied her perfect, rosy-complexioned face and found no scars whatsoever on it. Her body appeared to be intact, and her beehive hairdo and her make-up were perfect.

I thanked her for making my trip possible and enabling me to meet many fine deaf people and artists. She was a little taken aback, as if she did not expect me to say this, and then started to tell me about her position with the Department of Care for the Disabled. I wished to know her attitude toward deaf people, the government, and herself, but she began to introduce me to her retinue of elderly gentlemen before I had the chance.

Paur had already told me something about them. They all were war veterans, army officers who had become crippled in combat. Some walked with canes, others had vision problems, and still others had hearing impairments. Because of their distinguished military careers and crippling injuries the government had placed them in charge of the rehabilitation and employment of the handicapped, which meant devising mostly make-believe jobs such as basket weaving and the making of plastic junk gewgaws. None of them had ever bothered to learn sign language. As for the regal blond herself, her ignorance of sign language was excusable by her lack of hands, I suppose, even though she was in charge of the Czechoslovak deaf. Still, I couldn't help but marvel at the irony—a person with no hands in charge of a community of people to whom hands were the sole means of communication.

By then I had realized that the reason for the presence of these big wheels in Brno was not some special benevolence toward the deaf but an opportunity to take a vacation and get the best food and special privileges. They had simply come to be honored. Nothing unusual about that, I thought; it happens everywhere.

Miss Hradnickova asked me to entertain the group with a pantomime sketch. Her tone was a little too commanding and it put me off, so I said I was too tired. She then informed me that we would meet again the next day at a banquet in Holokin, a country resort, and offered me a ride in her chauffeured car. I bowed my head to indicate my acceptance; to decline twice would have been rude.

The next morning I packed my carry-on bag, since this was to be only an overnight trip, and waited with Paur for the car.

A black Zil pulled up at the same time as a large chartered bus, which the deaf artists began to board. Paur and I sat in the back of the Zil with Miss Hradnickova. We spent the next two hours gazing at the mountain scenery and chatting. Actually, communication is the wrong word, I asked many questions and from her responses, transmitted to me by Paur, I gathered that she knew very little about deafness and hardly ever mingled with deaf people, except to handle paperwork about them. Now and then during our conversation she asked me personal questions. She smelled of an exquisite and expensive perfume, probably from Paris, which, combined with her deformity, only added to my acute feeling of discomfort. She told me I would stay overnight at the lodge, but when I asked her whether other deaf people would do the same, a soft expression came over her face as she answered, "No, only you."

Finally we arrived. Paur showed me to my room and left. I washed up and got ready to go down to the foyer. Downstairs in the foyer the deaf people who had just arrived on the chartered bus were streaming inside. They were coming only for the banquet and would be driven back to Brno later, while the VIPs and I would stay overnight. We all went into the large dining room, gesticulating, laughing, excited and happy, like schoolchildren on an outing. I spotted Matilda and walked over to talk to her.

All sorts of tempting delicacies sat on the tables, but no one touched them. We all remained standing. I asked what we were waiting for and was told the VIPs had to come down first.

Finally they came in. How I wish I had filmed this scene! Bozena Hradnickova strode in wearing a purple silk dress that revealed the perfect shape of her body. Her blond hair fell in a mane around her shoulders. In her wake came her subordinates, some trotting, some limping, gray-haired, bald, paunchy, thin, tall, short. The little group advanced to the dais and sat down, whereupon we all sat down at our tables. I sat between Matilda and Paur.

But we could not eat yet. The obligatory speeches came first. With Paur interpreting, the blond Venus delivered a speech that was so self-congratulatory and replete with platitudes that I was mentally transported to a business convention in the United States. By the time she finished, we were ravenous. We devoured dinner with gusto. This was the best meal I had in Czechoslovakia.

After dinner, someone turned on a phonograph and dancing began. Matilda and I got up and began to glide around the floor. I could not hear the music, so I followed the rhythmic movements of the other dancers. I was suddenly awakened from this lovely, swaying dream when the music stopped. Paur tapped me on the shoulder. He apologized for cutting in, but Miss Hradnickova wanted to dance with me.

I led Matilda back to her chair, bowed in the best European manner and thanked her. Then I approached the blond woman, who kept eyeing me with a secretive smile. I bowed and motioned to her as if to say, "May I have this dance?" She rose and walked with me to the dance floor. I had been wondering how I would dance with a woman without hands, but quickly found out. She raised her stumps into the air and placed them on my shoulders. I held her by the waist, and in that position we began to do a slow fox-trot.

She pressed her body tightly to mine, squirming and swaying her hips. I was taken aback by her directness but accepted it with good grace. Her face was pressed against my cheek, and over her shoulder I watched Matilda, who was signing animatedly with Paur and now and then threw me an amused glance. I could see that most of the others were watching us. And indeed in her elegant silk dress with her lush blond mane, my partner stood out like a plumed bird among sparrows.

She moved away from me and started to dance a kind of fandango by herself, turning round and round, circling me, tapping the floor hard with her feet, and swaying her stumps as if her missing fingers were clicking castanets. Each time she faced me at the end of a turn, she stared at me with a passionate intensity. Her dance became wilder and I began to suspect that she was a little drunk. I began to feel uneasy, especially when the space around us on the dance floor cleared and we found ourselves in the middle of a silent circle of onlookers. She again rested her stumps on my shoulders; again I grasped her waist with both hands, but I stayed completely passive in her hold. There was something possessive about her that turned me off. She pressed against me without tenderness, as if she were trying to crush my body. Her brows were knitted and she looked infuriated by my passivity.

I could hardly wait for the music to stop. Finally, when it did, I escorted the goddess back to her chair, thanked her, and hurried to take my leave. But as I was about to turn away, she grasped my elbow with her surviving index finger and thumb to hold me back. She picked up her purse and indicated that I should hold it. With that finger and thumb she then unclasped her purse and took out a mirror, which she deftly balanced on the stump of her completely fingerless hand. With the finger and thumb of her other hand she removed her lipstick, and painted her lips while licking them sensuously now and then. When she finished, she put the mirror and lipstick back in the purse, which I was still holding, and thanked me. Finally, I was free to go.

I ran upstairs to my room. From the window, which faced the front of the lodge, I saw the chartered bus from Brno parked in the driveway. I packed my carry-on, opened the window, and flung the bag and my raincoat into the bushes. I then ran down to the first floor. To reach the foyer entrance, I had to pass the open door to the dining room, through which I saw Hradnickova chatting with one of her companions. She did not see me, but the old men on the dais did.

I walked on toward the door. Retrieving my bag and raincoat from behind the bush, I approached the bus. The driver was inside, smoking. I knocked on the door, which he opened, put my bag on a seat and, so that he would remember my face, asked him in gestures if I could leave it there until I came back. He responded with a gesture of welcome.

I went back to the lodge to have a drink. I found Matilda, who told me the bus would leave in half an hour so she better say good-bye to me soon. Fine, I responded, but no good-bye because I was going to leave with her. We looked at each other conspiratorially, and I asked her to save me the seat next to her on the bus. From the corner of my eye I watched Miss Hradnickova and her retinue. It struck me that not once had I seen them chat with any of the deaf people in the room other than me—yet they were officially in charge of these people.

Matilda and I had a last dance. Then it was over and people started to leave. I shook Matilda's hand, too, as if I were staying at the lodge overnight. But after the room had emptied and only I, Miss Hradnickova, and the old men remained, I watched from the big picture window as the last trippers got on the bus. I excused myself as if I were going to the lavatory, walked slowly out of the room and, once in the foyer, raced toward the bus just as it was about to leave.

The day-trippers were surprised to see me inside the bus and clapped to show their pleasure. I retrieved my belongings and sat down on the seat that Matilda had saved for me. We talked all the way back to Brno, in fact, we stayed together until her bus left for Prague later that day.

I returned to my hotel room and packed, and then I walked in the drizzle in that dreary and sad city until dark, when my train for Vienna was to depart. The taxi for the train station came on time, but once it brought me to the station, I looked around helplessly, having no idea which track to go to. A man in his late fifties suddenly appeared. It was the same mysterious stranger who had given me a ride to Hotel Slovan from this station. As if he already knew where I was going, he beckoned to me to follow him and took me to Platform 2. We stood in the cold, waiting and waiting. Abruptly, the man motioned for me to follow him to the next platform. We waited for forty-five minutes, then he suddenly picked up my suitcase and lead me back to Platform 2. The train pulled in and he motioned for me to board. As the train pulled away I watched his retreating figure, still wondering who he was.

That night I had a nightmare. I was alone on a brightly lit stage, rehearsing a monologue. The house lights came up and I saw the blond woman with the deformed hands rise from a seat and walk toward me menacingly, up the steps onto the stage, closer, closer, till I could feel her hot breath on my face and see nothing but her furious tiger's eyes. I awoke with a feeling of terror just as the train stopped at Břeclav. Once more I went through the search and show-the-passport routine. I was able to breathe a little more freely only after the train entered Austria.

At dawn the train reached the Vienna station. But even here in the West, among the bright lights and colorfully dressed crowd at the station, the oppressed feeling did not leave me completely until I saw Felizitas anxiously scanning the crowd for me.

From Europe I traveled east. To Teheran, India, Bangkok, Singapore, Hong Kong, Taiwan, Manila, and finally Tokyo. But it was in Hong Kong that I received a letter from David Hays that forced me to face reality.

The letter I received from David Hays stated that he and Linda Bove were arriving in Tokyo in January 1978, two weeks after I would be leaving. They were scheduled to appear on a television program there. David wrote, "One point that you can make for us, very strongly, is that the deaf must work very hard to make our [NTD's] appearance a success, but they must allow it to be seen as something that is presented by hearing people. You must very carefully explain the subtle problem that we have always had: that if an appearance is totally sponsored by the deaf, hearing people do not understand it as professional entertainment, but rather as 'help for the handicapped.' Therefore, you must say that for the ultimate benefit of deaf people, they must play a large role, but if they want the full benefit, they must be modest and defer to the concept of the fully professional international company that plays in all situations. I know that you understand this, and that you will help enormously here."

As I read that letter, I rationalized that I was too involved to see the whole picture. It even dawned on me that David was right. Until then I had thought that the idea was for me, a deaf man, and for him, a hearing man, to jointly make deaf theater popular in the world. In fact, that was my understanding when David and I jointly established the NTD way back in 1966. His letter made me realize that the world was not ready to accept deaf professional theater on its own unless it were led by a hearing person, a man like David. He hit the nail on the head, and I was touched by his confidence in me, by his straightforward approach without mincing any words. I did not misunderstand his intentions and I appreciated the truth as he told it, though it hurt. I still believed in myself and in a deaf professional theater that would stand on its own, without hearing directors, but clearly the time was not yet right for it.

Subsequently, after I had returned home to the States, Linda Bove talked to me of her experience with David on the Japanese television program. She had signed some poems and, in between, David had talked about the NTD. The Japanese, who usually keep their distance from handicapped persons, saw on television a lovely, young deaf actress who signed with such beauty and grace that their views on deaf people were altered. David felt this contributed greatly to making the NTD's performances in Japan so successful.

Before I left Japan I did an interview with the *Asahi Shimbun*, a leading Japanese newspaper. I also gave several lectures in which I continued to praise the NTD; in short, I did as David wanted. At the end of my tour I received several letters from American embassy staff congratulating me on my ability to "establish a deep rapport with your audience, both hearing and deaf people alike." They also told me that my visit was "an important step in paving the way for a major tour of the NTD" to Japan.

On my way home I spent a couple of days in San Diego with Ursula Bellugi, a longtime friend. I poured out my troubled feelings to her, and she convinced me that my decision to leave the NTD and strike out on my own was up to me alone. "You are the Shakespeare of Sign. I have faith in you!" she exclaimed, and reminded me of one of her favorite stories. She told me she often cited it in seminars on sign language at the Salk Institute. As part of her research, she had wanted to see whether sign language could stand on its own without being reinforced by facial expressions. She asked me to sign a story about catching a fish without once moving my facial features. I was to sign successive emotions of excitement, disappointment, and elation while my face remained composed. I did as she asked, and when it was over, I sat down groaning and holding my face with my hands. When she asked me what was wrong, I exclaimed, "Ouch, my face hurts!" She told the story with such good cheer that I felt much better.

I thought about David's letter for months after I returned home. I began to realize that we had a fundamental disagreement about the potential of deaf theater. The only solution I could see was to leave the NTD for good.

In the spring of 1978 I had lunch with Dr. Edward Merrill, the president of Gallaudet College. During the course of our conversation, he dropped a hint that I would be welcome as artist-in-residence at the college. This gave me the impetus I needed to leave NTD. As soon as I returned home I wrote David Hays a letter.

My long letter to David explained my motives for leaving the NTD. By return mail I received from him an angry reply containing questions which I answered point by point in my next letter to him. His subsequent replies grew milder, until finally he agreed to part amicably. We agreed that I would continue working for the NTD as a summer-school lecturer. He even threw a farewell party for me.

The surprise party was held in the living room of the O'Neill mansion. Everybody came—the staff, the administrators, and the actors. The last to enter was David, bearing a huge cake on which was emblazoned, "Good Luck Bernard. With Love from the Company." I cut the cake and distributed pieces to everyone. We all chatted and exchanged reminiscences. Then gradually the room emptied until only David and I were left. Two slices of the cake still remained on the tray. I was going to save one for a friend, Tim, who could not be at the party, and David was going to save the other for his son Danny. We wrapped the cake in napkins and wished each other well. As we got up to leave, David stumbled in freeing his leg from under a bench, fell against me, and dropped his cake. The sudden impact caused me to drop mine too. Both pieces of cake splattered as they struck the floor. That was the note on which we parted, a note symbolizing our opposite viewpoints and philosophies of theater. We parted with as much dignity and respect as the cake incident let us retain.

As I left Waterford I thought back on the last twelve years—the confrontations, the ordeals, the triumphs, and the little successes. I thought, too, of the wonderful people I had met and worked with. If it hadn't been for NTD, I would not have met one of my most cherished friends. Our friendship began with a letter I received in 1974.

Dear Bernard Bragg:

I was born deaf but never thought myself deaf, at least not until recently. I had never gone to a deaf school and knew nothing about deaf culture. The first time I saw deaf people was at age thirteen when I happened to walk with my mother and saw three or four deaf men gesticulating across the street. I wondered at the strange manner in which they moved their hands, and at their animated faces. When I asked my mother why they kept waving their hands, she said, "Oh, they're deaf and talk with their hands. They don't speak with each other."

I felt the same way as she. I could not relate to them. My father is a professor of social work at Columbia University and my mother is a social worker, a former student of my father. I have a brother whose hearing also is normal. But my own is not. Even so, I had always been treated like a hearing person in the environment I grew up in. I am a good lipreader and my speech, while not perfect, is understandable. Since it is not so clear to outsiders, however, I had a speech tutor all my life, until my college years. Even so, growing up sheltered in a small world with a few friends, in an upper class neighborhood in New Rochelle, I did not consider myself deaf.

When I was fifteen going on sixteen, I went through an identity crisis, a normal one, the kind hearing adolescents also have, or so I thought. At high school I skipped a class so that I graduated early and went on to Brandeis where my older brother also is studying. I am very close to him here at Brandeis, so that I am almost never on my own. Or rather, I was never on my own, because I feel that my life has changed after my first exposure to the National Theatre of the Deaf. I saw a play being enacted by deaf actors, and I saw deaf people in the audience sign to each other. Talk about the shock of recognition! I had never realized till then how beautiful sign language is, and now finally I feel that I found my identity.

In the program of the play I saw your picture and a brief biography which mentioned that you are a former student of Marcel Marceau. I was stunned, because I worship Marceau. He had influenced me so deeply that last summer I studied with the American Mime Theatre in New York. I felt and still feel that in you I have found a role model, that you and I share the same love and admiration for Marceau. Perhaps because we both are deaf and both desire to express ourselves. Mime is my compensation, a kind of surrogate bridge linking me to the world. Next fall I am going to major in Drama at Northwestern University, and this coming summer I ardently desire to attend the summer school at your theater, the National Theatre of the Deaf. Could you help me get in?

P.S. I'm twenty years old.

The letter was signed Michael Schwartz and bore a Brandeis University address. I passed it on to the head of the summer school, but he said no. I argued that Mr. Schwartz was someone special because he came from neither of the two major constituencies supplying our theater with the new generation of actors—residential schools for the deaf and mainstreamed schools. But he was unyielding. Why? "Because," he said, "Mr. Schwartz knows no sign language. He has to learn it before he can attend the school." It did make sense, and I had to agree with it. We wrote Michael, informing him of the director's decision, and shortly afterward we received a reply from him notifying us that he was going to take sign language classes at Northwestern University, as part of his master's program in drama.

In due time he completed these classes, applied again to our summer school, and was admitted in 1976.

On the Friday before the first week of summer school at the O'Neill Theater Center in Connecticut, a tall, dark, young man with finely chiseled features appeared at the school office to register. I happened to be there just then, and he recognized me from my picture in the play program. I signed to him, "Welcome to the deaf world." He was pleased but also appeared to be confused. He said he had been on the theater's grounds already for a few hours and he could not understand anyone's signs. I questioned him and found out the sad, ludicrous truth: the sign language courses he had taken at Northwestern were taught in SEE, Signing Exact English, a sign language system that aims to be an exact reproduction of English. In the SEE system, signs have been created for definite and indefinite articles, which do not have signs in ASL, as well as various prefixes, suffixes, and tenses. Users of American Sign Language generally find SEE signs artificial and a hindrance to the fluidity and grace of their language. Michael had realized it himself by then and he asked me desperately, "Could you tell me how to drop the 'the' and 'a'?"

"You'll have to go out and mix with the other students. There is no other way."

He took my words to heart. The environment there was congenial for this kind of learning by socializing. The students were together all day long, sleeping in the same dormitory, eating breakfast in the same dining room, attending all the same classes, and spending their after-class time together. Michael struck up quite a few friendships, particularly with Jimmy Turner, a cheerful young black man from the Mystic, Connecticut, School for the Deaf. Although it was an oral school, Jimmy was a master at signing, catching every expression on the wing as it were. At the same time, like so many other deaf people, his English was poor.

There could be no greater contrast than that between Michael and Jimmy, one extremely literate in English but signing like an illiterate, and the other practically illiterate in English but signing with extreme fluency and a dramatic, gripping flourish. Yet this odd couple seemed to complement each other. From Jimmy, Michael learned to limber up his signing, while Jimmy learned how to improve and broaden his command of English.

With me, Michael discussed things at a more intellectual level. He especially loved trying to define deafness and the place of the deaf in the world. "Deafness is not a physical handicap," he said. "It is a state of mind, and we deaf are Cain's children, condemned to expiate a sin of which we ourselves are not guilty."

The time came for the theater's director to choose new members of the troupe for the fall. He was impressed with Michael's stage presence, personality, and acting skills and decided to offer him a job. Michael was both happy and sad. He asked for a year's delay because of a medical problem doctors had assured him would be gone in a year. And so we parted.

The following winter I got a letter from a school for the deaf in the South which shall remain nameless. Its superintendent asked me to recommend to him a temporary drama teacher. I immediately thought of Michael. This would be a great experience for him, getting to know real deaf children and real deaf people in large numbers. I contacted him, and he was willing to try it out.

From the school he wrote me long letters. His initial euphoria, however, soon turned to depression. He was upset to see how some of the hearing teachers at the school treated the deaf pupils, and the few deaf teachers there as well, with such condescension. What shocked him particularly was that a number of hearing teachers who had spent years at the school still had not bothered to learn sign language properly, thus keeping communication between themselves and deaf pupils at an extremely low level. They were "time-servers," people who taught only for the sake of money and civil-service seniority. The had no interest in teaching, and many of them were there because they were too "content" to find jobs out in the real world. They expected the deaf children to sit in class like sheep, and they hammered into their heads the idea that they always had to be humble. They disciplined children without explaining why and called it the "silent treatment." Michael was also angry because some hearing teachers selected only the few children with real proficiency in speech to give demonstrations to visiting state officials, who came away impressed with the supposed accomplishments of the teachers. I smiled when I read this and I could not help thinking of the "decoys" mentioned in *The Deafmute Howls*, the autobiography of Albert Ballin. The more things change, the more they remain the same.

I wrote back asking him to be more charitable in his judgments, if only because otherwise he would make enemies and would not last long at the school, and the children needed him. He refused to listen to my advice. In his later letters he described to me how he had begun to rebel, to teach deaf children how to think creatively and express themselves, release their powers of self-expression.

In one letter he told to me how, the previous Sunday, he had watched dormitory supervisors escort the children to buses waiting to take them to religious classes. One bus was for Catholics, and two for Protestants. He saw a few Jewish children being shepherded into the bus for Catholics. He ran outside and told the supervisor it must be a mistake, these kids were not Catholics—they had names like Cohen, Rubin, and Levy. But the supervisor answered, "Mind your own business. We have been doing this for years and we ain't gonna stop now." When Michael insisted, he was told, "How else can they be cared for? We can't leave them unsupervised in the dormitory. And besides they never complain about it."

"Because they have no choice," answered Michael.

"Even if they had a choice, we still can't leave them unsupervised. You're concerned 'cause you're Jewish yourself."

"Even if I weren't Jewish, the principle of it would be the same. This violates the children's rights."

"That's enough. I'll thank you to mind your own goddamned business," the supervisor answered impatiently and told the driver to go ahead.

Michael returned to his room feeling outraged by the oppression of the deaf and their religious rights. He himself had grown up within the civil rights movement, so to speak, through the influence of his father. Until then he had thought that only black Americans had problems. Now he knew better. He opened the phone directory to find the address of the local American Civil Liberties Union and wrote them a detailed letter about the event he had witnessed.

Several weeks later an ACLU investigator appeared on the campus. He talked with many people, including the superintendent and his assistants, whose legs literally quaked, and prepared a report reprimanding the school for forcing children to undergo instruction in a religion other than their own, in the absence of parental permission to boot.

The school was never the same after that. From the superintendent down, the hearing teachers and staff members became openly hostile toward Michael. He was completely isolated, since even the few other deaf teachers were afraid to speak to him. This was a new experience for him. But let it be said that this was also a new experience for the hearing teachers—it was the first time a deaf man had stood up to them.

He reflected on his experience in his letters to me, comparing deaf people with black people in the South. When school closed for the summer, he packed his bags, said good-bye to the children, and did not return in the fall.

He drove to Connecticut to reenter the NTD summer school. Once there, at my invitation he moved into my house shortly before I left on my world trip. He said that he could hardly wait for me to come back so that we could work together.

When I returned to my house in Connecticut, we had a long chat about our experiences. Michael told me that he was ready to work with me, now that he was accepted as a member of the NTD troupe. But I, standing at the window, shook my head, no.

He noticed that I was not being myself and asked, "What happened?"

"Unfortunately, now that you are joining the troupe I have to leave it."

"You are quitting?"

"Yes, I came home a changed man." When he looked at me wonderingly, I explained, "I have decided to leave the NTD. I gave it ten years of my life. Enough is enough."

"Why this sudden decision?"

"I feel it's time for me to move on."

"It's so sudden."

"No," I admitted. "I have been thinking about it for a long time."

"Level with me. Tell me why?"

So I began to explain. "For ten years I went along with the NTD's orientation toward mainly hearing audiences because they are so much larger than deaf ones. Generally, NTD chooses to stage signed versions of contemporary and classical plays by hearing playwrights. Hearing audiences find beautifully acted plays in sign language an artistically moving experience. It is a new and different kind of theater, a synchronization of sign and speech. Wonderful for the NTD and magnificent for placing the power of sign language in the limelight, but what about us deaf? Of the scores of plays staged by the NTD since its founding, only two—*My Third Eye* and *Parade*—dealt with deaf culture, with the lives, joys, and miseries of the deaf. I helped build up the NTD, and I am happy about its success, but it is time for me to move on and try to fulfill the dream of my father, Professor Hughes, and Bob Panara, the dream of a theater of and by the deaf."

Michael asked, "Do you have any backing yet?"

"No, I'll have to start from scratch."

"That takes courage! Where will you go from here?"

I told him that I had been offered the post of artist-in-residence at Gallaudet and had decided to accept it.

A few days later, the day I was to leave for Washington, rehearsals began of a new comic version of *The Three Musketeers*. In the morning Michael and I said our farewells, then he hurried off to the rehearsal. I had already packed everything and was about to get into my car when I saw Michael return, slowly dragging his feet. He exclaimed, "You can't imagine what happened!" There followed a flood of rapid signs from which I gathered that when Michael arrived for the rehearsal he a saw a sign on the bulletin board announcing a meeting for the entire cast at 4:00 P.M. He asked around for the reason and found out that some new book on sign language was being developed and the director wanted to include in it photographs of NTD actors. Michael found it strange because there was no mention of this in his contract nor, as he determined upon inquiry, in the contracts of his fellow actors. He therefore asked them to attend a special meeting to discuss this topic later in the afternoon following rehearsal. Somehow, David Hays found out about it and summoned Michael to his office.

When Michael walked in, David asked, "What is this about, that meeting you want to call?"

Michael answered, "We'd like to know why we were asked to pose for pictures. That is not in our contracts."

David smiled, "That's something new. Do we have a locker room lawyer here?" He said that there was indeed no such clause in the contract but he expected the cast to show elementary courtesy and respond to his request. Patting Michael on the shoulder, he signed, "Now go home and rest."

I listened to, or rather watched Michael's story with interest. We looked at each other silently. Then I signed, "You made one mistake."

"What's that?"

"You shouldn't have taken it upon yourself to call the meeting. You should have asked the cast spokesperson to do it."

"All right. So it was a mistake, my calling the special meeting myself, but the idea of that meeting was right and I won't retract it."

"I never told you otherwise."

"I'll take your advice and go back, but not for long. So I am a locker room lawyer? Fine, I'll step out of my locker some day soon and try my hand at law school."

"Are you serious?"

"Why not? You don't think it's a bad idea?"

"No," I answered. "Just let me know when you make it."

We shook hands and I drove off. Four years later, in 1982, I was working in my office at Gallaudet when the TDD light flashed. I lifted the receiver, placed it on the TDD, and typed, "Hello, this is Bernard Bragg."

The row of glowing red letters rapidly disappeared to the left and was followed by my caller's greeting—"Assistant District Attorney Michael Schwartz speaking. . . ."

CHAPTER SEVEN

New Scripts

Soon after I moved to Washington, D.C., I called Mike Bortman, a scriptwriter I had first met in Philadelphia during my last year with the NTD. He had introduced himself and told me of his desire to write the teleplay And Your Name Is Jonah. *He wanted to write about a deaf boy who is misdiagnosed as mentally retarded by "experts" who know nothing about deafness. We had kept in touch since then and, now that I was home, I called to find out about the progress of his play.*

Mike and I agreed to meet at The Ginger Man, a popular restaurant near Lincoln Center.

He signed slowly, but clearly, "I have good news and bad. Which do you want to know first?"

"Good news, because, after all, bad news can always be worked out."

"CBS has agreed to produce *Jonah*. Charles Fries and Company will be in charge."

"That's great!" I exclaimed. "When do we start?"

"In three or four months."·

"Okay. What's the bad news?"

"They want a young hearing actor to play Jonah."

"Oh, no!" I groaned. "The same old story. They never give deaf roles to deaf actors. How ironic, because your play tries to enlighten hearing people about deafness yet hearing producers remain unenlightened."

"I know," Mike agreed. "But the producer isn't convinced. He feels he can't communicate with a deaf boy. Do you know any deaf actors who have played deaf roles in movies?"

"No, no major roles ever. They have always used hearing actors for these roles, like Tony Curtis who played a boxer."

"And don't forget Jane Wyman playing the illiterate deaf girl in *Johnny Belinda*." Mike interjected. "And what about Peter Falk as a derelict and rapist? It does sound like the deaf are portrayed as either morons or rapists."

"Not exactly," I pointed out. Falk's show was on TV, not on the big screen. Speaking of TV, a few deaf actors have gotten roles. My friend Audree Norton did a guest appearance on 'Mannix,' and Linda Bove appeared in 'Search for Tomorrow.' PBS taped *My Third Eye* and CBS taped *A Child's Christmas in Wales*, both done by the NTD. But that is about all, unfortunately."

Mike observed, "You forgot to mention your own show, 'The Quiet Man,' on KQED in San Francisco, which was later broadcast nationwide."

"Ah yes, but that was years ago. Wait, there was also the NBC program, 'Experiment in TV,' the one that the A. G. Bell Association tried to suppress because it was signed."

"But a deaf actor has never played a major role in a big screen movie or a film made for TV. If we succeed in getting a deaf actor to play Jonah, it will be a first in TV history."

"Okay," Mike signed, "can you find a deaf actor, nine, ten, eleven, or twelve years old, it doesn't matter as long as he looks nine. Let's find him quickly because the producer has done a nationwide search and has found two candidates, both in California. One is hearing and the other slightly hearing impaired. We need to act fast."

I closed my eyes, thinking of deaf kids I had met while giving workshops. One picture zoomed in my mind. "Yes, I have him."

Mike leaned forward, "Who?"

"Jeff Bravin. I first met him two years ago after the commencement address I gave at the New York School for the Deaf. Somebody tapped me on the back. I turned around but saw no one. The second time it happened, I saw a little boy. He introduced himself and told me what he thought of my speech. That's how I remember him. Plus, his parents, Judy and Phil are good friends of mine. Yes, Jeff Bravin. He'd be just right for the part."

"Sure?" Mike asked. I nodded firmly. He added, "Grab him and I'll arrange a screen test in Central Park."

Two weeks later, when I introduced Jeff to him, Mike's immediate reaction was, "That's Jonah. That's exactly how I pictured him when I wrote the play."

With the camera filming, Jeff and a specially hired New York actress played for a few minutes and then sat down on a bench and signed to each other to display a range of emotions.

All seemed to go well, but when I next met Mike he told me, "Trouble. The producer and director both have their hearts set on the hearing boy actor. But don't worry, I'm sure they'll change their minds when they audition Jeff."

A week later we were waiting in a hotel suite for the producer and director to come witness the audition.

"What are you doing with that corkscrew?" Mike asked. "Why are you fidgeting with it?"

"Mike, can't you see that you are as nervous as I? What are you doing with that script? You are fidgeting with it too."

Mike laughed and put the script down on the coffee table, signing to me, "Leave that corkscrew alone. You make too much noise."

Mike got up and walked toward the door. He opened the door to Jeff and his parents. After I performed mutual introductions, they sat down. Jeff grabbed the corkscrew and began to fiddle with it. I asked him, "How do you feel? Are you ready for the audition?"

"I guess so," he answered uncertainly. "I feel fine but probably a little nervous."

I signed, "Mike and I are nervous too. But you are going to make it. You are going to show them."

"Yes, but why do they insist on a hearing boy?"

"They're afraid; they don't know how to deal with the deaf, but we persuaded them to give you a chance. I know you'll make the best of it."

Mike joined in, signing slowly, "We're going to convince them that we work as a team. I'll interpret for you and Bernard."

Jeff looked at his watch, "What time will they be here?"

Just as I was going to say, "Anytime now," Mike got up to open the door, signing, "Right on the dot." The producer, Stanley Kaufman, and the director, Richard Michaels, came in. Mike introduced us to them, whereupon Jeff's parents wished him luck and then excused themselves.

After Jeff's parents left, we all sat down. Michaels said, "Go ahead." Turning to me he asked, "Can you say something bad, some sad news, to Jeff?"

We were sort of huddling together so that Jeff could not see Mike's signing. I got up and approached Jeff, who was back to fiddling with the corkscrew. "Let's improvise a scene for these gentlemen. I'll leave the room and reenter in a jiffy. Watch and respond to what I do. Okay?"

"Fine."

I left the room, waited a moment, then opened the door and walked in.

Jeff looked up and signed, "Hello."

I answered, "Hello, I'm sorry, but I . . ."

He was puzzled. "But what?"

"Your dog was hit by a car and instantly killed."

He had a dog. I happened to know it because of my friendship with his parents. He opened his mouth and shook his head slowly as if in disbelief. He looked down at the corkscrew in his hand and stayed quiet for a while, with his eyes downcast. Then he started to breathe heavily, as if he were about to burst into tears.

I decided to put a stop to it. I touched his shoulder and said, "That's all for now."

I glanced at the others. Michaels was staring straight ahead, frozen-faced. Kaufman was wiping his nose with a handkerchief and sniffling. I asked Jeff how he had felt when I first broke the news to him, and what was his initial reaction.

Jeff smiled and signed, "To be honest with you, I hardly felt anything."

I was puzzled. "But you did feel something, didn't you?"

"No. Not really."

I wished I had never asked him. "Oh, come on. Your feelings surely were touched."

"Yes," he answered. "I knew what you wanted of me—to see how I would respond. I tried very hard to believe, to imagine, that it was true, but that was not easy."

Aware that our conversation was being interpreted to Kaufman and Michaels by Mike, I once again asked, "But you surely must have felt something?"

Jeff did not answer. I glanced at the others. They too were waiting. I continued, "Did you really imagine this situation? Your own dog?"

"Yes. Maybe it was just me who struggled to believe it was true, much as I refused to believe it."

I turned to the others and exclaimed, "I don't think you could find a more honest actor in the world than Jeff."

They signed him up on the spot. I also got a part in the movie. But my main role was to coach Jeff and advise the director on the realities of deafness.

It was not easy for Jeff, a lively nine-year old boy, to identify with Jonah, a character who was supposed to be severely depressed by his environment, by the years he spent at an institution for the mentally retarded and by living with hearing parents with whom he could not communicate. Jeff's parents were deaf, so he lived in an environment in which communication by sign was natural and accepted. But Jeff was an apt pupil.

The rapport between us was just great. I never told him what emotions to display in front of the camera; that was something he just seemed naturally to know. Things did not always go smoothly, however. At one point in the rehearsals Jonah was to witness his grandfather's death from a heart attack. As

Jonah, Jeff was not supposed to understand the meaning of death; he was to look puzzled, yet placid, while his grandfather died. Jeff and I worked on the scene until he felt ready. Just before the camera started rolling, Sally Struthers, who was playing Jonah's mother and was unaware that shooting was about to begin, sneaked up behind Jeff and pinched him. Flabbergasted, I hollered, "Sally!" She realized her mistake and quickly drew away. I tried to stop the camera by shouting, "Jeff is not ready. He was just snapped out of the mood!" But Dick Michaels, the director, was already behind schedule, so he decided to go ahead. The grandfather clutched his heart and dropped while Jeff looked on with a slight smile on his face. This was not the right reaction, as Dick realized, so he interrupted the shooting while I tried to get Jeff into the right mood again. Jeff was perfect on the next take.

I worked closely with Jeff and the other cast members throughout the filming. Communication was usually not a problem, though by necessity we used some circuitous routes. Mike Bortman would usually interpret for me what the director wanted Jeff to do, and then I would relay the message to Jeff in clearer more graphic signs.

Mike would also interpret for me when Sally Struthers and James Woods, who played Jonah's parents, asked for suggestions on the "right" emotions to show. On one particular occasion, near the end of the filming, James Woods asked Mike to rewrite the end of the film so that his character would go back to his wife and son. Mike told him to talk to me about it. I told him that many marriages ended up in divorce when a hearing-impaired child was born into the family. It was unfortunate but true. James was insistent that the father should return because he loved his family, but I stood firm. I suggested, though, that he show more feeling during the parting scene. When they shot the scene James did express his feelings deeply and sincerely; his eyes glistened with the tears, and the rest of us watched with lumps in our throats.

I was still shaken up by my career change. At the same time I was excited by the new vistas and new prospects I was about to face. I also thought of Gene Bergman, my good friend from college days, the man I trusted most, and the man with whom I was going to pool my talent in service of deaf theater. He was now a professor at Gallaudet, so I would be seeing him often.

I settled into life in Washington, made new friends, and developed new routines. Every Thursday I went to Gene Bergman's home for dinner. Gene's delightful wife, Claire, made me feel part of the family.

Gene and I discussed my reasons for leaving the NTD, and we agreed that we should establish our own theater. During my ten years at the NTD only once, and partially at that, was a play ever staged by a deaf director, and after I left this happened only rarely. When I once asked David Hays for the chance to direct a play, he replied that the choice of director was "his prerogative." The next time I asked him was after he had chosen a hearing member of our troupe to direct a play. I asked why him and not me, what did he have over me, considering that we had joined the NTD at the same time? David's response was, "You're challenging me but, well, I am just following my intuition." The play folded after a very short run.

In our dreamed-of theater, deaf members of the troupe would be participants, not puppets, unlike at the NTD whose board members and administrators were all hearing except for the token deaf member. Gene and I wanted to work together to make our dream come true, and soon the opportunity arose. The National Association of the Deaf was to celebrate its centenary in the spring of 1980, so I asked Fred Schreiber, the head of the association, to let me be part of its entertainment program. When Fred agreed I asked Gene to coauthor with me a play for the deaf, about the deaf, and by the deaf, a play that the association would sponsor.

"I have it!" Gene exclaimed. "Let me ask you what the heart of the deaf world is?" He paused, then continued, "The deaf club. That's where the deaf meet. It's their gathering place, the heart of their world, their ballroom, their bar, their theater, their community center—all rolled into one. It is a piece of their own land in exile—an oasis in the desert of a world dominated by the hearing."

I liked the idea, and starting with the club, we fleshed out our play, *Tales from a Clubroom*. We created the characters first, always keeping in mind that they should be realistic, that the whole play should be a slice of life among the deaf.

We were in business. I organized a play production workshop with some forty-five volunteer deaf actors, members of the Hughes Memorial Theatre, Washington's longtime community theater of the deaf. I discussed with them their ideas of what typical deaf characters were like and how they should live. The idea was that these characters and the "Metro Club of the Deaf" should be representative of the deaf and their clubs throughout the United States and, as such, would be accepted as authentic by deaf audiences anywhere.

Through improvisations we developed such characters as the cigar-chomping club president, a crusty and bluff official to whom the club bylaws are a second bible. The club treasurer is enormously popular among the club members; they go to him for advice in finding jobs, writing letters, resolving quarrels and other personal problems. For him, we created a matronly wife who was in charge of the coffee urn and sandwiches at the club. We also came up with a sexpot, a divorcée to whom men gravitate; a henpecked TDD repairman and his gossipy busybody of a wife; a bartender-bouncer who uses earthy sign language; a roguish ABC card peddler whom the club members tolerate; a pompous college graduate who gets his comeuppance; the star of the club's basketball team ("Golden Lightnings"); the club's wisecracking film projectionist who is never without his bow tie; a naive young woman who has recently graduated from the local school for the deaf and is being seduced by the ABC card peddler, who intends to exploit her in his business; a college dropout—a loner who is too brilliant for her own good; an angelic young man with tunnel vision; a hearing woman who devotes herself to the club because she has once been in love with a deaf man; an ex-oralist convert to sign language; and the club pariah, a reticent and mysterious character.

The main plot, in short, was about embezzlement of funds by the club treasurer. But it wasn't the usual small-time embezzlement. It was a crime that took on an added significance against the background of the customs and attitudes of the deaf club members. The simple act of embezzlement leads to the complication of social ostracism—the worst punishment that the deaf can mete out to a fellow deaf person.

Tales from a Clubroom premiered in June 1980, in Cincinnati, Ohio, at the convention of the National Association of the Deaf. During the performance I sat in the middle of the auditorium so I could observe the reactions of the audience. I had never before seen an audience that was so stirred and totally absorbed by what was occurring on stage. When the curtain fell, the spectators practically stormed the stage to congratulate the players.

While I was backstage congratulating the actors, somebody tapped me on the shoulder. I turned to find David Hays. He signed, "Congratulations. Frankly, I did not understand the play, but I loved the set."

I answered, "That should be enough."

Inwardly, I wondered whether he meant that the play was just "too deaf," that it contained too many allusions and references to things that only the deaf understood? Could it be also that what he revealed was that after ten years of working with deaf people, his understanding of them was still deficient?

Gene and I wanted *Tales from a Clubroom* to be a realistic play, but it appears we got more than we bargained for; wherever it was staged, in Boston, New York, Philadelphia, and Washington, D.C., deaf audiences related so much to it that some spectators believed the characters portrayed were real people. After the curtain fell, the actors were often approached by spectators who related their personal stories in sympathy with what had happened to the character. One night, for example, a man told Bob Dillman, the actor who played the club treasurer and embezzler Yakubski, "I was through it myself. They caught me, and they did not let me stay in the club as a member. I think they treated you right." And when Bob protested, "But don't you realize I am only an actor?" he was nonplussed by the man's answer: "Oh, I keep forgetting. But you sure understand how I feel, because you went through it yourself."

I had never before in my life seen such an enthusiastic response to a play. Gene and I were wondering where it would lead us. The play was produced in New York, Philadelphia, and Boston. Yet, once its last performance ended in Washington, a year after its premiere in Cincinnati, *Tales* was revived only once, for a couple of performances in Delavan, Wisconsin. And to this day its sudden demise after such spectacular success remains a mystery to me. Perhaps David Hays was right after all. If he did not understand *Tales*, how could hearing audiences understand it? The sad truth that sank into me is that deaf audiences are simply too small, the deaf being too small a minority, to sustain a thriving deaf professional theater. To survive, plays about the deaf must be geared to hearing audiences by focusing on universal experiences and conflicts between the hearing and the deaf worlds. This accounts for the success of such plays as Mark Medoff's *Children of a Lesser God*.

Once I settled down at Gallaudet I began to receive a stream of invitations to direct workshops, give one-man performances and luncheon and after-dinner speeches, appear on television, and speak on the lecture circuit. Among other things, I also began to serve as a master of ceremonies at various national functions within the deaf community. In the summer of 1986 I received an invitation to emcee a deaf beauty pageant in California. What surprised me this visit was how much closer California had come to being a paradise for the deaf in a world emphatically not made for them.

It was amazing to see Linda Bove sign with one hand and shuffle pots and pans dexterously with the other. The grace of her movements fascinated me, and the gist of her lecture amused me as I was sitting at the kitchen counter watching her. There was something charming in her outrage at learning that sometimes I skipped breakfast. "Never, never skip breakfast," she signed gravely, and set down before me a bowl of cold cereal with all sorts of garnishes—nuts, bran, banana—laced with lactose milk, and a stack of thick heavy whole wheat toast, enough to last me for a week.

I looked up at her slender figure. She clearly took good care of herself. A moment ago she had finished exercising to a videocassette workout. My eyes took in the large sunny kitchen, part of the luxurious home in North Hollywood where Linda and her husband, Ed Waterstreet, lived. Times have clearly changed, I thought, now that deaf actors can afford to live like this.

"Time for me to move to the hotel so I can start rehearsing," I commented. "It's a fancy hotel, all right, but even fancy hotel living does not compare to your ritzy Hollywood place. To say nothing," I added ironically, "of the delicious breakfasts you have been fixing for me all week."

She laughed, "Well, only for three days and then you come back to us."

"Yes, yes, and then I'll return home to the East doubly healthy."

She lapped up what I was saying, then grew serious. "Careful. Be sure to eat your breakfast every day at the hotel."

"I promise," I answered. "You know, there are three things that would make me want to move back to California—the climate, your breakfasts, and, last but not least, California Relay Service. I still can't get over this marvelous telephone service for the deaf."

"Yes," she answered and went on to recount how happy she was with the CRS herself. She often got calls from agents regarding movie and television commitments, and thanks to the CRS she was not missing these calls. Deaf people never had it so good. All this was due to a California law that enabled any deaf person to use the CRS without charge to make and receive calls inside California from hearing people. Only a few other states have adopted similar laws.

I left Linda's and drove to the brand-new theater auditorium of the Concourse Stouffer, a fancy hotel where I was to attend rehearsals of the Miss GLAD (Greater Los Angeles Association of the Deaf) Pageant of 1987. There, I met some GLAD officials who introduced me to the contestants, some of the prettiest deaf young women in California, and discussed the program of events with me. All day I was busy blocking out the movements of the contestants, watching them rehearse their spiels and parade across the stage in their evening gowns, and meshing their appearances with my emceeing. By the evening I was so exhausted that I went straight up to my room to catch up on my sleep, but not before a GLAD official had loaned me his TDD.

Once in my room I saw a card saying that guests who wanted their shoes polished could have them back by ten o'clock the next morning. I had two pairs of shoes, both needed polishing. So I picked them up and took the elevator down to the lobby in order to give them to the bell captain, who assured me that they would indeed be delivered to my room by ten.

Once back in the elevator, a bulb lit up in my head and I began to curse myself for my stupidity. I didn't have to make this trip—I could have used the CRS. Too late, but I was certainly going to use it in the morning.

The next morning ten o'clock came and went, but still no shoes. I was already dressed, ready to go down, when I noticed the shoes were not there. I grew nervous, as I had only my sandals on hand and they would not do for the formal lunch I was to attend at noon. I consulted the hotel card for the bell captain's number, then dialed the CRS.

A reply appeared at once on the paper roll: "Station 37. California Relay Service. May I help you? GA (go ahead.) I identified myself, my hotel and my room telephone number, and gave the bell captain's extension number, asking the CRS to call him about my shoes. The operator asked me to hold while she dialed the bell captain, who must have been flabbergasted to get the message, "This is the California Relay Service. We are calling for a deaf man, Mr. Bragg, Room 1012. He is waiting for his shoes." He apologized and said he would bring them up in an instant. My reply, as relayed by the CRS, was, "Wonderful. Remember, don't knock on the door as I'm deaf. That would be a waste of time and energy." He answered, "Sure. No problem. I've got the key." I thanked the bell captain and the CRS operator, and no sooner did I replace the receiver than the door opened and the bell captain entered carrying my highly polished shoes.

I tipped him generously. I had never had it so good in all my life. The CRS became my Open Sesame to saving time and avoiding the frustrations, no, the vexations, connected with deafness, thanks to the generosity of the great state of California. I did not have to depend on the often snarling kindness of strangers to make phone calls for me. I felt equal to hearing people and luxuriated in this newfound freedom. And it was in this upbeat mood that I fell asleep after spending another busy day at dress rehearsals.

When I woke up, it was Saturday morning. A shaft of sunlight had penetrated a chink in the draperies and landed on my eyes. I still felt sleepy and needed more rest in order to be at my best for the pageant that night, but that sunlight bothered me like Linda's admonitory finger wagging in my face. And then, too, I felt hungry and missed Linda's breakfasts. Linda Bove, my sunshine! At the same time, I felt too lazy to get up and dress, go down for breakfast, then come back up to my room, undress, and again plop down onto my bed for a snooze. I settled down to sleep again, but I only tossed restlessly. Hunger won. I swung my feet over the bed's edge and suddenly a serendipitous thought hit me. Eureka! The CRS! I could use it to call room service! I was going to act just like a man with normal hearing. Super, super!

I jumped gleefully out of bed, wide awake, and dialed the CRS. The operator responded at once, and I asked her to call room service and order breakfast for me—freshly squeezed orange juice, two scrambled eggs with crisp bacon, raisin toast, hot tea, and milk for the tea. My mouth watered in anticipation, knowing Linda would have squawked if she had known what I ordered.

Then a hitch developed. The operator said she was sorry, but CRS could not do it. CRS had a policy not to call the same number twice, even though the extension numbers were different.

So the whole thing was, after all, too good to be true. All the same, I got into a heated argument with the CRS. I pointed out to the operator that the day before I had had no problem in getting CRS to call the bell captain, but she answered that the operator the day before must have made a mistake; this was definitely against CRS policy. I answered that I was very upset, to put it mildly. I told her I could very easily call my deaf friend who lives in North Hollywood and ask her to make the call for me through the CRS, "and she would give you this hotel number and you would have to call room service and have it bring up breakfast to my room. How about that? GA."

To my surprise, the operator excitedly exclaimed in print, "Very ingenious and a great idea. Go ahead. You can call her direct TDD to TDD and then she can call in here. Okay? GA." I said I would do that, but did she not think it also was a ridiculous thing to do, and she answered, "Yes. But I have to go by the rules. Sorry, Sir. It is not my decision. GA." But a devil got hold of me and I launched into a long and involved discussion with her about the CRS's policy. I questioned whether it was a written rule or something made up on the spot by her supervisor and demanded to speak directly with her supervisor. "Yes, Sir. She is on her way. Please hold. This is Mrs. Hobbs. No I did not invent the rule. That is the practice as set up by the Public Utilities Commission. GA." I finally got from her the acknowledgment that it was indeed a written rule not to call the same number twice. I thanked her for her patience, and she said I could call my friend now and wished me bon appetit, and I answered, "Merci beaucoup, Mademoiselle Hobbs. You probably can hear my stomach growling. SK." (SK indicates the end of the conversation.)

I hung up and called Linda, typing, "This is Bernard. You have been fixing breakfasts for me all week. How about this time ordering it for me from room service? GA."

"Hi, Bernard. Yep. Half a minute to get myself awake. Smile. GA."

I then explained the whole thing to her. She typed back, "I never heard of that but it must be so new to them. Okay. How many people would want to order breakfast from their home anyway? GA." She also typed that she was mortified and, of course, ready to help at once. So I gave her all the details and asked her to make sure the room service people knew I was deaf so they would just come in, without knocking. She called me a bad boy for ordering all those fattening goodies but added that she would comply with my request. I thanked her and said if she did not hear from me, that would mean things were okay. She said she was happy that at least I heeded her advice and would not let the day pass without breakfast, fattening or not, so I answered, "Don't start another lecture on me. I love you. Bye. SK."

She typed back, "We must fight the CRS for our privileges. Love. Bye. SK." I answered, "Don't worry, Mary Max Brown, the CRS supervisor, will be at the pageant and I will talk with her. Love. Bye. SK SK."

Half an hour later the door opened. A bellhop came in pushing a cart loaded with my breakfast, a stiff, snowy white napkin, and silver cutlery. I thanked him and tipped him. I felt as though I were in the lap of luxury.

It goes without saying that after this experience I was too stirred up to fall asleep again. At any rate, I saved the TDD paper with the record of my morning conversation.

The pageant was a smashing success. At the reception I found Mary Max Brown, the CRS trainer and supervisor I had expected to be there. I unrolled the strip of TDD paper with the record of my conversation. It was so long that it reached my raised hand to the floor. "Have I got a story to tell you!" I exclaimed in sign.

A small group surrounded us, looking on curiously. I said, "Look!" and, pointing at the strip of TDD paper, added, "It took me that long to get my breakfast!" Then I told them my story.

The reactions of the onlookers were varied. Some opened their mouths with wonder, some laughed, and still others looked horrified, among them Marcella Myers, a woman who was and is the guiding spirit behind GLAD. A middle-aged, cheerful woman, full of energy and wit, who knows how to pull strings, she's made GLAD the most successful deaf community organization in this country, if not the world. She also had helped make the CRS possible.

By this time I could laugh at the whole incident.

"You think it's funny?" asked Marcella.

"Sure, I can laugh now, after the fact."

She shook her head and chided me. "You have an Easterner's mentality. We out here in the West fight for our rights. Let me have that paper; the fur is going to fly."

I signed back, "I can't wait till the next time I come to California, to order breakfast."

Mary Max Brown interrupted, "The strip of paper will be much shorter, only about six inches long, I promise you. If you let her borrow that paper."

"Sure," I answered, "But what are you going to do with it?"

"Discuss it with the CRS committee, for a policy change."

"Wonderful, if you promise to return it."

"Why? Are you going to frame it? Or use it for publication?"

"You're darn right," I answered. "I want to add it to my book."

A week later I got a letter from the CRS. It was the most courteous letter I had ever received from a public agency. It said they had "resolved the matter of handling customers' requests to call an extension number in any in-house call." And they concluded, "Thank you for sharing your experience with us. Customer satisfaction is uppermost in our mind."

Now if only the deaf in the other states would receive this kind of treatment. We have come a long way, at least in California, since we were first permitted to drive cars.

As artist-in-residence at Gallaudet I not only videotaped stories for children and gave guest lectures in various college departments but also authored a romantic comedy, That Makes Two of Us, *about the relationship between a deaf woman who is an oralist and a deaf man who signs. It is a story about love and compromise. And in response to various requests, I traveled across the country, giving speeches and one-man performances.*

Then suddenly one day in 1984 I got a TDD call from my mother in Florida. She called to say that Father was sick. I dropped everything and flew to Miami on the next plane, feeling worried about my father and at the same time astounded by the thought that for the first time he needed me.

My parents met me at the airport. I asked my father what was wrong with him, and he signed that he just did not feel well. Had he called a doctor? I asked. No, not yet. Strange. I told him I would call a doctor for him and he signed, "Yes, please." That soft answer, coming from him, alarmed me.

I brought him to a doctor who diagnosed the problem as an aneurysm and said he must be hospitalized for tests next month. It did not seem serious as yet, so I flew back to Washington, planning to return three weeks later during the Christmas vacation. But once I was back home, my mother called, saying that Father had changed his mind and did not want to go to the hospital. I called Father on the TDD, urging him to keep his appointment and telling him that I would fly back to Florida to be with him then, but he answered, "No. Let us not discuss this anymore."

Three months later he was dead. I have only sad memories of him, except for that one shining moment when I saw him use the box of paints I had given him. Ours was never a father-son relationship. His last words, or rather signs, to me when I flew home were, "It's no use."

Yet when I look back I feel a warm sympathy for him. After my father's death my mother began to lead the life of an independent woman. She had waited on my father hand and foot for fifty-six years, and enjoyed her newfound freedom. She flew everywhere, to see friends in California and to play the slot machines in Nevada, and she took cruises in the Caribbean.

The summer of 1986 she came to visit me in Maryland. After a while I had to leave for Montana on a business trip. In my absence her friend Helen drove her around. I was not prepared for what I found when I returned home.

When I got home I was surprised that my mother and her friend Helen were not waiting for me. After several hours I began to worry. I went next door and asked my neighbor if he had seen them. When he said no, I asked him to please call the area hospitals to see if Mother and Helen had been admitted to any of them. My hunch proved correct. I got to the hospital as quickly as I could.

My mother was in the intensive care unit. Her face was swollen and misshapened from cuts and bruises; she was hooked up to oxygen and straw-like tubes ran from her nostrils. Her neck was enclosed in a brace and her hair was in disarray. Her right arm and leg were in splints. Life and hope seemed to ebb from her open eyes.

There was a lump in my throat but I held back my tears. I leaned toward her and gently kissed her brow. I signed, "Mother, you'll be fine. You'll be fine. Don't worry. I'm with you. I'm here now." She blinked and nodded slowly.

A nurse came in and wrote a note asking me if my mother could lipread. She also apologized because she knew no sign language. She then described my mother's injuries to me. Now I understood why Mother's left hand was bent so unnaturally; the wrist was broken but bandaged instead of being in a cast because a perceptive physician ordered it to be left alone so that she could sign. Her right arm was broken and she had a fractured pelvis, a dented kneecap, and a possible neck injury, which only a subsequent X ray could determine. The nurse was worried because there seemed to be no way for my mother to communicate. Her speech was difficult for strangers to understand. I assured the nurse that I would stay at the hospital to make sure Mother had someone to communicate with.

The nurse nodded. Then, at her request, I showed her how to make the signs for "pain," "medicine," "sleep," and "injection."

Suddenly I thought of Helen, Mother's eighty-year-old friend who had been driving the car. I asked the nurse where and how she was and whether I could see her. She led me to Helen's room. Mother's friend also had cuts and bruises on her swollen face. Her leg was in traction and her arm, ankle, and pelvis were broken. All the same, she seemed to be more alert than my mother. I approached her and tried to comfort her. She looked guiltily at me and signed with her unbroken hand, "How's your mother? I'm sorry I did that to her. I promised you I'd take care of her while you were away, but I didn't do a very good job."

I grasped her free hand, then signed, "Don't worry. Mom is alive and alert. I'm thankful you both are alive."

The time limit on a visit to the intensive care unit was ten minutes, but the supervisor broke the rule and let me stay with my mother and Helen all day long because I was the only one who could interpret for them.

The first night I slept at home I felt awful. I could not sleep; again and again I replayed the nightmarish accident in my mind. I tossed and turned for hours and then finally gave up trying to sleep.

I took a cold shower hoping it would wash away all the pain, suffering, and bitterness, and drove straight to the hospital.

I did not know if the road to my mother's recovery would be downhill or uphill. If it were downhill, that would be her end. After all, she was eighty-one years old. If uphill, the road would be long and hard. My greatest fear was that my mother's deafness, her inability to communicate, would make things worse for her in the hospital. Even the best interpreter in the world would have had difficulty understanding her immediate needs. I was the only person who could.

After three days in intensive care my mother improved sufficiently to be moved to a regular hospital room. She would recover, according to the doctor, but she would be hospitalized for eight to twelve weeks. The X ray showed no neck injury and her neck brace was removed.

Helen had to stay in intensive care one more day because her injuries were even more severe. When the nurses asked me whether Helen should be moved to my mother's room, I told them to let me ask Mother first. "I'd rather not," said Mother, shaking her head. "Afraid not. . . . I don't want to." I had known in advance that was what she would say, as she would feel uncomfortable sharing a room with the person she blamed for the accident. For that matter, Helen would feel awkward too. Then I went to Helen and told her the ostensible reason for their separation—one nurse could not care for two seriously injured persons in the same room. She smiled and accepted my explanation but made no comment.

After my mother was transferred to her new room we went through a series of nurses. The nurses in intensive care had been sensitive, attentive, and concerned. We didn't realize how spoiled Mother had been until we dealt with the floor nurses. When they learned that Mother could not speak or lipread they became exasperated. I was afraid they would not give Mother the care she needed, so I went to the head nurse and the hospital administrator.

They seemed to understand my concern and promised to do everything they could to make Mother's nurses aware of her communication needs.

Things improved a little after this meeting. Still, I found myself reminding nurses that just because Mother couldn't talk, it didn't mean she couldn't communicate. I had two particularly nasty run-ins with nurses who showed no compassion for Mother's inability to talk. They seemed to take it for carte blanche to ignore her call button. These experiences reaffirmed my belief that hospitals are not prepared to care for deaf patients.

In addition to our skirmishes with the nurses, Mother had a difficult recovery. The doctors had refused to operate on her broken right arm until her gashes and bruises healed. But when these wounds finally healed, she developed fluid in her lungs, with the attendant danger of pneumonia. The doctors inserted a needle in her back to drain the fluid. Then she developed phlebitis in one leg, a result of her prolonged stay in bed. And all the while she had to keep wearing an oxygen mask.

I sat watching her while she eyed the ceiling. I was determined not to let her regress. If she had to go, it must be from natural causes, not from that stupid car accident, especially since she had just started to enjoy life as a widow.

After several weeks, the doctors finally pronounced her fit for surgery. They screwed two metal plates onto bones in her right arm, but they did not do anything about her fractured knee and pelvis. They told me that prolonged surgery would be too dangerous at her age, so they decided to keep the leg in a splint and let it as well as the left wrist and the pelvis knit themselves, since these fractures were stable. We began a new recovery period.

Every morning after seeing my mother I stopped by Helen's room. Her daughter lived about fifty miles away, so she didn't get to visit as often as I did. Every time I saw Helen, she was just as guilt-ridden as the first day and she kept asking me to forgive her. I always said I did.

The routine of staying with Mother all day and consoling and telling Helen not to feel guilty began to take its toll on me. I was nearing a breakdown, which my drawn face with bags under my eyes showed.

One day as I was napping in the visitors' lounge, the head nurse stopped to talk to me. She wrote me that she was worried about my health because I had spent so much time at the hospital for more than a month. She suggested that I stay home or otherwise I would collapse from stress and worry. She added that she knew of many instances of relatives who had collapsed and that I should not worry, that the hospital would take good care of my mother.

I told her that if I had to go home I *would* collapse from stress and worry because I could not leave my mother in the hands of people I could not trust and who could not communicate with her. So I was doing myself a favor and avoiding a collapse by staying here and seeing with my own eyes that my mother got the proper care.

She did not answer. I could see she was mulling it over. Then I added, "I appreciate your concern, but from what I've observed, none of the nurses has made an effort to get to know my mother. It's easier for them to ignore her. I worry about her. You said you would learn sign language, but you never did. You are too busy. You don't know what it is to be deaf and left alone. You never bother to communicate with her. I'm worried that her mind will atrophy unless I am here. I'd appreciate it if you were more worried about my mother's health than about mine."

She looked exasperated and she left wordlessly.

The surgery on Mother's arm weakened her still further. I could see that, in her helpless state, her memory was starting to go. I tried to combat this new development. I phoned my friends from all over and asked them to come visit her. Her room was filled with flowers and one wall was completely covered with postcards.

My friends were wonderful during this time. They came to the hospital often, talked to Mother and tried to cheer her up. But she never answered them; she only smiled. That scared me and I wondered if her mind were going.

Then one morning a nurse brought in Mother's breakfast tray, but was suddenly called away for an emergency. As she was leaving the room she asked me to please feed my mother. There was hot oatmeal in the bowl. I asked my mother if I could feed her, and she nodded. I tried to be careful, but as I brought the spoon to her lips, I spilled some oatmeal. I said I was sorry and wiped my mother's chin. She assumed a watchful expression. I tried again to feed her, thinking how odd it was for me to do this to my own mother. Again I spilled some oatmeal.

Mother wrinkled her forehead. She started to sign with her bandaged wrist and mouthed, "You don't know how to feed me."

This was the first time since her transfer from intensive care that she had signed a coherent sentence. I was thrilled. I raised my eyebrows theatrically and signed, "I'm not your mother." She smiled. I smiled too. Now I knew for sure her mind was sound.

As time went by, we started to talk more and more. She began to complain about the discomfort of her bed, the terrible hospital food, the poor quality of the television set and the caption decoder, the slowness of the nurses. I thought her complaining wonderful.

My friends said I looked like a ghost and needed a break. Occasionally they would tell me to go home and would offer to stay with my mother, saying they felt she was like their own. Most of the time I accepted their offers gratefully because they too were deaf and could communicate with her.

One day when I was especially tired I told a friend who had come, "If only I had a brother like you to take turns. Too bad I'm an only son."

Just then, to my delight, my mother waved her hand to catch my attention and signed, "I'm your only mother."

That characteristic flash of one-upmanship on her part was, after the oatmeal incident, the best thing that had happened to me since the accident. Her sense of humor was intact!

The more Mother and I talked, the more it became clear that she either did not remember the accident or didn't want to. For a long time, she didn't ask about Helen. When she finally did, I described to her Helen's injuries and reminded her of her decision not to let Helen stay in the same room with her. I told her how Helen was always asking about her and begging her forgiveness. Her face froze and she turned her head toward the window. After that, she did not ask me again about Helen and would say nothing whenever I mentioned the subject. I got no reaction out of her either when I told her that Helen was about to be moved to a hospital closer to her daughter's home.

One day, six weeks after our ordeal began, the doctors decided that my mother was ready to be transferred to a nursing home for physical therapy. I was elated, and my friends were so happy for me, they threw a party to celebrate Mother's transfer.

The morning after the party I got up and found I could not relieve my bladder. Something was obstructing it. Doubled over with pain, I knocked at a neighbor's door. He drove me to the emergency room of a nearby hospital, where the doctor on duty diagnosed acute prostatitis and ordered my hospitalization. I resisted because the timing was all wrong. That day was my mother's birthday and the day she was going to be moved to the nursing home. The nurse in the emergency room gave me the same old spiel about my not having to worry because my mother would be well taken care of. I agreed to stay on one condition, that I get a TDD so I wouldn't be cut off from my mother and the world.

I spent a week in the hospital and another week recovering at home. During all that time some wonderful friends, angels from heaven, took good care of my mother. They kept me informed about her progress daily via the TDD.

As soon as I felt strong enough, I drove out to the nursing home. I found Mother sitting in a wheelchair, looking like herself again. Her brown eyes lit up and she gave me a warm smile. I also met her physical therapist, Ellen. She had learned the rudiments of sign language just to be able to communicate with my mother. She signed to me, awkwardly but legibly, "Your mother will walk again today."

I could not believe it. "Will she make it?"

"It won't be easy, but she will make it."

She wheeled Mother to the therapy room, and I followed them. Once in the room, she put a walker in front of Mother. She then raised Mother to her feet. The walker had special arm supports because Mother's right arm was still in a cast and her left wrist was still mending. What is more, her left knee was badly swollen and she wore a steel brace on it.

I watched Ellen give Mother a hands-on lesson in lifting the walker, moving it forward, putting it down after making a step, and then repeating this sequence.

It took Mother a long time to make that first step. I could see she was grimacing with pain. After three steps she shook her head. Ellen signed, "That's enough. Now you can sit down." She helped Mother to sit down in the wheelchair. Then Ellen gave me a big smile, "She did it!"

But Mother broke down and cried. I asked her, "What's wrong?" And she answered, "It's terrible. I watched you take your first steps when you were a little baby, and now you're watching me."

Days passed and Mother slowly improved. She kept on practicing how to walk. She also learned to feed herself with her left hand. Her progress was slow but evident.

One morning her doctor and the nursing home director came to watch her exercise. Ellen asked her to walk by herself with a cane.

"No, no. I must have the walker," my mother objected.

But Ellen said, "No, you can walk. Come on, try it," and handed her a cane.

Mother made a tentative slow step, then another and another. I counted ten. She started to laugh and cry.

Two weeks passed and finally the nursing home director came up to us, smiling, and wrote me, "Your mother can go home after Labor Day weekend." I showed the note to Mother and she signed uncertainly, "Really? I can't believe it. Am I ready?" It was hard work reassuring her.

While Mother stayed with me, she relearned how to walk up and down stairs, how to cook, how to use the TDD, and how to do needlepoint—her former favorite occupation. Finally, the doctor pronounced her fit to return home to Florida. We were unsure yet whether she would make it and be able to live on her own again. If the experiment failed, I was going to take her back to my home in Maryland.

Before we left, I asked my mother whether she wanted to visit Helen, who was then in another nursing home, and say good-bye to her. Mother was uncertain at first, but she nodded slightly, so I drove her to the reunion.

When we arrived, I left Mother sitting in a chair in the hallway while I opened Helen's door. Helen asked me expectantly, "Where is she?" "Here," I said as I opened the door and Mother shuffled in on a cane. She walked up to Helen's bed and they embraced. Then, after Mother sat down, the two old friends talked and talked. At one point Helen blurted out in sign, "I'm so happy you can walk again." Mother reassured her, "I'm sure you'll walk again too."

A nurse came in with a wheelchair and announced she was going to take Helen out for physical therapy. Mother got up and said, "Good-bye. Take care of yourself. Let me know how you're doing." They embraced again, and I saw one's guilt and the other's bitterness dissolve. Helen signed, "Yes, and when I'm on my feet again let's take a boat cruise together."

"I'd love that," Mother answered. "Like in the good old times." They parted, signing to each other, "I love you."

Once we arrived in Florida, I stayed with my mother until I was sure she could manage for herself. I got her a visiting nurse and a cleaning woman, stocked her kitchen with food, and spent all my time talking with her, gaining a new intimacy with her.

I felt increasingly confident that I could leave her on her own and fly back home to Maryland. When I asked her if she thought she could take care of herself, she said not to worry and that I could go home. But there was one last important hurdle to be cleared that I was anxious about—cards. Playing cards had been her ruling passion. There was nothing she loved more than meeting with her friends for a card game at the deaf club. What worried me was that playing cards well requires skill, memory, and concentration, and I wasn't sure if Mother was still capable of it. I asked her outright if we could go to the club to play cards, and her answer was far from reassuring. "No, I don't think I should," she said.

The day before I was scheduled to fly home, I took her to the club of the deaf near Fort Lauderdale. When we entered, her many friends flocked to her, hugged her, and told her how wonderful it was to see her.

Then card-playing time arrived. The card tables were set up and every-one sat down to play the club's favorite game, "500," a variety of gin rummy. Mother gave me an uncertain look and said she was not sure if she could remember how to play. I said, "Please, at least try." Some of her good friends approached and invited her to play.

She finally agreed and sat at a table with three men. I was jittery and worried about her, but I tried not to show it; I winked when she looked at me. The man on her right started to deal. Mother picked up her cards, held them like a fan and slowly rearranged them in her hand. As she inspected her cards, there was a hesitant look in her eyes and she raised her hand as if to quit.

"Oh, no," I groaned, and closed my eyes. When I opened them, I saw the three men ask, "What?" and Mother declare, "I think one card is missing."

The dealer said, "Oops," and offered her the deck, from which she was to select a card, but she threw her cards down and smilingly asked to be dealt a new hand.

What a pro, I thought. But that was only the beginning. Mother bid the seven of hearts and went on playing. The pile of cards in front of her kept growing. She was winning all the hands in her very first game.

The next day I flew home to Maryland. On the plane, I relaxed for the first time in ages. When I looked through the window, the sky seemed more blue than ever before.

Sometimes, when I look back on my life, I feel gratified knowing deaf people have come a long way since I was a small boy and my teacher told me to keep my hands down and sign modestly because sign language was ugly and alien. That experience confused and shocked me, and it left me wondering who I was supposed to be; sign language was part of my deafness. Did this mean that my deafness was to be kept an ugly secret? I could have developed a schizoid attitude about my deafness had not it been for the time I spent at home with my family and deaf friends, who signed and to whom sign language was a perfectly normal and acceptable way of communicating.

Nowadays sign language is accepted more widely and some universities even give credit for it as a foreign language requirement. I smile at the thought that people even pay to see me sign. I have even had the honor of performing a play written especially for me—The White Hawk by John Basinger. Other productions have been designed with me in mind.

I glanced at my appointment book. I had a ten o'clock meeting with Bettina Cox from the American Film Institute. It was already ten. She was late. My thoughts flew back to 1952, when I had begun to teach at the California School for the Deaf at Berkeley. Then also I was sitting behind a desk, before my first pupils entered, and I had wondered what lay ahead of me, where my future would lead me.

My thoughts were interrupted when the door opened and Ms. Cox walked in accompanied by Donna, a sign language interpreter. Donna had interpreted for me many times; she was professional, unobtrusive.

Ms. Cox, on the other hand, was very definitely not unobtrusive. A petite, elegantly dressed, perfectly coiffed blond in her thirties, she displayed great self-assurance, a self-assurance which I, willy-nilly, was fated to dent again and again.

I asked them to sit down, feeling not quite certain of the reasons for Ms. Cox's visit, and began to listen to what she said.

In brief, she said that she had heard a lot about me. She had seen me on television many times and thought I would be perfect for her studio's new program, called "Designing a Language," which was to part of a series with the overall title, "Thinkabout."

This sounded exciting. I asked, "How long will it be? What exactly do you want me to do?"

"You'll love it. This will be a fifteen-minute program divided into three segments, and you'll appear in the last segment."

"Really? That means I'll perform for about five minutes?"

"Yes. You'll talk about sign language, show the viewers what signs look like."

"Oh, I see. I only hope I can do a good job compressing a description of sign language into five minutes."

"Oh, I'm sure you can do it."

"You must have plenty of confidence in me. We've barely met."

"Don't forget, I've seen you on television many times. I've always thought of you as a marvelous actor."

"Thank you, but I'm curious what the other two segments are about."

"Remember the title, 'Designing a Language'? The first segment will show chimpanzees using sign language."

I called on my years of acting experience to keep a straight face, but inwardly I was aghast. Without blinking an eye, I asked her what the second segment was about.

"Whales. How they communicate and sing underwater."

"Oh, I see." In my mind I quickly saw chimpanzees signing "Want banana, me," by making peeling movements with their fingers and then pointing at their chests. Then I saw monstrous whales communing in the water. And lastly, I saw myself signing poems by Rilke or Blake in that company. I took a deep breath and answered, "I thank you for wanting to include me in this show, but I'm afraid that apes and whales would be a tough act to follow."

I said that to make her laugh, but she took it seriously and answered, "I'm sure you'll perform brilliantly."

"Yes, but I fail to see any resemblance or similarity between my language and that of apes and whales. Sign language is a conceptual language that lends itself to abstractions, just like English."

"Yes, but remember, research into simian and cetacean languages is still young, in an early stage of its development."

"Yes, but putting sign language in the same category with these would not, I'm afraid, make a favorable impression on the public. This would spoil the image of the deaf. I'm sorry, but I prefer not to be involved in this project. I'm sure you understand."

Her face fell. She said, "What a shame. What a pity. I'll discuss this with my producers to see what they say. I'll be in touch with you."

I opened the door for her and Donna. She asked me the sign for good-bye. Donna, the faithful interpreter, relayed the question to me instead of answering it herself. I answered, "You've been using it all your life long. Just wave your hand."

She covered her mouth and blushed. "Of course, I should have known. I've seen chimpanzees making that sign."

I managed a chuckle, hoping this was just a dream. She left, and I closed the door very slowly, feeling amazed at my self-control.

Within a week Ms. Cox returned with Donna in tow. Restraining myself, I politely welcomed her. She asked me how to sign "hello." I saluted. She said, "Oh, I must practice that. I have good news for you."

I held my breath, wondering what would come next.

"After a lengthy discussion with my producers, we finally agreed that the chimpanzees and whales must go."

I let my breath out, hoping she did not notice, and said, "I only hope that the chimps and whales won't be disappointed."

She laughed. "No, they won't know the difference."

"That's right. Good thing you never told them."

She laughed again. "Instead of three segments we'll have only two. This means you'll have seven and a half minutes to tell the story of sign language."

"That's generous of you. But tell me what's the other segment about?"

"You'll be thrilled to hear about it. It's a young language, even younger than yours."

"Well, mine is about two hundred years old. How old is this young language?"

"Oh, I'd say about three or five years old. It's called Bliss Symbolics."

I had never heard of it. "Please tell me about it. Is it like sign language in any way?"

"No, no. It's very different." She sat on the edge of her chair, talking excitedly. "You take a block of wood covered by a checkerboard of small squares, with a different symbol in each square. Put the block on a table or on your knees and with a wooden stick point to a symbol. Then pass the stick to the other person, who'll point to another symbol. By passing the stick back and forth you make conversation."

"I'll have to see it for myself. But who uses it? Who's it designed for?"

"It's for brain-damaged persons or for mentally retarded persons who can't talk. It also is good for individuals with severe cerebral palsy."

It seems this time my face betrayed my feelings, because she discerned them. "What's wrong?"

"Well, at first I was happy because the chimps and whales 'bowed out.' But now I'm not so sure about sharing the program with Bliss Symbolics. You see, sign language is a highly advanced language. It is part of deaf culture. It's a way of life for us deaf people, very much a part of who we are. The National Theatre of the Deaf was established because of the beauty, grace, and power of sign language. The very theatricality of sign language elevates it to a high level as an art form. Let me illustrate."

I stood up and gave a vigorous sign language rendition of Blake's "The Tyger." From the corner of my eye I could see that she was entranced. When I finished, she sat motionless. Finally she got up and said, "Thank you, Mr. Bragg. I'm going to see the producers again. Then I'll get back to you."

She and Donna left. I closed the door, thinking that, under the circumstances, I did not regret the loss of an opportunity to appear on nationwide television.

I was wrong. Ms. Cox returned a few days later with a broad smile on her face. What is it this time? I wondered.

She said, "I have a surprise for you."

Resignedly, I answered that I loved surprises. She explained that, after a lengthy conversation with her producers they had at last agreed that Bliss Symbolics must go and I would have the entire fifteen-minute show to myself. "How do you feel about that?" she asked.

"All to myself? No other languages to compare?"

"That's right. Sign language, as I now see it, stands out. Nothing in the world compares to it." She asked me the sign for "thank you," saying, "I learn slowly, but ultimately I do learn."

I taught her this gesture, which resembles blowing a kiss to someone. She blew me that kiss and left.

I sighed and wondered what else lay in store for me.

Just when I thought I had an appropriate ending for my book, life caught me by surprise again. From my haven of relative calm I was swept along by a torrential whirlwind of events that brought me both pain and joy and led to an unforeseen finale.

In February 1988 Dr. Nancy Kensicki, the chair of the English Department, called me to her office. The moment I arrived she congratulated me because the faculty committee at Gallaudet had just approved my reappointment as Visiting Professor, one of my many and varied assignments at Gallaudet. I had been teaching a course in poetry and was planning to teach a course on deaf characters in literature, which my colleague Gene Bergman had offered me.

As I was leaving her office, Nancy stopped me and clasped her hands to sign "Congratulations!" for a second time. I wondered why. Perhaps this was her way of reiterating her goodwill. She must have noticed the bafflement on my face because she asked, "Haven't you heard yet? There's more good news for you."

"What is it?" I asked. "It can't be. Two good things happening to me at the same time?"

"Yes, they did happen. The Faculty Senate just recommended you to the Board of Trustees for an honorary doctoral degree."

I was stunned. "The Faculty Senate?"

"Yes. The entire university faculty recommended two people, you and Dr. Stokoe."

I collapsed into a chair. The honor was all the greater because Dr. Stokoe is the man who first proved that sign language was as much a language as English. Later, Jack Gannon, the author of *Deaf Heritage* and *The Week the World Heard Gallaudet*, also was awarded this honor. I was in good company.

This honorary degree would mean a great deal to my mother, and I couldn't wait to tell her. "All right if I call my mother?" I asked.

"I think you better wait until the Board of Trustees makes it official. Although chances are it will approve."

For days after, friends dropped by my office to congratulate me on this honor. Finally, I figured that since the doctorate was already common knowledge on the campus, and since the deaf grapevine operates very fast, I might as well call my mother. I broke the news to her on the TDD. "How about calling me Dr. Bernard Bragg?" I asked, and then I explained to her what happened. She was so excited we began to make plans right away for her to come to D.C.

That was early in March 1988, a month that became memorable in the history of deaf people. The Board of Trustees was seeking a new president for Gallaudet University, and by March it had selected three finalists, two of them deaf and one hearing. When the student community learned of this, it started a heated campaign for a "Deaf President Now." Students distributed flyers and organized petitions and rallies. The first rally, on March 1, was attended by three thousand people. Soon afterward I joined a candlelight procession in front of the President's House where the Board of Trustees was then deliberating. We saw one of the two deaf finalists, Dr. I. King Jordan, pass us on his way to a fraternity banquet. He told me and two other faculty members that he had met with Jane Spilman, the chair of the Board of Trustees, and she told him she was impressed by the student demonstrations. I thought this encouraging; it looked like we would finally have a deaf president, the first in the one hundred and twenty-four years of Gallaudet's existence. I wished him good luck. He thanked me and left. We kept parading in front of the President's House, hot wax from the candles dripping on our fingers.

On Sunday March 6 the Board was to announce its selection at eight o'clock in the evening. I ate out with friends and returned to the campus a little before eight. As I was driving on Florida Avenue toward the Field House, where the student rally was being held, we could see students streaming out onto the street in a chaotic but well-behaved mass. Police officers were vainly trying to restore order.

I turned into a side street, parked, got out of the car and stopped one student who told me that the Board had chosen the hearing candidate, Dr. Zinser. I was flabbergasted and angered. They were marching to the White House to protest, he told me.

I could never have believed this sight—the deaf, usually so tame, in revolt. However, by then I was no longer able to be with them. I had to pack and get ready to fly to Chicago the next morning to speak at a teachers' convention. But when I returned home, a new emergency arose. The lights began to flash at midnight. It was a call from my friend Ruth, who told me that my mother had suffered a mild stroke and showed some weakness in her left side. However, she assured me that Mother was resting comfortably and she would watch over her. She urged me to go ahead with my trip to Chicago. I called another friend and asked him to send a dozen roses, my mother's favorite flower, to her hospital room. I remained wide-awake all night, silently praying for my mother's recovery.

Once in Chicago, I canceled all my other commitments and arranged to fly to Florida right after my speech. Even before I left Chicago, several other teachers from Gallaudet who were attending the convention told me that exciting things were happening on the campus. On the plane to Florida I opened the newspaper and saw articles about the student protest on the front page. Gallaudet in national news! This had never happened before!

I desperately wanted to be there, where deaf history was in the making, but right now my mother was foremost in my mind. When my plane landed in Fort Lauderdale at around ten o'clock in the evening I rented a car and drove straight to the hospital.

I entered my mother's room. She was sleeping. On the night table was a vase of flowers—the roses I had ordered through my friend—and an envelope addressed to me. I opened it. The message inside said that my mother had recently suffered another stroke, a massive one this time, with complete paralysis of her left side.

I crumpled the note and walked to my mother's bed. I touched her hand, and she opened her eyes and looked sleepily at me, smiling a crooked smile. She signed feebly, "I'm so happy you came" and, with her good right hand, pulled me gently by the lapel toward her so that I could kiss her. I asked her how she felt, and she said she was fine and wanted to get up. I objected, "No, not yet. You'll have to get better first."

She then complained that there was something wrong with her vision. She added, "Maybe my glasses are dirty." I steamed them with my breath and polished them with a tissue. She blinked, "No, it is still there."

I realized that the stroke had in some way skewed her vision and I assured her that the doctor would fix it tomorrow. I tried to cheer her up, like two years ago when she had been in the car accident. "You'll be fine. Don't worry. I'll help you. You will get better." She fretted, "I knew you would. But you always are so busy."

"Never too busy for you," I reassured her. I felt better knowing that she was mentally alert. I reminded her about my forthcoming Ph.D. She nodded weakly and fingerspelled very clearly, "Hello, Dr. Bernard Bragg." She added, with a touch of her old deviltry, "What about me? Am I still a Mrs.?" "Oh come on, Mother," I answered, "I'll get it for both of us." She held my hand in hers and suddenly began to look very tired, so I left for the night.

In what felt like a repeat performance of two years ago, I spent my days with Mother at the hospital. My evenings, however, were different; that was the only time I could keep up with the incredible events at Gallaudet. I watched the television in my mother's apartment and read the newspapers, from which I learned that on Sunday, March 6, a thousand students had marched to the Mayflower Hotel, where the board was cloistered, to protest its decision. On Monday the students closed the university and barricaded the campus gates with cars, vans, and school buses whose tires they let out. On

Wednesday the faculty and staff met and voted to support the students and their demands that a deaf president be selected and the Board of Trustees have a fifty-one percent majority of deaf members. I wondered if we could win this time. Was it possible?

Every evening I watched the news on television and saw scenes of students guarding the closed campus gates, cheering on the speakers, waving banners and posters, and exclaiming and signing in unison, "Deaf President Now." Familiar faces appeared on the screen. I recognized deaf people from across the country who had gone to Washington to join the protest. The event attracted such national attention that it was even featured on ABC's *Nightline* with Ted Koppel.

Wednesday morning I visited my mother at the nursing home where she had been transferred. She was slumped over in a wheelchair and was frantically scribbling something with a marking pen on her left, paralyzed arm. She was so intent that she did not notice me. I walked up to her and saw that she had written on her arm, over and over again, "I'm thirsty. Please bring water."

My temples throbbed with anger and outrage. I ran out into the hallway and yelled. As nurses and aides clustered around me, I pointed at my mother. They rushed toward her, started cleaning her arm, and brought her water. I asked why they had left my mother alone in the middle of the room, away from the buzzer. They answered they were sorry, but they were busy. I pointed out that my mother was deaf and asked why they didn't even leave her some paper to write on, paper that I had brought for this purpose the night before. They seemed somewhat irritated by the scene I was making. The impression they gave me was that they were impatient and uncaring.

What made things somewhat better was that Mother's friends—Bernie, Frieda, Ann, and Sanford—came every day to cheer her up and help feed her. But there still were problems. Mother was reluctant to accept food and medication.

One evening that week she again asked me to help her get up. I explained to her that she was paralyzed on her left side and could not move or look to the left. She would not believe me. I placed her right hand on her left arm and asked, "Can you feel it?"

"Oh, that hand? Whose is it?" she asked.

Heartbroken, I told her, "No. It's your own hand."

She still would not believe me and shook her head. So I pulled her limp left hand closer toward her limited field of vision. She saw it for the first time. When Frieda and Bernie came to visit that day, my mother signed to them, "My left side is paralyzed. I had a stroke."

Thursday night I sat in Mother's apartment all by myself, watching on television more scenes of the student protest at Gallaudet. Suddenly, there was an announcement that Dr. Zinser had resigned. Now the board will choose a deaf president, I thought. Having no one to celebrate this great news with, I clapped weakly.

Next morning I told my mother the news. She closed her eyes for a moment, then signed, "Oh, wonderful, wonderful." A few minutes later a physical therapist came in. She stared at me and asked, "Who are you? What's your relationship to Mrs. Bragg?"

I said, "I am her son. She is deaf and so am I."

She said, "Oh, I have a deaf cousin. I never had trouble communicating with him."

I told her I could see that for myself because she was so easy to lipread.

The therapist walked to my mother's left side, tapped her on the left shoulder, wrote something on a piece of paper, and shoved it in Mother's face, startling her. I could not believe it. Was it possible the therapist did not know that Mother's left side was paralyzed? I said, "I beg your pardon. It would be better if you walked over to her right side so that she could see you."

She glowered at me, "Don't you tell me what to do."

"But," I started to say. She interrupted me, "I know what I am doing."

"She can't see to the left," I protested.

"Leave me alone. I know what to do. I have worked with many stroke patients. I can train her to move her eye to the left."

In desperation, I said, "She is deaf. She can't hear you. When you tapped her on the left shoulder she could not feel it. And you did not even turn on the lamp for her to read the note. How did you expect her to see it?"

She began to talk so fast and furiously that I could not lipread her anymore, but I did catch one last sentence, "Deaf or hearing makes no difference."

I yelled at the top of my voice, "Yes, it does! You have to stand to the right of her so that she can see who you are and understand what you are trying to do instead of talking to her back, instead of shoving that paper right in front of her face. That was a terrible thing to do to her. She did not know where the paper came from."

She kept shouting angrily, pointing her finger at me. "She is the problem!"

I shouted back, pointing my finger at her, "No! You are the problem."

All that time my mother sat placidly, looking away to the right, not knowing what was happening.

A nurse entered and tried to calm me and the therapist. She made us go down the hallway to the social worker's office where we were joined by a hastily called interpreter and the head nurse. The head nurse reproved the therapist for being too abrupt toward visitors. The therapist defended herself by launching into an involved explanation, and I in my turn complained that, though I distributed alphabet cards among the nursing home personnel, no one had bothered to learn how to fingerspell. I was emotionally drained.

The problem with the nursing home was cleared up but I still felt uneasy. On my next visit to my mother I asked her if she was content there. She shook her head. "You want to move?" I asked. She nodded. "Where?" She did not answer. I knew she wanted to live with me, but by then even that was no longer possible. "Do you want to move to Columbus?" I asked. She knew what I meant. In Columbus, Ohio, was a nursing home especially designed for deaf patients, the only one of its kind in this country if not in the world. My Aunt Lena, Mother's sister, lived there. All the staff knew sign language and readily communicated with deaf patients.

I repeated, "Columbus?"

She nodded. I asked her why. She signed firmly, "Deaf."

That very evening I called Jessie Gurney, the director of the Columbus Colony for Care of the Elderly. She was very cooperative and said she had a room available and would make arrangements for flying Mother to Columbus. Her quick response made me feel a little more relaxed.

Afterward, I sat down in the front of the TV set and turned it on. I watched a press conference with Philip Bravin, the newly elected deaf chair of the Gallaudet Board of Trustees, announcing that Irving King Jordan had been selected as the new president. I felt a double pleasure at this—Phil was an old friend and the father of Jeff, who I had coached for the TV film *And Your Name Is Jonah*, and Gallaudet was installing its first deaf president. The screen showed Dr. Jordan signing his acceptance speech and students jumping up and down, cheering, and embracing each other. The protest was over; the deaf community had won an enormous victory.

A week passed before my mother was placed in an air ambulance for the flight to Columbus. Now she would be among people who cared and who understood her, and I could have peace of mind. I flew ahead of her to Columbus and waited for her to arrive.

When she woke up from her sedation, she asked, "Where am I?"

"In Columbus, among friends, people who can communicate with you."

She looked so relieved. I stayed all week with her to make sure she was comfortable.

One day Jessie came to me and said, "I think it's about time for you to go. You did everything a son can do for his mother, and more. You must go on with your life. You look tired, and I know you are tired. We'll take good care of your mother. Trust us."

I answered, "Of course, I do."

I told my mother that I was going to fly out the next day. She accepted the news quietly.

The following afternoon I visited my mother to tell her once more that I was leaving and to say good-bye. She nodded, "Yes, I know. You told me." I signed, "I only wanted to make sure you remembered."

"Yes, I do remember."

"It means so much to me knowing that you are in good hands. The nurses, nurses' aides, and even therapists here can sign. Are you happy now?"

She nodded.

I continued, "I'll visit you as often as I can."

"Yes, I am sure you will."

I still was reluctant to leave her alone. "I'll write. Sarah, the volunteer aide, will read my letters to you and answer them for you. I'll keep in close touch with you."

Smiling, she again raised her right hand, "Go home, you pest."

A touch of her inimitable wit and love. I said, "Thanks, Mother."

She placed a finger on her lips, beckoning me to kiss her. She did it again, and again, and each time I kissed her.

I left the room for a moment, then returned. She lay asleep on her bed. I watched her for a long time and then left.

Once I was back on the Gallaudet campus, I became aware of the changed atmosphere there. Everyone, students, faculty, and staff, seemed to be walking tall and rejoicing in the victory of the "Deaf President Now" movement. I called Jessie every day to inquire about my mother. The last time I did so, late on a Tuesday afternoon, she told me Mother was resting comfortably. But at around midnight that same day the TDD lights flashed. As I lifted the phone receiver to place it on the TDD, I had a premonition. It was Jessie. Even as her words moved across the TDD screen, a cold shock gripped my body. My mother had passed away peacefully. A nurse was with her all the time.

Regaining my composure, I asked her to please arrange for the funeral home to have me view her the next day and then to have her cremated—a wish she had expressed to me. Even though it was midnight, I called Gene and Claire to tell them the sad news. Their words of consolation meant much to me.

I lay awake most of the night. The next day I flew to Columbus. Jessie met me and drove me to the funeral home. I felt another chill as Jessie introduced me to the funeral home director who then led us to the chapel. My mother looked like she was asleep; I wanted to shake her awake.

Jessie and the funeral home director left the room. Once Mother and I were alone, I found myself signing the Twenty-third Psalm. Then I said good-bye to her. I touched my lips with a finger and placed it on her lips.

May arrived, and with it Commencement Day. As my name was announced I rose to receive my honorary diploma. Merv Garretson, special assistant to Dr. Jordan, signed the text of the citation: "All through the years, Bernard Bragg has crossed the country and the oceans performing, lecturing, appearing on television. The continuing stream of his knowledge and talent entertains and communicates to an appreciative world a message no one needs to hear to understand and enjoy." As he continued reading, I thought of how proud my mother would have been to witness this day.

When Merv finished reading, "Gallaudet University is pleased and honored to recognize Bernard N. Bragg for his many contributions to the world of art, education, and communication." Phil Bravin slipped the doctoral hood over my head and Dr. Jordan handed me my diploma and shook my hand.

In June I drove to Connecticut to scatter my mother's ashes. I picked up Michael Schwartz in New York City, and from there we drove to my grandfather's farm where my family and I had spent so many happy summers. We drove through the Sharon Valley until we found a knoll that offered a majestic view of the valley.

Until then it had been a windless day, but when we got out of the car we both felt the wind rising. We had agreed beforehand that Michael would scatter Mother's ashes. I watched him walk down the hill and open the urn. Just as he was about to let it go, a sudden gust of wind swiftly bore the contents upward in an awesome plume. I felt the gentle presence of my mother in that great white blossom as it soared and slowly dissipated in the gray sky.

CHAPTER EIGHT

Denouement

As Michael and I drove away from the Sharon Valley, I signed to him with one hand, keeping the other hand on the steering wheel, "This is where I want my ashes scattered, too. Will you do me that service?" And when he answered, "Yes, do let me have the honor," I quipped, "If you promise me not to let me outlive you."

"Fine," he signed. "It's a deal," and extended a hand to be shaken, but I stopped him.

"I'm afraid I am in trouble." Michael looked puzzled, so I explained, "Some other friends may want to share the privilege with you."

Mike responded, "No problem. We'll divide the ashes into three parts."

"Why not four, to spread in all directions?" I winked.

Chatting in this spirit, we drove on looking for a place to eat. Just before Danbury we saw a chalet-like house with the sign "Fox Restaurant. Food and Drink With Care." It looked inviting, so we parked and went inside. It was eight o'clock, just before closing time, but when the proprietor saw us sign, he smiled and motioned us to a corner table near a window.

Our timing was perfect because right after we sat down the skies darkened and a rainstorm began. A waitress brought us drinks and Michael proposed a toast "To your mother's flight." I drank, recalling that soaring plume back in Sharon.

The waitress spoke clearly and distinctly to us when she took our order. I mentioned this to Michael, so when she came back we told her, "You speak so clearly. You must know some deaf people." She nodded and told us that the proprietor had a twelve-year-old deaf son. He was the only deaf child at his public school, but he had an interpreter for every class. He was a very lively and clever boy. After she left to get our food I commented that all this sounded fine but it was a pity the boy didn't have deaf role models. His experience was very similar to Michael's. Michael nodded.

In the meantime, Beth, the waitress talked with the proprietor, who had been observing us the whole time. He came over and introduced himself, then he asked if we would be willing to meet his deaf son. We answered, "of course." He called his wife and while we waited he offered us a brandy. He was easy to lipread.

Dessert arrived at the same time as the boy, Adam Fox, and his mother. He was indeed alert and lively as Beth had said. He knew some basic sign language. He told us about himself: how he was doing fine at school even though he had some problems with teachers who talked too fast for him to lipread; how it was a good thing he had an "oral" interpreter, that is, a man who mouthed to him more clearly the words uttered by teachers; and how he got along fine with the other kids at school. His favorite subjects were math and science, and right now he was reading Thomas Wolfe's *Look Homeward, Angel*. He then started to question us about ourselves. Who were we? And what were we doing? I introduced Michael and told Adam he was an assistant district attorney in Manhattan and that he had the same background as Adam. Michael introduced me as an actor, teacher, and lecturer at Gallaudet. Adam was fascinated by our backgrounds. His eyes opened wide as he asked me, "Are you really an actor?" I nodded yes and asked him if he had ever seen a deaf actor perform. He answered excitedly that he had just seen the movie *Children of a Lesser God*, with Marlee Matlin. I smiled and told him that I had first met Marlee when she was about his age. I had conducted an acting workshop for children at Traveling Hands Troupe, a theater in Chicago run by my friend Pat Scherer, and Marlee was one of the workshop participants. When it was over, she came up to me and asked, "Can I become an actress?" I winked at her and said, "Why sure! Just do it."

Before we knew it, it was after ten. The restaurant was long closed and we were the only customers left. It was time for us to leave as well. We exchanged addresses with Adam, then he and his parents, who had sat at a neighboring table and watched us, accompanied us to the door.

The night sky was clear and bright with stars. Adam waved to us as we drove away. Michael signed to me, "He'll never be the same now that he has been exposed to people like us. He's going to be one of the growing number of deaf writers and scientists."

I answered, "You just signed a handful." As we drove on in the darkness, a sense of peace and contentment came over me.

This book was set in 10/13 Caslon 540 by Robey Graphics, Inc. of Washington, D.C. It was printed on 60 lb. Glatfelter White, an acid-free paper. Text design by Robey Graphics, Inc.; jacket design by Jane Berman of Washington, D.C.